PORTRAITS *of*
RIGHTEOUSNESS

FREE GRACE SANCTIFICATION IN ROMANS 5-8

DAVE ANDERSON & JIM REITMAN

FOREWORD

The relationship between Justification and Sanctification has been the center of debate among theologians since the beginning of the Reformation. The early Reformers put their emphasis on Justification. The Pietists who followed them put their emphasis on Sanctification. For the purposes of this book we will define **Justification** as Deliverance from the Penalty of Sin and **Sanctification** as Deliverance from the Power of Sin in order to conform to the righteousness of Christ. Early within their respective movements, Martin Luther and John Calvin viewed Sanctification as a work subsequent to Justification, highly desired but not guaranteed. Under pressure from Rome they linked the two in such a fashion that if Sanctification did not follow Justification, one's Justification was in question. As a result, both Calvin and Luther wound up with theological systems that were inherently unstable.

Both Calvin and Luther initially taught the view of justification set forth by Melanchthon that by faith alone (no works involved) in Christ alone (trusting no other source of life) the sinner is declared righteous in the courtroom of God in heaven. As such, all one's sins (past, present, and future) are wiped away by the blood of the Lamb. If it is true that even future sins are washed away by Justification, then no future sins, either individually or collectively, can cause one to lose their standing before God (i.e., "I cannot lose my destiny in heaven because of future sins"). But forgiveness for future sins had never been taught in the Church, either East or West. The Church of Rome cried foul: Why, then, would anyone try to avoid sin in the future? They held that this dangerous teaching on Justification would only promote loose (licentious) living.

Consequently, most of the early Reformers succumbed to this fear of promoting licentiousness and began to teach that Justification and Sanctification must be linked; that is, a Christian cannot have one without the other. The two main ways they explained an obvious lack of Sanctification in people who claimed to be believers were: (1) they had never been justified in the first place (as the Calvinists hold), or (2) they could lose their salvation after they were first justified (as the Arminians claim). But this invariable linkage of Justification with Sanctification produces an unstable theological system, as R. C. Zachman (a Reformed scholar himself) recognizes and with whom this author agrees:[1] One cannot claim that Justification *wipes away* future sins and then claim that future sins can *nullify* our Justification. The result is a paralyzing of lack of assurance.

While Western Christianity *à la* Augustine has labored over the issue of Justification, the issue of Sanctification too often sits on a side-road of theology that doesn't get much ink. In many churches, for every sermon we hear on getting sanctified, we must hear *ten* on "getting saved." But "getting saved" (by which we mean courtroom justification, not full-orbed salvation) only deals with the penalty for our sins (eternal separation from God) and not with how we are conformed to the image of Christ *after* we are saved or how sin in our lives *subverts* that calling. As a result, many Christians experience the death mentioned repeatedly in Romans 5-8, where "death" does not mean separation from God for eternity but spiritual defeat and disillusionment on earth. Yet we were not called to this. So Paul emphasizes God's present offer of *righteous life* through the Spirit to replace the Sin and "death" we have incurred in Adam through the flesh.

I[2] have already written a textbook called *Free Grace Soteriology* for the introductory course on soteriology (our Justification and its implications) at Grace School of Theology (gsot.edu) in Houston. However, a proper understanding of how Justification and Sanctification are related is essential to any prospect of deliverance from our sinfulness in Adam to fulfill our calling in Christ. The present book therefore draws from Romans 5–8 to elucidate this critical relationship. Since the book is based on an earlier sermon series designed to help people in the pew navigate the choppy waters of recurring sin after they become Christians, it bears much of the original homiletic tone and is not intended to offer a full scholarly treatment of the issues. However, we have expanded the original exposition to better reflect Paul's emphasis on our calling to *reveal God's righteousness* from the inside out and not merely to "manage sin" from the outside in. Moreover, we offer additional exegetical support in the notes wherever needed to substantiate the Free Grace perspective outlined above.

I wish to extend my gratitude to Grace School of Theology for sponsoring the writing of this book. A special thanks goes to Dr. Jim Reitman who began as an editor for this book but wound up as a co-author. His insights into the argument of Romans as well as his literary gifts provided invaluable input for a more holistic and synthetic approach to the text that has greatly improved the cohesiveness of our argument.

David R. Anderson, PhD
The Woodlands, Texas
August, 2012

---

1 R. C. Zachman, *The Assurance of Faith* (Louisville, KY: John Knox Press, 2005), 221-22.
2 All first person accounts hereinafter are those of the first author, David Anderson.

 viii

PREFACE

An artist once decided he would paint some "street people." Finding an appropriate location to spy out some homeless subjects, he sat down to position his easel. It didn't take long before he spotted a likely prospect. After awhile, the beggar noticed the artist staring at him and decided to come over for a look. The artist introduced himself and asked the beggar if he recognized the man in the painting. After squinting for awhile, he shook his head. The artist invited him to look more closely. After further scrutiny the beggar asked haltingly, "Is that . . . is that me?" The artist's reply was almost mystical. He said, "That's the man I see in you." Shocked but curiously inspired by the artist's "interpretation," the beggar said, "If that's the man you see, then that's the man I'll be."

That story graphically portrays God's intention as expressed through Paul in the Book of Romans that we need God's Holy Spirit to live out our **Position** in Christ (*declared* righteous) and **New Identity** ("righteous ones") in our daily **Condition** (Christ's righteousness *exemplified in us*). Christ's righteousness credited to us in the courtroom of heaven has given us a new nature, yet as long as we tread planet earth we are all bound by some level of sin. None of us in this life can fully escape our fallen nature inherited from Adam which Paul calls "Sin" and which dwells in our unredeemed "flesh." Not until Jesus returns will we be fully released from the Presence of Sin. But we don't have to remain incarcerated by Sin in this life. Paul reassures us as believers that we can have progressive deliverance from the Power of Sin to *live out our New Identity on earth.* As long as we focus on our Condition, it gets worse; but as we focus more consistently on our Position, our righteous Condition begins to conform to our righteous Position and Identity in Christ (2 Cor 3:18; Rom 5:21).

By "righteousness of God" we mean both His attitudes and actions — in other words, His character and its outworking in our lives. The Book of Romans is about a lot more than just getting to heaven when we die. Mankind was created "a little lower than the angels" (Ps 8:4-5; Heb 2:6-7) in order to demonstrate to the angels (both fallen and unfallen) that God has the right to rule the universe (He is sovereign) and to show the world that He is worthy of being known and loved. Romans is about the unveiling of God's redemptive character and purposes to the created universe, including the angels (1 Cor 11:10; 1 Pet 1:12). Therefore, as the righteousness of God is revealed in us (Rom 1:17) through progressive sanctification, we participate in God's sovereign restoration of the world and show Him as worthy of being known and loved. So when we use the term "righteousness of God" in this book we are referring to the open display before the created universe of God's character and its outworking in our lives.

Thus, Paul's good news, the "gospel of God" (Rom 1:1-4), is that our Position secured by **Christ's death** can indeed be matched by our Condition through **Christ's life.** As affirmed in Romans 3:21–4:25, believers have been set free from the Penalty of Sin — they are *justified*, declared righteous in heaven's court by faith alone in Christ alone. Their new Position and true Identity is **Righteous in Christ.** But their Condition on earth does not yet match their Position in heaven: they are free from the Penalty of Sin by Christ's *death* but not yet released from the Power of Sin by His *life*. The gospel of God assures us that by appropriating Christ's resurrection life by faith, we are delivered from the Power of Sin to reign in righteousness (5:17, 21) and thus reveal the righteousness of God (1:16-18; 3:21-22). The gospel is therefore not "complete" until the Power of God in Christ's life releases us from the power of Sin to reveal the Righteousness of God to the world and thereby to display the Glory of God in us as "sons of God" (8:14-21).

We desperately long to break the shackles of Sin so that we can be free to enjoy our relationship with God; but in the process we become more like God's beloved Son, and we bring more glory to the Father and the Son by demonstrating His righteousness in our lives. This is what *sanctifies us — sets us apart —* in the eyes of God and the world. As we further explore this invitation to more life in Him, may we be moved like the beggar to say to our Savior, "If that's the man you see, then that's the man I'll be."

CHAPTER 1

"WHO YOU GONNA CALL?"

Romans 5:1-5a

The second highest grossing film in America in 1984 was the comedy "Ghost Busters." The film was about three guys who lost their jobs at the university because of their preoccupation with spiritual things, namely ghosts. So they set up a company for hire to help people get rid of ghosts in their homes or apartments. They wore sci-fi suits and carried nuclear accelerator proton packs to get rid of the ghosts. Of course it was only a spoof on obsession with "paranormal" activity.

But, oh that we *could* call someone in the midst of real life spiritual battles! Spiritual warfare is no joke in the Christian life. We may not battle with unseen demons on a daily basis, but we do battle every day with something Paul calls Sin, often referred to as our Sin Nature.[1] And what we learn in the Bible also is that even after Salvation from the Penalty of Sin, a born-again Christian can still be in bondage to Sin. The Sin Nature is very powerful.

Lying, cheating, addictions, jealousy, anger, self-righteousness and judgment, pride — all these and many more are manufactured on a regular basis by our Sin Nature. Some of these things can dominate us our entire lives. Once sin has us in its clutches, it never wants to let go. If only we could call the "Sin Busters" to bring their spiritual accelerator power packs to zap our Sin Nature and make it go away, never to return.

---

[1] The NIV often translates the word *sarx* as "sinful nature," especially in Romans 5–8. We believe this is mistaken, though the error has been partially corrected in the latest NIV revision (2011). See Earl Radmacher and Zane C. Hodges, *The NIV Reconsidered* (Dallas, TX: Redención Viva, 1990), 113-30. In these instances, the *sarx* (literally, the "flesh") only *houses* the sin nature, as Paul depicts so graphically in Rom 7:14-25. Thus, the term Sin Nature in *this* book refers to Paul's main Greek word for *sin* in Romans, used with the definite article: *hē hamartia*. "Sin" is inherited from Adam, whose disobedience *constituted* us *sinful* (Rom 5:12, 19a).

Few things discourage the believer as much as the ongoing struggle in life with *Sin* and *Suffering*, two punches that can knock the serious Christian down and out. Sadly, this Sin Nature will afflict us until Jesus comes (1 Jn 3:1-3). But fortunately, there *is* Someone we can call to *deliver us* from the power of the Sin Nature in our lives today. And that is what we want to explore in this book. What follows is an explanation of how we can be delivered from the power of sin in our lives, as expounded by Paul in Romans 5–8. Here is a brief outline of the first half of Romans to help guide us through this rich portion of Scripture (the shaded levels cover chapters 1-3 of this book):

    I. **SIN**   **(1:1–3:20)**

    II. **SALVATION**   **(3:21–4:25)**

    III. SANCTIFICATION   **(5–8)**

        A. **Freedom from Wrath**   **(5)**

            1. **Our Deliverance *from* Wrath**   **(5:1-11)**

            2. **Our Deliverance *to* Righteousness**   **(5:12-21)**

        B. **Freedom from Sin**   **(6)**

        C. **Freedom from Law**   **(7)**

        D. **Freedom from Despair**   **(8)**

The end of Romans 4 concludes Paul's discussion of Justification, or Salvation from the *Penalty* of Sin. Romans 4:25 is thus a transitional verse that leads us out of Justification and into Sanctification, the main topic of Romans 5–8. The process of Sanctification delivers us from the Power of Sin through suffering to reveal the Righteousness of God in us in *this life* and glorify us together with Christ in *the life to come*. The two clauses of Romans 4:25 summarize how *justification* and *sanctification* are accomplished in our accepting the gift of Christ's gracious work in *death* and *resurrection*, respectively, by faith: our Justification was accomplished *once for all* by Christ's *death* (Rom 4:25a); our Sanctification will now depend on our *ongoing* appropriation of Christ's righteous *life* in us by faith (4:25b; compare 5:10):

    4:25a: He died "because of" our *sins*

        (*summarizing* **3:21–4:25**: our Justification)

    4:25b: He was raised "with a view to" our ultimate *vindication*[2]

        (*anticipating* **5:1–8:39**: our Sanctification, leading to Glorification)

---

2 Both clauses in 4:25 end with the preposition *dia* + <u>accusative noun</u>, which can be read as either *retrospective* ("because of___") or *prospective* ("for [with a view to]___"). The accusative noun *dikaiōsin* in 4:25b can mean "justification"; "absolution, acquittal"; or "vindication." If *dia* is read "because of," then both of the clauses look *backward*: Christ's death was *because of our sins*; his resurrection was *because of our justification (acquittal, absolution)*. In other words, our *sins* made Christ's *death* necessary to acquit us before God; however because Sin still works "death" in us through our unredeemed flesh from Adam (see n. 1 above), this *acquittal* (*dikaiōsin*) in turn made Christ's *resurrection life* necessary for us to *actually live* a righteous life now (Rom 5:9-10, 12-21). This preserves the symmetry in Paul's use of *dia* + <u>accusative</u> and portends the intended sense of *dikaiōsin zōēs* in 5:18 ("absolution that leads to

So as we leave Romans 4 and enter Romans 5, Paul is moving from the subject of our Justification in heaven to explain our Sanctification on earth as we look forward to our ultimate Glorification at the Judgment Seat of Christ.

1. What We Need to Know about PEACE with God 5:1

Therefore, having been justified by faith, we have peace with God through our Lord Jesus Christ.

When we are justified we have switched sides; we used to be the enemies of God (see 5:10), but now we have peace with Him. And this peace is not just future tranquility in heaven after we die. The word "have" (*echōmen*) is in the present tense and means to have *now*. Paul is talking about a calm that we have in the midst of today's hurricane pressures, and the basis of this peace is our justification by faith. We do not have to keep looking over our shoulder wondering when God is going to "get" us. He is not our enemy; we don't have to fear Him. He is *with* us and He is *for* us; He is on His team, and we are on His team.

When I was a senior in high school, one of my teachers asked the class, "Do you have peace?" I knew the answer for me was "No." I had no inner peace; I reveled in breaking the school rules. My flagrant fouls seemed harmless enough: skipping school to go to the golf course or the pool hall. But I always wondered when I would get caught. I still had an inner turmoil from doing things I knew were wrong. And then I was born again: justified by faith. At that moment I caught a glimpse of what hymn writer Horatio Gates Spafford must have experienced when he received a cablegram from his wife that his four children had gone down to a watery grave in the mid-Atlantic as the family was going to rejoin their beloved husband and father. The cablegram said, "Saved, alone." But in his great sorrow, from the depths of his soul, Spafford poured forth a song which would ring through the corridors of Christ's church forever:

> When peace, like a river, attendeth my way;
> When sorrows like sea billows roll;
> Whatever my lot, thou hast taught me to say,
> It is well, it is well, with my soul.

---

life"). But many expositors (e.g., Moo, N. T. Wright, Cranfield, Hodge, Murray) read the second clause as *prospective* (as in Matt 24:22; Mk 2:27; Jn 11:42; 12:30; 1 Cor 11:9): Christ was raised *with a view to* our *final* "justification" or "vindication" in glory (as emphasized in Rom 8:18-23, 29-30).

Whichever sense is intended for *dikaiōsin* in 4:25b, it launches the main topic of *progressive sanctification* or "righteous living" in Romans 5–8. Romans 4:25 thus frames these chapters as Paul's explanation for how Christ's death and resurrection fulfill our present calling to reveal God's righteousness *in this life* and thereby vindicate us at Christ's return; for only as we appropriate Christ's resurrection life by faith to display God's righteousness *in this life* (5:17-21) do we warrant our ultimate vindication before the world as righteous "children" and "sons" of God *in glory* (8:14-21). Thus, the *retrospective* and *prospective* views of 4:25b both enhance this understanding.

As it did for Spafford, a wave of inner peace sent me soaring twenty feet above the surface of life with all its problems and complexities. There I found a peace that passes all understanding: peace with God. But this peace is meant to foster an *abiding relationship* with God through Christ that can bolster our *present* hope and confidence through trials, as we are progressively conformed to Christ's righteous image — *sanctified* — in this life.

How could we describe that peace? We recently vacationed in the beautiful Smokies of North Carolina. Our grandchildren were with us, so one afternoon my grandson and I went on a hike. Drew, being all of six, didn't just want to hike; he also wanted to lead. So, as we headed into the forest, he confidently appointed himself the leader. But as we ambled along, the forest got darker and the trail got steeper. Finally, Drew came back a few paces to me and slipped his hand in mine. "We can lead together," he announced. Of course, there was no one to lead, just the two of us hiking. But the Christian life is a lot like that. And as we start up the mountain, we instinctively want to be in the lead. But when the trail gets rough and the sun starts going down, there is *great peace* in knowing that He is there to take our hand, and we can "lead together," just as Jesus invited us (Matt 11:28-30).

It is shocking that these days peace is just as lacking among Christians as non-Christians. Much of this can be ascribed to our penchant for rugged self-sufficiency. Perhaps you are saying, "Yes, I too experienced that peace when I became a believer; but that was, oh, so long ago. Since that time, so much anxiety and stress has come along to stab me that I've lost that peace. Now my life is full of bitterness toward people I should love. How can I regain that peace?" Well, that leads us to the second thing we need to understand before we can have freedom from the Power of Sin to display God's righteousness in this life: we need to actively exploit our access to God.

2. What We Need to Know about ACCESS to God   5:2

Through whom we also have access by faith into this grace in which we stand, and rejoice in the hope of the glory of God.

Romans 5–8 begins and ends with the assurance of two provisions of God that are crucial for us to secure freedom from the power of sin when we go through trials and suffering: our access to God's grace and the promise of sharing His glory. Paul introduces these two concepts in 5:2, and the reason is very simple: Access to God's grace enables us to be delivered from sin to the life he has for us *now*; the hope of His glory provides us with the incentive to endure trials and suffering until we receive the life he has for us *then*. Here we cover the first provision, our present access to God. The second provision, the promise of sharing His glory, will be covered in our study of Romans 5:11 (Chapter 3). Our assurance of these two provisions is based on our relationship with the Holy Spirit, and Paul will make this final connection gloriously secure in Romans 8.

Many in their quest for peace turn everywhere but to the arms of God and then rationalize away the true source of their anxiety and stress. Freud sanctioned the unrestrained pursuit of pleasure by proposing that the way to find peace is simply to forget the mixed-up conscience (1:19-20) and indulge oneself. Freud thus reneged on all personal responsibility, blaming most of our problems on the sins of our fathers. Indeed, some ministers today are taught to say nothing in the pulpit that might make people feel guilty. People have too much guilt already, young ministers are told; if they talk about sin and guilt and moral responsibility from the pulpit they only increase the risk of "neurosis." However, Paul says the way to relieve anxiety and stress is to come to God and confess to Him. John elaborates, "If any man sins, we have an advocate with the father, Jesus Christ the righteous" (1 Jn 2:1). He ever lives to make intercession for us.

The grammar of Romans 5:2 confirms our permanent access in him. The word "have" in verse 2 is the same Greek verb for "have" used in v. 1, where it is in the *present* tense. In this case, however, the *perfect* tense (*eschēkamen*) indicates *established* and *permanent* access. The word for "access" here is *prosagōgēn*, which denotes the entrance to the Holy of Holies in the heavenly temple. We desperately need to know we have ongoing access to the throne of grace, because though our *Position* is perfect, our *Condition* is not. We gained this access the moment we were justified by faith, and it is *still available* to us so that we might live fully in the power of Christ's resurrection (4:25b). While our Position is secure when we first believe, our Condition improves with time only as we avail ourselves of the power of His resurrection (Phil 3:10).

Moreover, the word "stand" in this verse (*estēkamen*) is also in the perfect tense, which implies a complete and ongoing standing in His grace. It answers the question, "But what about when I slip and fall? Will He receive me?" There will be times we are so ashamed of our failures that we instinctively think God has shut the door on us. We may pray repeatedly for deliverance from a particular besetting sin. When we do not get immediate deliverance, we assume that God has denied us access. Paul assures us we have a permanent standing before the Lord. Through His grace-tinted glasses He always sees us standing before Him. And He says, "Be anxious for nothing, but in everything by prayer and supplication, with thanksgiving, let your requests be made known to God; and the peace of God, which surpasses all understanding, will guard your hearts and minds through Christ Jesus" (Phil 4:6-7).

This concept of a permanent open-door policy must be understood before we have any assurance of freedom from the Power of Sin. That is why Paul mentions *grace* in the promise of permanent access — there is no other way to have permanent access to Him. By grace He has saved us from the penalty of sin, and by grace He will save us from the Power of Sin. If our *performance* saves us from the Penalty of Sin, then any slip-up after justification and we're back in our handcuffs, incarcerated by sin. But God knows how sinful we are and He knows that our sins cause great guilt, stress, and anxiety. Without permanent access to Him and His grace we could never have peace in this present life. Permanent access. It is God's Open Door Policy. You can *always* come in! But we also need a heavenly perspective on our *suffering*.

3. What We Need to Know about HOPE in God   5:3-4

3And not only that, but we also glory in tribulations, knowing that tribulation produces perseverance; 4and perseverance, character; and character, hope.

In his book *Terminal Generation* Hal Lindsey claimed, "Man can live about forty days without food, about three days without water, about eight minutes without air . . . but only about one second without hope."[3] He adds, "There is nothing more essential to life than hope. Without it man may be breathing, but he's dead."[4]

Hope is an elixir of life. Harold G. Wolff once conducted an investigation into the effects of hope on the body at Cornell University Medial School. Dr. Wolff reported that when a man has hope, he is "capable of incredible burdens and taking cruel punishments."[5] He investigated 25,000 American soldiers imprisoned by the Japanese in WWII. Under terrible conditions, inhumane treatment, and forced labor many died and almost all became sick. But Dr. Wolff discovered a few who showed only slight physical change during their nightmarish months in prison. One key characteristic stood out among these men: their above-average ability to hope. While in prison they organized seminars in business management, planned the homes they would live in, and even wrote word pictures describing the girls they wanted to marry. In effect, *they lived in light of their future release to go home.* Dr. Wolff concluded that this joyous, confident expectation (hope) kept them well and, in some cases, even kept them alive.

So what is the Christian's hope? This principle of hope is no less true for the Christian today. The blessed hope for the Christian, of course, is the day Christ will return for His own. In the Greek text there is no definite article ("the") before "hope," which emphasizes a *quality* in life that hopes for the glory of God.

---

3   Hal Lindsey with C. C. Carlson, *The Terminal Generation* (New York: Bantam, 1977), xi.

4   Ibid., ix.

5   Harold G. Wolff, "What Hope Can Do For Man," *Saturday Review* 40 (January, 1957), 42.

However, hope was given for today, not just tomorrow; for the present, not just the future. The glory of God refers to public manifestation and magnification of His attributes and characteristics: the righteousness of God revealed in us by faith (Rom 1:17; 3:21-22). So when the Christian hopes for the future glory of God (8:18-23, 29-30), he should be motivated to be more like Christ *now* by his joyous expectation *then*: no more Sin Nature; having perfect love; no pride; no anger; being just like Him. As John explains, "Beloved, now we are children of God; and it has not yet appeared what we shall be, but we know that when He is revealed, we shall be like Him, for we shall see Him as He is. And everyone who has this hope in Him purifies himself, just as He is pure" (1 Jn 3:1-3).

But how is this hope sustained? Specifically, by embracing God's process, that is, His working in our lives to develop Christ-like character. And how does He do that? Through *trials* of every kind. What we can so easily miss is God's purpose for trials in making us more like His Son. Our trials are His tools to purify us. Ironically, without the trials we have no hope of becoming like Him — that's why Paul says he glories or rejoices in tribulations (trials), because he knows it is God's process. The trials have an objective: Trials → Endurance → Character → Hope. The Greek word in the text for *character* is *dokimē*, which refers to the smelting process by which impurities were removed from silver or gold. Without the heat, these metals could never be purged of impurities.

We should note that the word "hope" in v. 2 is repeated at the end of v. 4. It is a cycle. As new Christians, we begin with great hope — hope of being like Jesus. In our failures we begin to get discouraged and lose hope. Nothing can be more discouraging to the believer who hopes to become more like Christ than to slip back into the habits of the Old Man or fail to be delivered from those habits to begin with. We might easily say to ourselves, "It's not working. I haven't changed. I'm just as rotten as I ever was." As the devil whispers these kinds of thoughts in our ears, we begin to lose hope of ever becoming more Christ-like. And we *may* lose *all* hope and conclude that Christianity does not work, or even that Christ is not coming back. So God brings along some trials to purify us in order to develop our Christ-like character. When we experience this process, it reminds us that God is not finished with us and it revives our hope.

Now it is important to recognize that God is not directly responsible for all the trials that come our way. Some of them, perhaps most of them, we bring on ourselves through our own foolish decisions or just plain sin. But whether self-inflicted or designed by God, trials can all serve to purify us into Christ-likeness, living a sanctified life in the power of *His* life.

Conclusion

As I reflected on our recent week of vacation with my grandkids in the Smokey Mountains — fishing, horses, hiking, boating — I had a great time watching my little grandchildren, Grace and Drew, try to ride the inner-tube behind a boat. They were adopted from different orphanages in Russia at nine and seven months but are now six years old. We asked Drew if he wanted to go first, but he is not quite as bold as his sister, so he declined. His father said, "Don't worry, Drew, daddy will go first." Drew quickly responded by saying, "We'll miss you," as he stepped away from the tube. Well, Grace didn't want to wait. She hopped on the tube right in front of daddy and had a great time.

Watching Grace gave Drew confidence, so when she finished, he was ready to give it a go. He nestled down right in front of his father, and we started moving, barely moving. Fear filled little Drew's face, so we went very slowly. He kept looking backward to make sure his dad was still there. Scot, my son-in-law, said, "Don't worry, Drew, daddy's got your back." Finally, Drew's smile spread across his face, his fear disappeared, and we picked up speed. What a time — all because Drew knew that "Daddy's got your back."

And that's what this passage is saying. Before we embark on the grand adventure of the abundant life of Salvation from the Power of Sin to realize our call to righteousness (2 Cor 5:21), we need to know that our heavenly Father has our back. Sure, we're going to ride the waves, but He's right there behind us all the way, on our side, on our team. We can ask Him whatever we want, and He will help guide us along the way. No matter how high the waves or how many times we fall, as long as Daddy has our back, there is hope, hope to become like His own Son. And when we make mistakes, His love never fails us.

So, who you gonna call? If we go into spiritual warfare on our own, we are doomed to slavery and failure. But when our Daddy's got our back, there is hope. And there is nothing to be ashamed of when we have hope. For us to progress down the trail toward Christ-likeness we need to know that God is on our side — that we have permanent access to Him, and that even the trials of life can be used to develop the character of Christ: Peace, prayer, and hope. But a fourth element in this passage is so absolutely essential for us to grasp, that it deserves its own chapter — why we need to know about the *love* of God.

CHAPTER 2

"WHAT THE WORLD NEEDS NOW"
Romans 5:5-10

People the world around are love-starved. Burt Bacharach wrote the words to the song "What the World Needs Now" in 1965 amid the turmoil of the Vietnam War. Since then the song has been recorded by over a hundred artists, and the need for love is even more obvious now with the advent of suicide bombing. The first modern suicide bombing occurred in Iran in 1980 when 13-year old Hussein Fahmideh detonated himself as he ran up to an Iraqi tank at a key point in a battle during the Iran-Iraq War. Since then suicide bombings and genocide have multiplied, each an expression of intensifying hate.

Our problem is that we have been "looking for love in all the wrong places." And we have been looking for the wrong *kind* of love. God's love is unique in our universe. The first time in Romans love of any kind is mentioned is 5:5; it is the word *agapē*, which Galatians 5:24 lists as the first fruit of the Holy Spirit. It is a divine love — its source is in God Himself. And we need to understand it if we are going to get very far down the road to becoming like Christ. Other than coming from God, the main trait of *agapē* is that it is *unconditional*, in contrast to emotional (*philē*) or erotic love (*eros*). We see this from four angles in Romans 5:5-10.

1. God's Love Is Unending   5:5

Now hope does not disappoint, because the love of God has been poured out in our hearts by the Holy Spirit who was given to us.

The gift of this divine love is a good reason for assurance that our hope of becoming more like Christ will not disappoint. Now that is quite a claim, one that needs further explanation. Much more is buried in Paul's comment about the love of God than may first meet the eye. By the time we get to the conclusion of Romans 8, it will become clear how crucial the Spirit really is in "pouring out the love of God in our hearts" in times of severe difficulty and suffering. By beginning and ending this major section (Rom 5–8) with this concept, Paul underscores exactly why "the gospel of God" (1:1, 16) is such good news: the "power of God to salvation" that trumps the power of Sin is *rooted in God's love*. This redemptive love poured out "completes" the revealing of the righteousness of God by faith (1:17; 3:21-22) in the face of His wrath against sin (1:18). The rest of this passage (5:5-11) explains *how* this love can overcome this wrath to reveal His righteousness.

Continuing the passage's emphasis on the *permanence* of God's work through Christ, the verb "poured out" (*ekkechutai*) is in the perfect tense. The emphasis here is not so much on the completed action in the past (at our conversion) as it is on our *current state* — we are loved with a complete outpouring that endures to the present. Especially important is the result that once we become believers and have received the Holy Spirit, there is nothing we can do to stop His love that was already poured out for us.

How different this is from human love. Do you remember the first time you fell in love? I do. I still remember her dark, brown hair. Dimples. Big brown eyes like Faline, Bambi's girlfriend. We did everything together — walked, talked, rode horses. And it lasted three years, all the way from third through fifth grade. The spell was broken in the beginning of sixth grade. She cut her pigtails. Yes, there was something about those pigtails. I don't know to this day if I loved her or her pigtails more, but when the pigtails were gone, so was my love.

We smile and say, "Well, that's just puppy love." Yeah, but it's real to the *puppy*. And I have seen more than one marriage break up over "cut pigtails." So it is with human love. In her book *Women Who Love Too Much* Robin Norwood describes the syndrome of people who are addicted to romantic love.[1] Very much like an addictive drug, its "high" cannot be sustained. It may last six months or a year and six months, but sooner or later, it will dissipate.

M. Scott Peck echoes Norwood's sentiments in his book *The Road Less Traveled:* [2]the "cloud nine" phase of a relationship lasts an average of two years. When the couple then "falls out of love" (if they are living together), they have to *choose* whether to love each other. Peck thus calls "falling in love" Nature's trick to get us to the altar. Most of us in our right minds, he says, would never make the kinds of promises usually heard in marriage vows. Why? Because we cannot sustain

---

1   Robin Norwood, *Women Who Love Too Much* (New York: Simon & Schuster, 1985).
2   M. Scott Peck, *The Road Less Traveled* (New York: Simon & Schuster, 1978), 86-110.

that kind of love. Sooner or later the beloved will do enough things to irritate or disillusion the lover that it will break the spell.

When my wife Betty and I were dating, we were so much in love we thought it could never stop. If you were on a Houston freeway in those days, you might have sworn you saw a car driven by a two-headed person. I owned the powerful thirty-six horse 1960 VW Beatle with stick shift and bucket seats. Buckets seats don't work when you are in love. So I had to teach Betty to squeeze into my seat and shift the gears while I worked the clutch, brakes, and accelerator with my feet. In love. We even had our own song: Ed Ames' "My Cup Runneth Over with Love." Whenever I needed some love, I'd just hold out my cup to Betty, and she would gladly fill it from her cup, and vice versa. Wonderful.

Then we got married. Our first year was easy, no problem, and most of the popular print said it was the toughest, so we thought we had it made. Then, due to no planning of our own, Betty got pregnant. We were not prepared for the changes that would bring into our marriage. One day I held out my love cup for Betty to fill only to find that her cup had a crack in it and was empty. Then I looked at my cup and, sure enough, it too had a crack in it and was empty. You can't fill someone else's cup if yours is empty. It took us years to discover that as humans we are incapable of keeping another's cup full. We are too needy, too selfish. That's when we found only one love that could keep our cup full.

God's unending love. He never stops pouring from His infinite supply. Only He can keep our cups full. We also discovered that when our own cup is overflowing with God's love, we can share from the surplus with others who need this same love. Yes, it is unending, but God's love is also *undeserved*.

2. God's Love Is Undeserved   5:6-8

6For when we were still without strength, in due time Christ died for the ungodly. 7For scarcely for a righteous man will one die; yet perhaps for a good man someone would even dare to die. 8But God demonstrates His own love toward us, in that while we were still sinners, Christ died for us.

Note carefully these descriptors: "without strength," "the ungodly," "still sinners." God is making it clear that we had nothing in ourselves to commend us to Him; we were destined for the wrath God reveals against "*all* ungodliness and unrighteousness of men" (1:18). There was nothing attractive about us. It was all repulsive to Him, but He loved us anyway. Because we tend to gloss over our sin, to compare ourselves with others we deem less godly than ourselves, we will probably never be able to comprehend what a powerful and outrageous statement is made in these verses — what a contrast to human love! We are drawn to the lovely and lovable, not to the ugly and fractious. So, Paul argues, there might be some good person we would die for — our spouse, our children, maybe even a fellow soldier or friend — but who of us would die for Jeffrey Dahmer, Pol Pot, bin Laden, or Hitler? None of us. And the fact that Christ died for *all* of us while we were ungodly and sinful is precisely what proves His love for us.

Are we *confident* of this undeserved love? A friend of mine lived for a time next to an unattached granddaughter of H. L. Hunt, the oil billionaire. After my friend became wealthy in his own right and had two unattached daughters of his own, he and his wife made the decision not to leave their money to their two daughters. When I asked him why, he said, "I watched the kind of guys that chased after Hunt's granddaughter. I would never want to leave my girls in that situation. They would never know if they were really loved." God's love demonstrated through Christ's death for us should have just the opposite effect for those who receive it — there should *never* be any doubt. He loved us when we were completely debt-ridden and poverty-stricken (spiritually).

This kind of love is evident in one of my favorite stories about the little girl who loved dollies. One evening the local pastor came for a visit. When the little girl's mother slipped into the kitchen to make some coffee, the little girl appeared before the honored guest and asked him if he liked dollies. "Of course," he responded, trying to be polite. "Well, then, would you like to see my dollies?" asked the little girl. "Why, of course I would," replied the pastor. So the little girl proceeded to bring her dolly collection from her room to the living room one by one until they were all arranged around the coffee table.

Very impressed, the pastor asked, "Now, which one is your favorite dolly?" The little girl hesitated and then asked, "Are you sure you like dollies?" "Yes, yes, of course," answered the pastor. "Then I will show you my favorite dolly," said the little girl. So she ran back to her room and came out with an old Raggedy Anne dolly which was missing one leg, half her hair, and her belly button. Astonished, the pastor asked, "Why is this doll your favorite when you have so many other beautiful dolls?" Clutching her Raggedy Anne dolly very close, the little girl looked down fondly and said, "If I didn't love this dolly, nobody would."

That is just like God's love. When sin had degraded us to our most unlovable condition, Christ came to woo us. Sin had "torn off one of my legs"; moral failure had "torn away half my hair"; duplicity had "ripped out my belly button." I was totally repulsive, but He loved me anyway. If God's love is unending and undeserved, it is also *unlimited*.

3. God's Love Is Unlimited   5:9-10

9Much more then, having now been justified by His blood, we shall be saved from wrath through Him. 10For if when we were enemies we were reconciled to God through the death of His Son, much more, having been reconciled, we shall be saved by His life.

There is a progression depicted in these verses that is matched step-for-step by the depth of God's love:

   a. "Ungodly" (v. 6) = *asebōn*: absence of God's character, a passive trait
   b. "Sinners" (v. 8) = *hamartōlōn*: missing the mark, an active trait
   c. "Enemies" (v. 10) = *echthroi*: in open rebellion

Paul's argument is simple but profound. The words "much more" jump out at us twice in these verses. If God loved us when we were *ungodly*, *sinners*, and now even *enemies*, how much more must He love us now that we are His children, justified and reconciled?

In reality, the depth of that kind of love is unfathomable. In the days of Nansen, the great arctic explorer, there was no sonar for ship captains to monitor the depth of the water where they were sailing. At one point in his voyages, Nansen wanted to know how deep the ocean was, so he lowered a plumb bob. It did not hit the bottom, so he wrote in his journal "Deeper than that." The next day he tied more line on the bob, but it still didn't reach bottom, so Nansen wrote in his log "Deeper than that." Finally, he tied all the line available on the ship and lowered the bob. No bottom. He wrote once again in his log "Deeper than that," and sailed away.

And so shall we sail away from this great passage on God's love, not knowing how deep His love is for us. We will simply have to be satisfied by saying, "Deeper than that." Young or old (whether by age or by experience in the faith), Christians need confidence of this kind of love. This is because in our flesh, our hearts are prone to wander. If, in the initial stages of our growth after we become believers, we are still uncertain as to whether our sins will prevent God's love for us, we may just collapse on the floor and quit.

Perhaps even harder to handle are the sins believers commit *after* they have been in the faith for decades. The divine love attested in these verses sets the stage for the incredible grace that Paul will describe by the end of the chapter: grace that is greater than all our sin. This grace grows out of His immeasurable love. If His love is "deeper than that," then it can still inundate any mountain of sin we could pile up.

The other idea that is difficult for us to humanly fathom is the notion of "substitution." One little girl was just beginning to memorize verses from the Bible and she was learning John 3:16. Half way through her memorizing, she came to her daddy with a question. "Daddy, if God loved us so much, why didn't

He die for us instead of sending His Son?" For a moment the father was stumped. Then the answer dawned on him, and he said, "Sweetheart, it took much more love for God the Father to send His Son than to die for us Himself, just as it would be easier for me to die to save our family than to send you in my place."

This idea of dying "for us" is conveyed by the Greek word *huper*, which occurs four times in 5:6-8, translated each time as "for." But "for" does not adequately convey the meaning of the Greek word: It literally means "in lieu of." Scarcely will anyone die *in lieu of* a righteous man; but Christ died *in lieu of* the ungodly. While we were still sinners, Christ died "in our place." This establishes another foundational principle for the victorious Christian life that theologians call the "substitutionary death" of Christ; He died "in our place." Paul presents this as a completed fact. He was our substitute on the cross. He took upon Himself the penalty for our sins. I would claim that the hardest thing in the world for an unbeliever to believe is that Jesus is his substitute in death.

But if the substitutionary Death of Christ is the hardest thing for the unbeliever to believe, then the hardest thing in the world for the *believer* to understand is the substitutionary *Life* of Christ — that is the overwhelming truth that Paul introduces in Romans 5:1-11. In fact, this is precisely the passage in which Paul transitions from the substitutionary Death of Christ (5:6-8) to the substitutionary Life of Christ (5:9-10), as portended by 4:25.[3] This is also the first time the word "saved" occurs in Romans, and in order to grasp the significance of this transition, we need to look closer at Paul's use of this concept in these two verses.

Digging Deeper: Paul's Use of "Wrath" and "Saved" in Romans 5–8

In these two verses the readers were *already* justified (5:9) and reconciled (5:10) but they have *not yet* been "saved." In both verses justification is in the *past* and reconciliation is in the *past*, but the tense of the saving action in both verses is *future*. If Paul's readers had died before reading the Book of Romans, they would go to heaven because they were *justified* and *reconciled* to God but they would not yet be "saved." What are we to make of this? Could the word "saved" here mean something *other* than their destiny in heaven when they die? The idea here is that of "deliverance." But it is not the same as justification, or deliverance from the Penalty of Sin. It is "much more": besides deliverance **from** *sin and death*, Paul also has in view deliverance **to** *a greater destiny,* both now and in the life to come.

---

3   See note 2 of the previous chapter and associated text dealing with the interpretation of Rom 4:25.

This is precisely the broader implication of Paul's use of the related noun *sōteria* ("salvation") in Romans 1:16 to explain the Power of God in light of what is being revealed (1:17-18): God's *righteousness* and His *wrath*. Many suggest that this "wrath" (*orgē*, in both 1:18 and 5:9) refers to God's judgment on unbelievers for eternity. However, the wrath of God in 1:18 is *presently being revealed* (the best sense for the Greek present tense, *apokaluptetai*). It is *not* referring to an event that will take place at the Great White Throne. (In fact, *no* use of *orgē* in the NT is linked directly with the Great White Throne.) So it appears that the wrath in Romans 1:18 is not connected with "getting to heaven." It is *present* judgment that culminates in the Day of Wrath at the end of the present age (2:5; compare Rev 6:16-17).

The wrath of Romans 1 is depicted as three stages of descending consequences of Sin, marked by the phrase "God gave them over" (*paredōken autous ho theos,* 1:24, 26, 28). The last stage is to have a mind that is "disapproved" (*adokimos*), "unable to tell right from wrong," the starkest possible contrast to our calling to reveal the righteousness of God by faith (1:17; 3:21-22). Hence, we are *incarcerated* by Sin, *unable* to fulfill the "gospel of God" (1:1, 16).

Let's plug this meaning into Romans 5:9 to see if it makes sense: "Much more, then, having now been justified by His blood, we shall be saved from *wrath* [incarceration by Sin] through Him." If this is what "wrath" means in 5:9, then "saved" in 5:9 must refer to our deliverance from this tyranny of Sin in our lives; we are *released* to reveal His righteousness now and share greater glory with Him in the life to come. Romans 5:10 says that we were **reconciled** (past tense) through the *death* of His Son, but we shall be **saved** (future tense) through His *life*. We were saved from the Penalty of sin by His death, but we shall be saved from the Power of sin by His life. Whereas we gained eternal life as He became our *substitute in death,* we shall enjoy a more abundant life now *and* in the life to come if we allow Him to become our *substitute in life,* so that we might *reign* in life through God's abundant gift of grace in Christ's righteous life (5:17, 21). This is totally consistent with the truth taught in summary form in Galatians, the "Shorter Romans": "I am crucified with Christ; nevertheless, I live; yet not I, but *Christ lives in me*" (Gal 2:20).

In this transitional section of Romans, Paul therefore shifts his focus from deliverance from the Penalty of sin (justification) to deliverance from the Power of sin (sanctification). Being "saved" is *to be delivered **from** the tyranny of Sin* (the *wrath*[4] of Rom 1:18; 5:9-10) **to** *a purified, righteous life now.* This definition

---

4 On Paul's use of "wrath" in Romans as *applicable to believers*, see René A. López, "Do Believers Experience the Wrath of God?" *Journal of the Grace Evangelical Society* 15, no. 2 (Autumn 2002): 45-66.

is crucial, since the salvation in Romans 5–8 is consistently seen to depend on the substitutionary *life*[5] of Christ (Rom 4:25b; 5:10).

[END OF EXCURSUS]

Several other foundational concepts also appear for the first time in Romans 5:1-11; concepts that unite chapters 5–8 and are key to a victorious Christian life. We have seen that divine love is mentioned for the first time in this passage. So too is the Holy Spirit, who literally pervades chapter eight as the key to revealing the righteousness of God in us. But before we leave what may be the greatest passage on God's love in the whole Bible, we need to observe another characteristic of His love which stares at us from each and every verse.

4. God's Love Is *Unselfish*   5:6-10

Notice all the figures in the verses above that refer to Christ's substitutionary act: "died" (vv. 6, 8); "blood" (v. 9); "death" (v. 10). These allusions to His death all point to His perfectly selfless sacrifice. As Paul acknowledges in v. 7, human analogies for such sacrificial love fall short, but the following narrative helps depict the "selflessness" entailed in the sacrifice.

Dale Galloway relates the story of Chad, a third grade boy who was new in the neighborhood.[6] He was a shy boy who did not make friends as quickly as most of the other boys. He went through the fall without making a single friend. Every day Chad's mother would stand at the window and watch as the kids got off the bus. Chad was always the last one off. The other kids came out laughing and skipping, some of them hand in hand. Then came Chad, always alone. Chad's mom had high hopes for the next semester. But it was the same story every day.

In the middle of January, Chad came to his mother and said, "Mom, you know Valentines Day will be coming in about a month. I have just enough time to make a valentine for every member of my class. I want each of them to know how much I love them." Chad's mother thought, *Oh, Chad, I wish you wouldn't do that. It will be a sad day for you.* But she couldn't bear to dampen his enthusiasm, so they went to the store and bought everything they would need to make the valentines. Each day Chad made a different valentine, a unique one for each member of his class. Valentines Day came with a freeze, but that didn't slow Chad down. He packed up his lunch box and valentines and marched out the front door.

---

5   "Since the term 'life' and its derivatives appear a mere three times from [*sic*] chapters 1–4 ... and twenty-five times in chapters 5–8 ..., this indicates the noun 'life' and the verb 'live' bind chapters 5–8." See René A. López, *Romans Unlocked: Power to Deliver,* Revised Edition (Springfield, MO: 21st Century, 2009), 103.

6   Dale E. Galloway, *Dream a New Dream* (London: Tyndale House, 1975), 78.

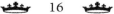

Through the window overlooking the front yard, Chad's mom watched him get on the bus. "This will be a tough day for Chad," she mused. "I better have some warm cookies and milk waiting for him when he gets home."

Chad's mother heard the squeaking of school bus brakes in time to go back to the window and looked at the kids getting off the bus. They were laughing and skipping as usual, some of them with big bags of valentines under their arms. And sure enough, there came Chad, by himself. Only his mom noticed that he was walking a little faster than usual. "Oh, he's about to cry," she imagined. Opening the front door to welcome him, she said, "Chad, welcome home. Mommy has some cookies and warm milk waiting for you on the kitchen table." But Chad traipsed right by the cookies and marched down the hall towards his bedroom. "Not one, Mom. Not a single one. I didn't miss a one. They all know now how much I love them." Chad's love was completely unselfish, just like God's love for us.

Divine love is like a magic penny. When you give it away, it just comes right back. Kids just seem to understand this truth. Apparently, they haven't lived long enough for their perspectives to become skewed or jaded. I think I first learned this truth from my daughter Christie. One day, after my shower, there was a light knock on the bathroom door. The next thing I observed was some folded up papers being shoved under the door. It was my five-year-old, who was just learning to read and write in kindergarten. I unfolded the three papers. On the first piece of paper she had scratched out "My Sinnes" on the top and wrote "Anderson, Christie" next to that. Then she listed her "sinnes": "I hid from my mother, I argued with my brother, I played chase in the house, I didin't pratise my peano, I realy sinned." *Man*, I thought, *we are raising a kid with an overly sensitive conscience.* She had two other sheets of paper, so I looked at the next one. It was a little more positive. It said, "I love my mommy, I love my daddy, I love Jimmy [her older brother], I love me, and I love you too." *Hmmm*, I thought, *how could she love her older brother who picks on her, and her parents, and herself, and you too? Where did she get that?*

Then I read the third piece of paper and had my answer. It read, "Jesus loves me, this sine O, for the bible tells me so. Letose oones to him be laling, they are week, but he is sraling. Yes, Jesus loves me; yes, Jesus loves me; yes, Jesus loves me, the bible tels me so." I looked at these three little sheets of paper and realized, "O my gosh. This is exactly what Romans is teaching us! We cannot love others until we first *recognize* our sinful condition, *realize* how much God loves us, and *receive* that sacrificial love through Jesus."

Burt Bacharach *was* right. What the world needs now is love, sweet love. The world needs it and we need it. But there's no shortage of God's mercy, and there's no shortage of His love. And when we have a cup full of God's love, which is

Unending, Undeserved, Unlimited, and Unselfish, amazingly, we can share His love with others out of the overflow.

CHAPTER 3

"BUSTED STRINGS AND BROKEN DREAMS"
Romans 5:11

*A*nd *not only that, but we also rejoice in God through our Lord Jesus Christ, through whom we have now received the reconciliation.*

Remember the four things we have to know in this passage: *peace, access, hope, love?* The Christian life goes beyond just *knowing* these things. In v. 11, we are urged not only to *know* these things but also to do something. One word in 5:1-11 is repeated three times: Rejoice. The Greek verb *kauchōmai* is important because it also occurs in 5:2 where it is translated "rejoice," and again in 5:3 where it is translated "glory" (NKJV) or "rejoice" (NIV). With the words "and not only that" in v. 3 and again in v. 11 the passage builds to a crescendo of joy. But this kind of rejoicing is a choice and a vital component of our freedom from the Power of Sin. Rejoicing in the face of our broken dreams is a conscious choice we must make in this life.

George Frederick Watts has a painting in the Tate Gallery in London labeled "Hope." It's the picture of a woman sitting on a globe, planet earth. And on her lap is a harp with every string in it broken except one. She sits blind-folded, bent over with her ear right next to the harp and her finger about to pluck that last, unbroken string. And that is her last hope. Stories abound about people who have been inspired by this painting. One gentleman headed out to a bridge over the Thames River to take his life. But as he passed by this painting, he thought of his little boy at home and said to himself, "He is my last string, my last hope." The depressed man went home to raise his son. "But," I thought, "what if his little boy grows up to be a big bust, a big disappointment? Then his last string is broken, and he has no hope."

Not so for the Christian. Broken dreams consist of unfulfilled expectations. If we tie up our hopes, our expectations in this world, then we are bound to be disappointed, disillusioned by busted strings and broken dreams. But God is writing a message in those broken dreams. The message is that this world is passing away. We have a hope — an expectation — that cannot be disappointed, a string which cannot be broken, a dream that can never be dashed. It is our hope in the glory of God. In good times or bad we can praise His name, we can rejoice — if we *choose* to. If we choose *not* to we can live just like the non-Christian, simply going through life as though Christ does not make any difference. That is, until we die.

It is said that everyone dreams of one life but gets to live out another. People who believe that chance or fate (or "karma") governs the universe and the fulfillment of their dreams will be left empty-handed. They don't get to live out their dreams and are forced to live some other life. Not much hope. However, even religious people, like Judas, can succumb to the disappointment of broken dreams. He was religious and he had a dream of ruling on one of the twelve thrones over the twelve tribes of Israel during the Kingdom that Jesus would one day establish (Matt 19:28). There was nothing wrong with that dream; the other disciples had the same dream, and Jesus even encouraged it. But Judas' dream did not quite work out as he intended. Just like a lot of Christians, his dream was tied to the here and now.

When Jesus failed to set up His kingdom at that time and was instead crucified on a cross, Judas' cherished dream went up in smoke, and he selfishly took his life rather than accept defeat. There is another option, another way to deal with broken dreams. Again, we are just laying the foundation for an abundant Christian life, a victorious life. So, it is critical at the outset on our journey to Christ-likeness that we are able to deal with broken dreams — we all have them. So did Jesus. The question is will we turn out like Jesus . . . or Judas?

Broken dreams can adversely affect our relationship with God through disillusionment, anger, and lack of trust, which is another way of saying *lack of faith*. In fact, broken dreams can make a shipwreck of our faith (1 Tim 1:19). When our faith crumbles, we often descend into a downward spiral of sin. So, in order to find *deliverance* in our lives as believers — freedom from the Power of Sin — we need to *choose* to rejoice. As we go through this passage again, we will find we are to rejoice in the right *Product*, the right *Process*, and the right *Person*. Many of our dreams are simply tied to the wrong product, or goals in life. Or we pursue them using the wrong methods. Or our dreams are tied to the wrong person: our mate, our children, our boss at work, our coach. If we tie our dreams to the wrong product, process, or person, they *beg* to be broken.

1. Rejoice in the Right *Product* 5:2

. . . through whom also we have access by faith into this grace in which we stand, and rejoice in hope of the glory of God.

This Greek word (*kauchōmai*) is not the usual word for rejoicing in the NT (*chairein*). It adds something beyond just a smile or simple joy — it includes the idea of celebration, even boasting (as we shall see in v. 11). It says we can rejoice, we can celebrate, we can even *boast* in the right *product*. So, what is this product? It is related to *hope* — hope of *becoming like* Christ, which leads to the glory of God. Remember, the glory of God refers to an open, public display of His character (8:18-21), especially the quality of *righteousness* (1:17; 3:21-22). The more we become like Christ, the more the character of God is on display for the universe (man and angels) to see in His *people*: perfected sons of God who look like Christ (8:29).

The best time to see His righteousness in us *now* is *in the very midst* of our broken dreams. When everything in life goes just according to script, even non-Christians can rejoice; yet, even gaining the whole world will not necessarily make us more like Christ. Ironically, it is through our broken dreams that we move closer to being like Christ.

Even Jesus had broken dreams. According to the first three Gospels, Jesus did not go around Israel preaching the cross or the resurrection. He preached the good news (the gospel) of the kingdom (Mk 1:16) as their very King, their Messiah. "Let's do it! I'm your King. Accept Me." But they didn't accept Him. They crucified Him. They broke His heart. They broke His dream. It may have been the greatest broken dream in history. But didn't Jesus turn His tragedy into a triumph? He wants us to do the same.

There is a little town in Alabama called Enterprise. It was a sharecropper's town, dependent on cotton, that is, until an uninvited guest came to town. His name was Boll Weevil. He ate up the entire cotton crop of Enterprise. He destroyed their livelihood. Not knowing what to do, the farmers scratched their heads and said, "Well, we could plant peanuts." So they planted peanuts, and the peanuts turned into a cash crop greater than cotton had ever been. So they went down town and made a monument to the boll weevil that still stands in Enterprise to this day. They were so grateful for the visit of the boll weevil, because the whole county wound up wealthier than they had been with cotton. You may have had a boll weevil visit your life. He has eaten up your funds or your health or your career. Have you ever thought of making a monument to *that* boll weevil?

Some of you are probably thinking, "Brother Dave, you've really lost it." Maybe so. But the Apostle Paul was playing the same tune when he wrote Romans and had lived long enough to experience lots of busted strings and broken dreams. Three times in our passage he encourages us to *rejoice* right in the midst of our frustrated expectations.

Not even the prelates of Rome during the Renaissance could figure it out. Their slaves cut marble out of the quarries; they dragged the marble to the rafts, floated it down the river, and set it before Michelangelo. But all he ever seemed to do was chip away at the precious marble. Chip, chip, chip, chip. As he chipped away, soon there was more marble on the floor than on the block. As the onlookers watched the marble block getting smaller day by day, they were tempted to say, "Hey, buddy, are you gonna leave any marble?" Michelangelo's reply was telling: "As the chips fall, the image emerges."

Our broken dreams are the chips. If we are bitter and disillusioned, it is because our focus is on the chips instead of the image that is emerging. The image will never disappoint us. That is why Christians can go through this life with its good times and bad (busted strings and broken dreams) and still rejoice. The good times are good, but the bad times are better, because through disillusionment (the death of our dreams), our "hearts" are edified (Eccl 7:1-14)[1] and we can make more progress toward our greatest hope, which is Christ-like righteousness.

This is the right Product, what will be left over at the end of your life, what will last, our greatest legacy: Christ-likeness. "And not only that, but we also rejoice" in the right *Process*.

2. Rejoicing in the Right *Process*   5:3-4

3And not only that, but we also glory in tribulations, knowing that tribulation produces perseverance; 4and perseverance, character; and character, hope.

Here the word "glory" is the same word (*kauchōmai*) that is translated "rejoice" in verses 2 and 11. This verse says to rejoice in tribulations. Howard Hendricks, Professor Emeritus of Dallas Theological Seminary, used to sit in class, look at us, and then say as only he could, "Gentlemen, you all want the product, don't you? But none of you wants the process. You can't have the product [Christ-likeness] without the process." In other words, we could not become like Jesus without going through what Jesus went through. Of course, we all just sat there nodding our heads, "Amen, Prof, preach it." But as the years go by and we experience some of the process, will we still rejoice?

---

1   On the benefits of disillusionment in Ecclesiastes, see James Reitman, *Unlocking Wisdom: Forming Agents of God in the House of Mourning* (Springfield, MO: 21st Century Press, 2008), 181-354; and "'God's Eye' for the *Imago Dei*: Wise Advocacy amid Disillusionment in Job and Ecclesiastes," *Trinity Journal* 31NS (2010), 115-34.

So, what is the process? Trials and tribulations produce perseverance or endurance. It sounds a lot like James 1:2-4 where we are also told to rejoice when we fall into various trials, since these trials will produce endurance. The word for endurance is *hupomonē*, which combines the Greek words for "under" and "remain." This is what endurance is. To *remain under* whatever the circumstances might be. In this case, to remain under God's will is to stay under the protective umbrella of His grace (Rom 5:1) when the storms of life hit. Don't lose hope. That's just what Satan is waiting for. He looks for those who have left the protection of the umbrella. There is no safer place for you than right in the center of God's will for your life.

As we remain under God's will during the storms of life, God works on us like a sculptor with a chisel to reproduce in us the image of His Son. If we step out from under the umbrella of grace and revert to the false appeal of *self*-protection we abort the process. Unlike the marble, of course, we are wounded by the cut of the chisel and we all try to avoid pain. However, while stepping out from under the umbrella may stop the *pain*, it will also stop the *process*. Paul says we can rejoice in these trials, even celebrate; indeed, even boast! Using the same word boast (*kauchōmai*) in another passage (2 Cor 12:1ff), Paul prefers *not* to boast in his supernatural revelations lest he get puffed up with pride, so he chooses rather to boast/rejoice/celebrate in his weaknesses.

When I think of perseverance, I remember the story of a little boy named Glenn growing up in Kansas. He lived out in the country with just a one-room schoolhouse for all the kids of all grades. It was his job to make sure the fire was lit before school started to keep everyone warm. One morning as he and his older brother Floyd came to light the fire, they did not realize there was gasoline in the can to pour on the logs instead of the normal kerosene. They lit the gasoline, and there was an explosion that ignited both boys' clothes. Glenn ran out, but his brother was still in the schoolhouse. To his own peril, Glenn ran back and dragged his brother out. Floyd died of his burns. Glenn survived, but his legs looked like burnt marshmallows. The doctors recommended amputation and thought he would never walk again. He was just eight years old.

After two years of skin grafts and exercises Glenn took his first step. He never learned to walk well, but he did find that he could at least lean on the plow as the horses pulled it along during the farming season. The horses would drag him along until one day he found he could lope along while he was leaning on the plow. Before long, he was running. He won his first race at age twelve and went to college at age twenty. Oddly enough, Glenn still could not walk very well, but he could run. He had the dream of becoming the fastest runner in the world. He was not that good at the sprints, but the ability to endure pain enabled him to become good at the mile. Glenn Cunningham set two world records in the mile and became the greatest miler of his era.

However, the Glenn Cunningham story is more than just about a man who, against all odds, became a great runner. It is also the story of a man of great faith in Jesus Christ. Most of us are familiar with the movie *Chariots of Fire,* the story of Eric Liddell and his stand for the Sabbath, but Cunningham's faith was even more public than Liddell's refusal to compete on Sunday. It was well known that Cunningham did not smoke or drink because of his faith. Since there was so much admiration for him among the spectators, no one smoked when he came to a track meet. He had that kind of impact and inspiration. Another great miler from Kansas, Jim Ryan, once said, "The key to becoming a great miler is one's ability to endure pain."

For the most part, all the world has to offer is busted strings and broken dreams. But if we live by faith in light of our future inheritance in God, He will enable us to endure our pain by the power of the Holy Spirit, as Paul will conclude in Rom 8:17-30. And if we endure, the process of suffering produces character: Christ-likeness. What legacy do you want to leave when your life is over? An inheritance for your kids? The best legacy we could ever leave is a model of Christ-likeness. If that is the right *Product,* a string that cannot be broken, then we can also rejoice in the right *Process.* The right Process that leads to the right Product will involve trials, but we can endure the pain when we remember that "all who desire to live godly in Christ Jesus will suffer" (2 Tim 3:12). If we try to avoid this pain and suffering by stepping out from under the umbrella of God's grace. In that case, of course, we will suffer anyway, but *that* suffering will be wasted since it does not display the righteous Christ-likeness that endures forever in the glory of God (1 Pet 2:20-25; 3:8-17; 4:12-19). And this "display" requires rejoicing in the right *Person.*

3. Rejoicing in the Right Person   5:11

And not only that, but we also rejoice in God through our Lord Jesus Christ, through whom we have now received the reconciliation.

Thus we come to the consummation of Paul's rejoicing, and it bears almost the same sense — i.e., *boasting* — that we discussed above. This verse also alludes to the same *reconciliation* mentioned in 5:1 ("we have peace with God"). This is a literary device known as *inclusio,* used to highlight the passage's main theme and to distinguish it from the preceding and following text. His summary point here is that because of our reconciliation to God in Christ, we can "boast" in God through Christ (5:1-2, 11), by whose death *and* life we are being delivered (5:3-10; compare 4:25).

How is God the source of our boasting? He is righteous. He is loving. He is faithful. He is not out to make us miserable. He is unchanging. He will not woo us one day and turn away the next. He is not out to trick us or deceive us. He does not derive pleasure from watching us suffer. But most importantly, all of these traits are rooted in God's grace and availed for us by faith (5:2). We can endure our present trials, not because of any natural ability to protect ourselves but by grace through faith, in light of the hope He gives us, in spite of suffering, so that we might escape wrath against sin and truly live, both now and in the world to come (5:9-10). It is because of our reconciliation to God through Christ that this life is even possible for us. And we dare not forget it, for *our life in His life is always at risk of reverting to that flesh-driven Adamic self-sufficiency from which we were released.*

In the literary transition to the present passage (4:25), Paul's main point was that we were **released from condemnation** by Christ's death *with a view to* **living a righteous life now** through His resurrection life *and* **sharing His glory** when He returns. Now that Paul has reminded us of our high privilege in being reconciled to God through His death, the remainder of Romans 5–8 will focus on *living out* our deliverance from sin and death in Adam (in the flesh) to righteousness and life in Christ (in the Spirit) in light of the glory to come. Since God's plan for us to escape His wrath against sin and to display His righteousness to the world by faith is at the core of the "gospel of God" (1:1, 16-18), Romans 5–8 thus constitutes Paul's extended exposition of this more abundant deliverance through Christ's resurrection life (4:25b).

CHAPTER 4

"HUMANITY, WE HAVE A PROBLEM"
Romans 5:12-21

[12]*Therefore, just as through one man sin entered the world, and death through sin, and thus death spread to all men, because all sinned —* [13](*For until the law sin was in the world, but sin is not imputed when there is no law.* [14]*Nevertheless death reigned from Adam to Moses, even over those who had not sinned according to the likeness of the transgression of Adam, who is a type of Him who was to come.* [15]*But the free gift is not like the offense. For if by the one man's offense many died, much more the grace of God and the gift by the grace of the one Man, Jesus Christ, abounded to many.* [16]*And the gift is not like that which came through the one who sinned. For the judgment which came from one offense resulted in condemnation, but the free gift which came from many offenses resulted in justification.* [17]*For if by the one man's offense death reigned through the one, much more those who receive abundance of grace and of the gift of righteousness will reign in life through the One, Jesus Christ.*)*

[18]*Therefore, as through one man's offense judgment came to all men, resulting in condemnation, even so through one Man's righteous act the free gift came to all men, resulting in justification of life.* [19]*For as by one man's disobedience many were made sinners, so also by one Man's obedience many will be made righteous.* [20]*Moreover the law entered that the offense might abound. But where sin abounded, grace abounded much more,* [21]*so that as sin reigned in death, even so grace might reign through righteousness to eternal life through Jesus Christ our Lord.*

I have seen all the hurricanes that have gone through Texas since 1963 but I have never seen one like Ike. It didn't take a meteorologist to look at the radar screen in early September 2008 and see Hurricane Ike occupying what appeared to be the entire Gulf of Mexico and heading straight toward Texas for one to be able to say, "Houston, we have a problem." About a week into the city's recovery, my wife met someone who was driving a truck, trying to help get electricity reestablished in our neighborhood. She asked where he was from, and he replied, "Virginia." We discovered that people came from all over to help in the recovery. Obviously, we needed outside resources to recover. Would Houston recover? Sure, but it was going to take some time and it was going to require outside resources.

In much the same way, "Hurricane Satan" blew into the Garden of Eden soon after God created Adam and Eve. And we have had a spiritual blackout in the human race ever since, such that one might well observe, "Humanity, we have a problem." But we do not have the resources to reverse the damage of that hurricane. Will humanity recover? The Bible says yes, but just as it did for Houston, it will take some time and some outside resources.

If spiritual recovery is needed for humanity, then it is needed in all our lives. The Bible teaches that we were all born in a spiritual blackout, a spiritual disconnect between ourselves and our Maker. Acts 17:27 says the unbeliever can *grope for* the light, but he cannot *create* the light — it is God who said, "Let there be light." Fortunately, God has brought light to every man who has come into the world (Jn 1:9). God is no respecter of persons; He gives every person the opportunity to know Him. But the light comes from God — it is an external resource. If the Bible says anything about man in his fallen condition, it is that he does not have the resources within himself ("in Adam") to solve the problems of humanity at large or those of any given individual.

Justification — being declared righteous in the courtroom of heaven — gives us access to heaven. But the goal of our redemption is not just to get us to heaven when we die. The goal is for us to display God's righteousness on earth and thereby bring Him glory for eternity. And to do this, we need *deliverance*, not only from the Penalty of sin but also from the Power of sin. So, as Paul has transitioned out of Justification (Rom 3:21-4:25, salvation from the Penalty of sin) into Progressive Sanctification (Rom 5–8, salvation from the Power of sin) he has provided us with powerful incentive toward sanctification by proposing five forward-looking dispositions necessary for us to finish the course with confidence (5:1-11):

1. **Peace**: God for us, not against us
2. **Prayer**: permanent, open access to the throne of grace
3. **Hope**: of God's glory in conforming to Christ, the ultimate goal of our salvation
4. **Love**: God's perfect, unconditional love, even after our repeated failures
5. **Joy**: true celebration in our trials because God uses them to help conform us to Christ.

Having grounded our confidence to move forward with these five truths, Paul is ready in Romans 5:12-21 to explain how the Power of God through Christ's work can deliver us from the Power of Sin in Adam to actually *reveal* in us the righteousness of God (Rom 1:1-4, 16-18; 4:20-25). The Sculptor wants to take pliable "clay" (the reconciled "children of God") and mold it into the righteous image of His Son. Here is an outline of where we are in context:

A. Freedom from Wrath		**(5)**
1.	**Our Deliverance *from* Wrath**	**(5:1-11)**
2.	**Our Deliverance *to* Righteousness**	**(5:12-21)**
	a. **Man's *Problem* with Death**	**(12-14)**
	b. **God's *Provision* for Life**	**(15-17)**
	c. **God's *Purpose* in Giving Life**	**(18-21)**

Paul must first show how the "law of sin and death" through Adam has "infected" all humanity in order to show how Christ's work reverses those consequences. After expounding Man's Problem with Death (12-14), Paul then explains God's Provision for Life (15-17) and finally introduces God's Purpose in Giving that Life (18-21) as a transition to Romans 6.

A. Man's PROBLEM with Death   5:12-14

[12]Therefore, just as through one man sin entered the world, and death through sin, and thus death spread to all men, because all sinned — [13](For until the law sin was in the world, but sin is not imputed when there is no law. [14]Nevertheless death reigned from Adam to Moses, even over those who had not sinned according to the likeness of the transgression of Adam, who is a type of Him who was to come. . . .

Romans 5:8 essentially recapitulated the conclusion of Paul's extensive argument about the need for Christ's **death** in 3:21-4:25a, but Paul has not yet explained what he meant in 4:25b by "was **raised** because of our justification."[1] This statement of prospective deliverance to a righteous life through Christ's resurrection was echoed in 5:9-10 but not further developed at that point in the argument. Now with the opening connective "Therefore" (*dia touto*, "for this reason"), Paul sets out to explain how this "righteous life" is actually accomplished in us — hence, Paul now begins an extended argument to explain just how, "having been justified by his blood, we shall be saved from wrath . . . by his life" (5:9, 10b).

Again, it is critical to remember throughout our exposition that Paul's use of "saved" in Romans 5–8 is not dealing with escaping from hell or getting to

---

1   See note 2, Chapter 1, "Who You Gonna Call?"

heaven but rather with delivering us **from** *wrath against sin* (the tyranny of our Sin Nature, 1:18-32) **to** a visibly *righteous life now* and the confidence of *greater glory in the life to come.*[2] Romans 5:12-21 shows that Christ's work accomplishes this salvation within us by *reversing* and *transcending* the ongoing devastation of Adam's "residue of sin."

1. The *Origin* of Sin   12a

Right at the outset we encounter difficulty. Paul says that sin entered the world through a man. But wasn't it Lucifer who first sinned in heaven before he was cast down to earth? Yes, that's true: before Adam sinned, Lucifer sinned. And before Adam sinned, his wife was seduced by the serpent. On the surface, it would appear that Eve dragged Adam into this whole mess. Why then does the text say "through one man"?

First Timothy 2:14 tells us Eve was deceived, but Adam was not. Apparently, Adam knew exactly what he was doing. So Eve did not rebel against God, *Adam* did — it was conscious, willful sin. People often tell me that all sin is sin: It's all black and all equal. Well, that is just not true. While all sin shares the common denominator of "total" lawbreaking (Gal 3:10; Jas 2:10), some sin is more serious. For example, some sin is "against the body" (1 Cor 6:18). Moreover, in Hebrews 10:26 the writer speaks of willful (or "presumptuous") sin (Num 15:30), or what Paul will shortly call "sin in the likeness of the offense of Adam" (Rom 5:14b). The consequences for that type of sin are more grievous — there is more "death" (6:23b) — than for unintentional sin.

Thus, because Adam knew what he was doing he bore the greater responsibility. Death was the Penalty for Adam's intentional sin. But this does not mean there are no consequences for unknown or inadvertent sin: Eve died, even though Adam was credited with bringing sin into the human race, for death spread to affect *all* humanity, including Eve, with no partiality — it was the consequence of Adam's single intentional sin *(di' enos . . . hē hamartia).*

2. The *Consequence* of Sin   12b-c

The "death" in view in Romans 5:12 mirrors Genesis 3, where death is depicted as *separation*, both physical and spiritual. *Physical* death is physical separation from man's spiritual being; spiritual death is the *spiritual* separation of man from God. This is what Paul means when he says we are "dead in trespasses and sins" (Eph 2:1) — we are not spiritual "corpses" that can do nothing, as many Reformed

---

2   See "Digging Deeper: Paul's Use of 'Wrath' and 'Saved' in Romans 5–8" in Chapter 2, "What the World Needs Now."

scholars teach.[3] The human spirit longs to be reunited with the Creator, and for the believer this occurs immediately after physical death. The body goes back to the elements of the earth from which it came, and the spirit goes back to God who gave it (Eccl 12:7).

After Adam sinned, he did not die physically — that is, not right away. But he *did* die spiritually in his spiritual separation from God. So did Eve. It was not until their sin was dealt with by faith in the promise of life in the "seed of the woman" (Gen 3:15, 20) that they were spiritually reunited with God. This same "death sentence" for Adam's sin has come upon the entire human race, as Paul says that *all sinned*. The point of "all sinned" seems to be that all humanity somehow "participated" in Adam's sin and received his "death sentence" even before they themselves deliberately chose to sin; in fact, that is exactly what Paul confirms in Romans 5:13-14. This hardly seems fair. How is it that all humanity is thus "tagged" with Adam's sin?

3. The *Inheritance* of Sin   12c-14

We prefer to translate "all sinned" (*hēmarton*) as a *gnomic* aorist: "all *sin*" rather than "all *have sinned*." The gnomic aorist denotes a "universal or timeless truth," a law.[4] This use of the aorist tense is consistent with Romans 3:23, which may also be translated, "All *sin* and come short of the glory of God." Somehow all of us "sin" and die in *Adam's one transgression* (*paraptōma*) (5:15a, 16a, 17a, 18a). Paul calls this "the law of sin and death" (7:24; 8:2b): since all men sin (timeless truth), all die. Sin began with Adam and was passed down to and through each generation. Some hold that we die because of the *personal* sins each of us commits. Yet it must encompass *more* than personal sin, as Paul goes on to elaborate in 5:13-14. For example, many children die before they have yet committed any personal sin, so it must be a more "direct" effect of Adam's sin. This is implicit in the notion of *original sin*, a "genetic" defect of some sort: spiritual or physical or both.

Augustine (d. 431) explained this "passing down" of Adam's sin with a theory of *inherited guilt* in Adam that ultimately led to a view known as "Federal Headship." Although this view has been adopted by most evangelical scholars, it is based on an inaccurate Latin translation of two little Greek words in 5:12 (*eph hō*). Instead of the normal meaning of *eph hō* (*because* all sinned), it was translated *in quo* (*in whom* all sinned) in the Latin Vulgate Bible, the only ancient translation in the history of Christianity to translate these two Greek words in

---

3   Genesis 41:8 is a clear refutation of such a notion when it says Pharaoh's spirit was troubled within him (see also Dan 2:1 and 3). Obviously Pharaoh was an unbeliever, but his spirit was not a corpse that could do nothing. It was alive and kicking but it was not well; it was troubled. And it was separated from God (spiritual death). So it is with every unbeliever.

4   Daniel B. Wallace, *Greek Grammar Beyond the Basics* (Grand Rapids, MI: Zondervan, 1996), 562.

this way. But this translation has influenced English translations of the New Testament and it is how Augustine justified his view of how we all sinned "in Adam" — when Adam "voted" for sin he acted as our "representative," so that *his sin* was imputed or credited to the entire human race. However, this would end up condemning infants or others who have *not yet sinned intentionally* — not yet committed *personal* sin; that is, who have not yet *consciously* sinned like Adam (5:14).

Paul thus offers an explanation of how "all sinned" that will extend all the way to 5:21. Even before the law entered to *impute* sin, sin was present and "death reigned" (5:13-14). Paul goes on to explain that *all* received a death sentence through Adam's *condemnation* (5:16a, 18a) because (*gar*) all were "*made [constituted*, not "declared"] sinners" by his one act of disobedience (5:19a). However, this condemnation is not the *verdict* (*krima*, 5:16a), but rather the *death sentence passed down* (**katakrima**) for Adam's sin. So it is not the *guilt* that Adam passed on (and here is where Augustine erred): it is only Adam's death sentence as an *inherited condition* (Sin Nature) that is passed down to and through the human race and that every child brings into the world. Thus, "all sin," in that a child is *naturally* prone to disobey and tell lies. Foolishness is bound up in the heart of a child (Prov 22:15) — we do not have to teach them to disobey and to lie; we have to teach them to obey and tell the truth.

Yet this does *not* mean that personal sin is *excluded* in 5:12c ("all sin[ned]"). Indeed, this is Paul's pretext for reintroducing the notion of Law (see 2:1–3:20) in 5:13-14 to reach his conclusion in 5:20: the law entered so that every person of mature conscience might know God's righteous standard and be held accountable for *personal sin*, "after the likeness of Adam's transgression." This is the sense implicit in 5:16 ("many offenses") and 5:20 ("that the offense might abound"). Therefore "all sin[ned]" in the sense of both our *inheritance* of a Sin Nature from Adam (5:19a) and the *imputation* of personal sin whenever conscience informs us (1:19-20; 2:14-15; 3:20b; 5:20a; 7:7-12) that we have failed to meet the standard (*dikaiōma*, 1:32; 5:16, 18; 8:4). Of course, it is the Sin Nature that *generates* personal sin, much like a factory produces individual units, yet Paul considers these two notions of sin separately.[5]

---

5   We will see that the Sin Nature is inherited from Adam *through the flesh* (6:19; 7:5, 14, 18, 25c; 8:3). While Christ *also* came "in the likeness of sinful flesh" (8:3b), this "second Adam" was "without sin" (Heb 4:15) and offered a *different kind* of "inheritance" (Rom 5:14c-17): his shed blood was a "free gift of grace" that paid the price to reverse the "death," including the Sin Nature ("original sin"), that came from *one offense* (5:15-19). To cover the "many offenses" of *personal* sin, the gift must be *voluntarily received* for life (5:15-17). However, since personal sin is *not imputed* to those without a mature conscience (5:13), the Sin Nature is *already covered* by the gift, and *they will live again* after physical death (5:18-19; compare John 5:28-29).

Conclusion

It is easy to see how "all sin" when we see blatant evidence of human depravity like terrorism and human trafficking. But a man like Mel brings the issue of personal sin closer to home. Around 1900 there was not a lot of teenage alcoholism, but Mel's father kept a saloon, and Mel became an alcoholic early in life. He married young but continued to binge. He once sold his horse and carriage for booze, and one version of his life story claims that he actually sold his sick daughter's medicine to buy liquor. When she died, he took the shoes right off her corpse at the funeral and sold them to buy more booze. Later, he was so ashamed, that he promised his wife he would never drink again. But just two hours later he was drunk. Having run out of options for controlling his addiction, Mel gave up trying. After selling his own shoes for more liquor, he headed for one of the Great Lakes, barefoot in the snow, to take his life.

I'll tell you what happened to Mel a little later, but after forty years of ministry I've concluded that given the right circumstances — or I should say, the *wrong* circumstances — we are all capable of almost anything and can be in real trouble without even going to this extreme. Humanity, we have a problem. Each and every one of us has this problem, and we need outside resources to overcome the problem. What in our lives do we really wrestle with? What is it that drags us down? Is it a problem with the tongue? Why can't we seem to stop being critical or argumentative or telling little lies? Is the problem with our emotions, so that we can't control our anger or get rid of bitterness or envy?

Whatever it is that keeps tearing us down is produced by this Sin Factory, this Sin Nature we've inherited from Adam (5:19a). It does not matter how many self-help books we read or seminars we go to, this thing is not going away. But for the Christian there is hope, and it shines through in vv. 15-17, where the consequences of this "law of sin and death" are not just *reversed* by Christ's death, they are abundantly *transcended* by his life, so that we might be delivered from wrath against Sin to reign righteously with Him in life.

B. God's PROVISION for Life   5:15-17

15*But the free gift is not like the offense. For if by the one man's offense many died, much more the grace of God and the gift by the grace of the one Man, Jesus Christ, abounded to many.* 16*And the gift is not like that which came through the one who sinned. For the judgment which came from one offense resulted in condemnation, but the free gift which came from many offenses resulted in justification.* 17*For if by the one man's offense death reigned through the one, much more those who receive abundance of grace and of the gift of righteousness will reign in life through the One, Jesus Christ.)*

1. The *Origin* of Free Grace   **15**

This is the greatest passage in the Bible on what we call "free grace." But wait, isn't that redundant? Isn't grace free *by definition*? Well, the word for "grace" (*charis*) is used in this passage six times, but three times we find the word "free gift" (*dōrea/dōrēma*).[6] The Bible puts the two words side by side here (see also Eph 2:8-9; 3:7) just to avoid confusing this issue of grace. While all Christian denominations stake a claim to grace, for many of these groups the "gift" of grace comes with strings attached — additional requirements to be met either before or after we are born again. But Paul insists that God's grace is *absolutely free* — there are no works we can do to *get it* or to *prove we have it* after the fact. It is a gift.

Paul starts with "But" to contrast the prevailing problem through Adam (death) with the free provision in Christ (life). If, as many NT scholars believe, Galatians was the first of Paul's epistles, then it was only a few years after their conversion that he was compelled to write, "I marvel that you are so soon removed from the gospel that I preached to you" (Gal 1:6). Apparently Paul's message of free grace was corrupted by legalists (Judaizers) who desperately wanted to keep works in the gospel, and it's been a struggle ever since. Like a great fog, legalism sweeps in to obscure our view of the shining light of God's marvelous grace. I run into people regularly who recoil at the notion that God's grace is absolutely free. It is our Sin Nature that reacts so violently, trying to convince us that we have to do something either to acquire the gift or prove that we have it. So Paul begins to clear the fog here by stating "But the *free gift* . . ."[7]

This is not a trivial matter. Paul says if anyone preaches a gospel other than the one he preached, he is to be *accursed* (Gal 1:8-9). This is strong language. (I wonder how long Paul would last in the average American church before he was encouraged by the leadership to become a foreign missionary!) T. F. Torrance contends that the notion of justification by faith without works was lost soon after the original apostles, not to be discovered again until the Reformation.[8] Nagging questions about the role of works led to a huge debate in about AD 400. The main players were Augustine, whom we met in the last section, and a man named Pelagius. While Pelagius thought one had to do something to *merit* God's grace, Augustine believed one had to do something to *prove possession* of God's grace — both views misunderstood how free God's grace really is. A lesser-

---

6   The same word occurs in adverbial form translated "freely" in Rev 21:6 and 22:17.

7   Not every translation reads this way: The NIV just reads "gift" and the NET says "gracious gift," but the idea is the same: God's gift to us is *absolutely free*. See Zane C. Hodges, *Absolutely Free* (Dallas, TX: Redención Viva, 1989).

8   Thomas F. Torrance, *The Doctrine of Grace in the Apostolic Fathers* (Eugene, OR: Wipf and Stock, 1996).

known Christian leader named John Cassian explained grace as a gift to be received *freely*, with no strings attached at all.[9]

If I see a man on the street in need of transportation and I decide to buy him a car, it is *my* decision. It is *my* work that pays for that car, so when I offer him the keys, I am offering him a free gift. He has done nothing to deserve or merit the car, but I won't force the car on him. I will offer him the keys. He still has to decide whether to accept my gift — to *receive* the keys. Would anyone argue that this beggar has earned the gift if he accepts my offer? No. That's why it is *gracious*. One's *will* is involved only insofar as a choice is made to receive it, but one cannot *work* for God's favor. Grace is something we simply *receive* (*lambanō*, Rom 5:17). That is why John defines believing as *receiving* (Jn 1:12). So also argued John Cassian. And this is why we, like Paul, emphasize "free" grace.

2. The *Goal* of Free Grace 16

The goal of free grace emerges for us here in the word *dikaiōma*, commonly translated "justification" (as in NKJV). However, this translation confuses courtroom justification with the *goal* of that justification in our lives. *Dikaiōma* does not refer to the courtroom; it is talking about *righteous living*. Courtroom justification takes place in heaven (our Position); *dikaiōma* refers to our Condition on earth. How can we be sure that this is the intended connection between *dikaiosunē* in 1:17 and *dikaiōma* in 5:16 in the context of Romans? One of the problems with beginning in the middle of a book (Rom 5–8) is our need to reconstruct the groundwork laid in earlier chapters for the subsequent logic of the argument. So, let's review how Paul develops and deploys the *dikaiosunē* word-group in Romans.

Digging Deeper: The Semantic Range of "Righteousness" in Romans 5–8

The NT use of "righteousness" (*dikaiosunē*) spans a wide semantic range. It most often denotes righteous behavior (Condition) but can also signify righteousness in Position. Likewise, Paul's use of *dikaiosunē* in Romans can denote a righteous *status credited* to our account in heaven's courtroom by faith (Rom 3:21-4:25) or a righteous *behavior* that leads to quality life on earth (Rom 5:17, 21; 6:13, 16-23; 8:10). God granted us a new Position in heaven, so that it might affect our Condition on earth: *heavenly righteousness should lead to earthly righteousness*. Paul makes the same point in Ephesians when he moves from Position (Eph 1–3)

---

9 See the more extended treatment of Cassian's views and of the Augustine-Pelagius debate over salvation and grace in David R. Anderson, *Free Grace Soteriology,* Revised Edition (Houston: Grace Theology Press, 2012), 34-38, 349-57.

to Condition (Eph 4–6): "to walk worthy of the calling to which you were called" (Eph 4:1, my translation).

Beginning in Romans 1:16-18, Paul tells us that the gospel is the power of God, intended to *lead to* (*eis*) salvation for all who believe (1:16), but this salvation was meant to *extend beyond* initial faith, conveyed in 1:17 by the phrase "from faith to faith." The repeated connective "for" (*gar*) in 1:17-18 tells us *why*: "*For* the righteousness of God *is being revealed* . . . . *For* the wrath of God *is being revealed* . . . ," as sin continues to incur God's wrath (1:19-32). The present tense here implies that the same faith that *initially* saved us from the Penalty of Sin is still needed to save us from God's ongoing wrath against sin so that we might *continue* to reveal the righteousness of God (1:16-18; 3:21). Thus, our "deliverance" by grace through faith is *also* to be ongoing: our *past* deliverance from the Penalty of Sin (Justification) is to continue in our *present* deliverance from the Power of Sin (Sanctification), all with a view to our *future* Glorification (8:18-39).

Our New Position "in Christ" — including a new *righteous identity* (2 Cor 5:17) — is conferred on us the moment we are *acquitted* of sin (*dikaioō*) by Christ's *death*; but our present and future *display* of that New Identity (righteous *behavior*) depends on incarnating His resurrection *life* (4:25b). Thus, *dikaiosunē* in Romans 4:3 mainly denotes *forensic* righteousness (*credited* to us once-for-all in heaven), but this new righteous Position (3:21-26) is meant to be lived out on earth by faith. God's righteousness is progressively revealed in us as *righteous acts* or *behavior* (*dikaiōma*, 5:16; 18) by ongoing faith (1:17; 3:22) as God conforms our Condition (*dikaioi*, righteous in *character*, 5:19b) to our Position in Christ. As G. Schrenk observes, "Thus without any sense of difficulty or contradiction, the thought of pardoning and forensic righteousness passes over into that of righteousness as the living power which overcomes sin."[10]

We could thus say that within the "genus" *dikaiosunē* are various "species" that point to the different aspects of righteousness which Paul develops in Romans, depending on the context. In order to distinguish these nuances, Paul uses different terms that all begin with the same root (dikaio-) as the word *dikaiosunē*: the verb *dikaioō* ("acquit, justify, vindicate, release," 14 times); the adjective *dikaios* ("righteous [one]," 5:19b; compare 1:17b); and the nouns *dikaiōsis* ("justification, absolution, acquittal [and release], vindication," 4:25; 5:18) and *dikaiōma* ("righteous act, acceptable standard of behavior," 5:16, 5:18; 8:4; compare 1:32).

---

10   G. Schrenk, "*dikaiosunē*," in *Theological Dictionary of the New Testament,* vol. 2 (Grand Rapids, MI: Eerdmans, 1964), 209.

Thus, the word *dikaiōma* moves us from heaven's courtroom to life experience. Just as *dikaiōma* in 5:18 denotes Christ's righteous work on earth, so also *dikaiōma* in the lives of believers denotes the righteous *acts* or *behavior* God intends for us to display on earth (5:16; 8:4). *This* is the "salvation" offered in Paul's "gospel of God" (Rom 1:1-4, 16-18).

So practically speaking, what does this righteousness "look" like as it is worked out in our lives? The answer to that is found in Romans 12–16. While Romans 1–11 focuses on our vertical relationship with God, Romans 12–16 describes our intended horizontal relationships with mankind. See also the Appendix, "What Does the Righteousness of God 'Look' Like?"

[END OF EXCURSUS]

Paul is therefore affirming in Romans 5:16 that our righteousness *declared* in heaven (Justification) is to be *lived out* on earth through the righteous life of Christ (Sanctification) — this is the thrust of *dikaiōma*.[11] This *righteous life* is the express purpose of the free gift of grace, as indicated by the preposition *eis* ("with a view to") before *dikaiōma*. The goal is not just to populate heaven when we die, though that is a sure promise to every believer; the goal is *higher* than heaven. It may help to think of heaven as only an *intermediate* goal.

The ultimate goal is to reveal God's righteousness by faith (1:17; 3:21-22) as the Holy Spirit within us fulfills God's standard of righteous behavior: *dikaiōma* (1:32; 2:26; 8:4). So God's grace not only secures our access to heaven but also transforms our character in this life on earth (12:2). Properly understood, free grace *teaches* us how to live righteously: "For the grace of God that brings salvation has appeared to all men, *teaching* us that, denying ungodliness and worldly lusts, we should live soberly, righteously, and godly in the present age" (Titus 2:11-12). However, for this righteous behavior to be displayed *outwardly*, we are to keep availing ourselves of this grace *abundantly* by faith (Rom 5:17).

3. The *Power* of Free Grace   17

The word "reign" (*basileuō*) implies *royalty*. The noun form (*basileus*) means "king." Sin reigns in death, but grace reigns in life. Death *was* reigning, but now, "O Death, where is your sting; O Hades, where is your victory?" (1 Cor 15:55). Christians were meant to *reign in life,* as Christ's righteousness overcomes not only the Penalty of Sin but also the Power of Sin, and free grace entails God's daily provision of Christ's righteous life to complete and sustain that reign. This

---

11   Walter Bauer, *A Greek-English Lexicon of the New Testament and Other Early Christian Literature,* rev. and ed. by Frederick William Danker (Chicago: University of Chicago Press, 2000), 249.

reign of righteousness is meant to yield eternal life, which as we shall see denotes a *quality* of life more than *quantity*, as Paul goes on to clarify in Rom 5:20-21 and 6:22-23.

This is power of free grace. But we "reign" only when the free gift of grace — Christ's righteous life in us — is freely and abundantly *received (lambanō)*. Since this is a daily choice, a righteous life after justification may not be externally evident. Critics of free grace often call this view "cheap grace" or "easy believism." The implication is that free grace lets one receive this gift of eternal life and then "live like hell" — exactly the criticism leveled against the Reformers by the Catholics at the Council of Trent (1545–1563). While this may be true in any individual believer, the fact that grace is free actually provides the greatest possible incentive for transformation.

While Mel Trotter was on the way to the lake to freeze himself to death, he walked by an old Rescue Mission next to a saloon, where someone saw him and invited him in for a hot meal. While he ate, Trotter listened to John Newton's magnificent hymn about God's amazing grace in Jesus Christ. Trotter trusted God's promises and was justified, declared righteous in heaven. But that's not all. He went on to complete deliverance from alcohol to actually *reign* over sin, and in fact, he was eventually appointed to run that very mission, which was highly successful. The saloon next door shut down and Mel went on to establish 67 more rescue missions. Whenever someone asked how he knew he was saved, he answered "I was there when it happened: January 19, 1897, ten minutes past nine, central time, Pacific Garden Mission, Chicago, Illinois, USA." That is the power of grace. He had tried everything until he was so exhausted he despaired of living at all. He ran headlong into the grace of God, and that is how he was saved from both the Penalty and the Power of sin to fulfill God's royal purpose in him: to *reign in life through Christ's righteousness.*

C. God's PURPOSE in Giving Life   5:18-21

1. From *Adam* to *Christ*: New Life Comes from a New Identity   18-19

18*Therefore, as through one man's offense judgment came to all men, resulting in condemnation, even so through one Man's righteous act the free gift came to all men, resulting in justification of life.* 19*For as by one man's disobedience many were made sinners, so also by one Man's obedience many will be made righteous.*

Having shown how Christ's work *transcended* Adam's work (5:15-17), Paul now resumes and completes the argument he began in 5:12 to show how the work of Adam is *abundantly reversed* by that of the Second Adam who was to come (5:14c); one act by Adam and one by Christ, each with its own results: Adam's act resulted in "condemnation," but Christ's act resulted in "justification of life"

(5:18). However, we need to carefully define these terms as they are used by Paul. Neither this "condemnation" nor its opposite "justification of life" refers to a *courtroom verdict* (our Position).

Paul's word for a courtroom *judgment* or *verdict* is *krima* but the word used here is ***kata*krima**. In 5:16a where the two words occur together, the prefix *kata*- marks a shift from Position (*krima* = the *judgment* of Adam's sin) to Condition (*katakrima* = the *death sentence handed down* to us, as also in 5:18a). By "death sentence" we mean not only the *physical* death we inherited from Adam (5:12) but also a *life enslaved* by Sin for the believer who chooses to live self-sufficiently by the flesh, bringing moral defeat, disillusionment, and despair. It is a life that is behaviorally indistinguishable from a nonbeliever "in Adam."

Likewise, *dikaiōsin zōēs* (the term that parallels *katakrima* in 5:18) also signifies Condition, not Position. The preposition *eis* in front of *dikaiōsin zōēs* indicates the intended goal of our justification/acquittal: "absolution *with a view* to righteous living."[12] The reversal secured for us by Christ's work in 5:18 thus achieves our Sanctification: *a righteous life* for believers that leads to Glorification. However in comparing 5:18-19 with 5:15-17, it is clear that this Righteous Condition ("will be made righteous," 5:19b) will prevail over the Sin Nature from Adam ("were made sinful," 5:19a) only in "the many" *who receive the abundance of the free gift of grace* in Christ's righteousness (5:15, 17) by faith (1:17; 3:22).

Paul's logic in 5:12, 18-19 tracks the sequence of Adam's work and Christ's work, respectively, to show how Christ's work (by its "much more" effects in 5:15-17) can produce visibly righteous behavior, even though the flesh still carries the sinful trappings of our old identity in Adam. We can trace **Adam's work** in the *first half* of each verse (from *one sinful act* leading to *death*), and then trace how **Christ's work** in the *second half* of each verse (from *one righteous act* leading to *life*) reverses and transcends Adam's work to bring righteous life:

Adam's work. Through Adam's one offense (5:12, 16a) *all mankind* has been sentenced to an **Inherited Condition** (*incarcerated* by Sin, *leading to* death) (5:12, 16a, 18a). This happens *because* (*gar*, "for") by Adam's disobedience they were *constituted* (*kathistēmi*) *sinful by nature* (*hamartōloi*, 5:19a), thus spawning sin and death. This Inherited Condition recurs many times in Romans 6–8: It is a life in believers still enslaved by the Power of Sin in the *unredeemed flesh*; hence, to be *fleshly minded* is "death" — physically alive, yet experiencing death (Rom 8:6). Thus, Paul says in 1 Tim 5:5 that the Christian widow who lives for pleasure

---

12   The phrase *dikaiōsin zōēs* ("acquittal of life") is very likely a *genitive of result*. See J. H. Moulton and G. Milligan, *Vocabulary of the Greek New Testament* (Peabody, MA: Hendrickson, 1997), 328 [hereafter MM], where it is defined as "a process of absolution, carrying with it life."

is dead even though she lives, and he pleads in Romans 7:24 from the vantage of law-keeping by the flesh: "Oh, wretched man that I am, who will deliver me from this body of death?"

Therefore, just because grace secured our entrance to heaven (4:25a) does not mean we no longer need grace to live the Christian life. Remember that this portion of Paul's argument is talking about our *ongoing life* as believers. Since we still carry forward our Sin Nature from our Old Identity in Adam through the flesh, we wrestle with it daily and need more grace to overcome it. We see this same point in James 4:1-6. He says the conflict in our lives comes from the lusts which war in our members *after* we become Christians.

Christ's work. In order to overcome those lusts (from our Sin Nature), we thus need "more grace"—and a *lot* of it. That's why Paul brings up *abundance of grace* as the free gift of Christ's righteousness in 5:17. For those who *freely accept* this abundant grace (5:17b), Christ's *righteous act* (*dikaiōma*, 5:18b) in death and resurrection (4:25) will progressively result in a New Condition: *overtly righteous behavior* in their lives on earth (5:18b). This is *because* (*gar*, "for") in receiving Christ's resurrection life (5:17b) by faith, they will be *constituted* (*kathistēmi*) *righteous by nature* (*dikaioi*, 5:19b). Paul thus cited Habakkuk 2:4 in the book's opening thematic statement to support his thesis: if the one who is saved is to "reveal the *righteousness* of God *from faith to faith*," then "the *righteous one* [*ho dikaios*] must *live by faith*" (1:17). That is, since we are incapable of *righteous life on our own,* it takes ongoing faith for us to appropriate the full grace we need in *Christ's gift of righteousness* (5:15b, 17b).[13]

We still carry the trappings of our Old Identity in Adam. Over years of ministry I have had the opportunity to work with alcoholics. Many of them attend AA and have invited me to their meetings. As I've observed a number of those meetings I have asked myself why this twelve step system seems to work. Although they invoke a "Higher Power," they never explicitly call upon Christ (at least not when

---

13   We can diagram this sequence of Paul's logic in 5:12-19 as the outcome, respectively, of: (1) the work of Adam, *inherited by all mankind;* and (2) the work of Christ (the "Second Adam," 5:14c), *appropriated by faith* (for an explanation of the Greek terms, see text on pp. 30-40):

1. ***Just as* Adam's** one *sinful act* (*paraptōma*, 15a, 17a, 18a, explains *hamartia*, 5:12a)
   a. led to Adam's **guilty** *verdict* (*krima*, 16a)
   b. *and* the resulting *sentence* was an **Inherited Condition** (*katakrima*, incarceration by **sin**, leading to **death**, 16a, 18a) that extended *to all (eis pantas)* humanity (12b, 18a)
   c. *because* all were **constituted Sinful** (*hamartōloi*, 19a, explains *hēmarton*, "all sinned," 12c)
2. *so also* **Christ's** one *righteous act* (*dikaiōma*, 18b) of grace to many (15b)
   a. made **absolution** (*dikaiōsin*) available *to all (eis pantas)* (18b)
   b. *and* will *release* to a **New Condition** (*dikaiōsin zōēs*, **righteous life**, 18b, explains *dikaiōma*, "righteous behavior," 16b) *those who receive the abundance of grace* as a free gift in Christ's righteous life (16b, 17b) by faith (see 1:17; 3:22)
   c. *because* in receiving this gracious gift they will be **constituted Righteous** (*dikaioi*, 5:19b)

I've attended). I finally read Bill Wilson's biography[14] to see if I could figure it out and saw the AA essentials that help a lot of men and women addicted to alcohol. One essential is the admission the moment they walk into the meeting that *they have a problem*. They never view themselves as having that problem completely eradicated. Although a member of AA may be delivered from alcohol for many years, he never speaks of himself as "healed." He says, "I am a recovering alcoholic the rest of my life." He knows he is just one drink away from the gutter.

I've often thought churches would be better off if they would adopt that principle. We will never get rid of our sinfulness in Adam in this life. We were *sin*-aholics when we met Christ. Now we are forgiven. We have a new righteous Identity from God: "Christ in you, the hope of glory" (Col 1:27). But in our fleshly Condition we will be recovering sin-aholics for the rest of our days. We are just one known sin away from the spiritual gutter—*let him who stands take heed lest he fall* (1 Cor 10:12). Our New Condition will take some time; no instantaneous deliverance. It is a recovery mission. He wants to completely redeem us, not just from the Penalty of sin but also from the Power and Presence of sin in our lives. We were created to *reign in life,* but that will require us to *keep appropriating* Christ's righteous life in us (Rom 5:17b).

2. From *Law* to *Grace*: New Life Comes from Righteous Living   20-21

20*Moreover the law entered that the offense might abound. But where sin abounded, grace abounded much more,* 21*so that as sin reigned in death, even so grace might reign through righteousness to eternal life through Jesus Christ our Lord.*

Paul now concludes the argument begun in 5:13-14 by explaining *why* personal sin is imputed. Sin was *there* before the Law of Moses, but the Law made us *recognize* it more clearly. Following Paul's prior logic (1:18-20; 2:14-15; 3:20), the Law entered that sin might "abound": by spelling out God's standard of holiness, the Law as our tutor *holds us,* like Adam, *personally accountable* for our sin (5:13-14; see Gal 3:24). But the Law not only enables us to *see* our sin, it also *incites* our Sin Nature (Rom 5:12, 19a), as Paul will elaborate in 7:7-25. Like the little boy walking along the sidewalk minding his own business until he sees a sign that says "Keep Off" beside some fresh cement, immediately he wants to put his hand or foot in the cement. He might not even have been tempted had he not seen the sign. By inciting our Sin Nature the Law *increases* our desperate need of a Savior, not only to *bring* us to Christ but also to *conform* us to His image (8:29). And this requires *grace — abundant* grace.

---

14 Francis Hartigan, *Bill W.—A Biography of Alcoholics Anonymous Co-founder Bill Wilson* (New York: St. Martin's, 2000).

To complete the argument Paul therefore draws on his prior notion of "abundance of grace" (5:17b): "But where sin abounds, grace *abounds even more*" (5:20b).[15] The Greek term is a compound word: *hyper* + *perisseuō* (the root verb of *perisseia* ["abundance"] in 5:17b) = *super* + *abound*. It describes overflowing liquids. Most people who believe a Christian can lose his salvation ascribe it to sinning *too much, too seriously,* or *both*; but this promise (5:20b) is one of the strongest affirmations of eternal security we will find in the entire Bible. It tells us that even if sin digs a Grand Canyon in our lives, God's grace is able to *overflow* that Canyon.

In fact, grace is so much greater than our sin that it can *reign over* sin (5:21) — a statement of Condition, not Position. God wants *us* to reign in life (5:17b), but here it is *grace* that reigns **in us** *with a view to* (*eis*) eternal life. This may *sound* like Position, but the Bible's main emphasis when eternal life is mentioned is *quality* not *quantity* (see Rom 6:23). "Death" in Romans 5–8 denotes a *rotten* quality of life, whereas "life" signifies a *rich* quality of life. Everyone — believer or unbeliever — will exist forever, but "eternal life" is much more than a *static destination* in heaven; this quality of life is meant to steadily improve in *this* life, as we grow more and more like Christ (8:29; compare Gal 6:8; 1 Tim 6:12; Titus 1:2; Jn 12:25). It is a *dynamic* concept that hopefully grows and expands in this life as we are delivered by grace from the tyranny ("reign") of sin and death in Adam to reign through the righteousness of Christ (Rom 5:21a).[16] Paul will go on to explain that this grace-empowered "eternal life" reign consummates in *a more*

---

15   Just like the *gnomic* aorist in 5:12 ("all *sin*") the aorist tense of the two verbs in 5:20b ("abound" and "super-abound") completes the comparison to also teach "a universal or timeless truth" (see above note 4 and associated text): grace abundantly received *reverses and transcends* the residual effect of Adam's one sin on all mankind.

16   Here, then, is the completion (shaded) of the linear sequence of Paul's logic in 5:12-21 (see note 13):

1. ***Just as* Adam's** one *sinful act* (*paraptōma*, 15a, 17a, 18a, explains *hamartia*, 5:12a)

   a. led to Adam's **guilty** *verdict* (*krima*, 16a)

   b. *and* the resulting *sentence* was an **Inherited Condition** (*katakrima*, incarceration by **sin**, leading to **death**, 16a, 18a) that extended *to all* (*eis pantas*) humanity (12b, 18a)

   c. *because* all were **constituted Sinful** (*hamartōloi*, 19a, explains *hēmarton*, "all sinned," 12c)

   d. *moreover* law entered to **make sin abound** (*credit* man *with personal sin* like Adam, 13-14, 20a)

   e. *so that* sin might **reign in death** (*have dominion through sin and death*, 21a) . . .

2. ***so also* Christ's** one *righteous act* (*dikaiōma*, 18b) of grace to many (15b)

   a. made **absolution** (*dikaiōsin*) available *to all* (*eis pantas*) (18b)

   b. *and* will *release* to a **New Condition** (*dikaiōsin zōēs*, **righteous life**, 18b, explains *dikaiōma*, "righteous behavior," 16b) *those who receive the abundance of grace* as a free gift in Christ's righteous life (16b, 17b) by faith (see 1:17; 3:22)

   c. *because* in receiving this gracious gift they will be **constituted Righteous** (*dikaioi*, 5:19b)

   d. *but* wherever sin abounds, **grace** [abundantly appropriated, 17b] **super-abounds** (20b)

   e. *so that* through Christ's righteousness grace might **reign to eternal life** "quality" (21b) *glorious co-inheritance* for royal "sons" who are led by the Spirit and suffer with Christ *in this life* so they may rule with Him *in the world to come* (8:14-19).

Christ can turn a pauper into a prince, a slave into a sovereign, both now and for eternity. None of us has any rightful claim to such a high calling, but that God has granted us *Free Grace*. It is God who builds trophies from the scrap-heap, who finds the clay to work with under the dung-hill, who makes instruments of beauty even from our most abysmal past failures. Our Father, great in grace, loved us when we were yet sinners (5:8): rebels, liars, drunks, druggies, brawlers, playboys, Pharisees, adulteresses, hypocrites, do-gooders, drop-outs. Looking for the sick and the sinner, He found us in desperate straits. And lifting us to the Position of His dear Son, he washed us, healed our wounds, and changed our direction. All our churchgoing, praise, worship, hymn-singing, long prayers, and pious looks never could erase the fact that we were dug out of a deep, dark, desperate pit — classic misfits that we are.

Yes, humanity, we *do* have a problem: *sin abounds*. Can we recover? Yes. But it requires *over-abounding* grace. God's grace raining down from heaven will overflow any gorge, any canyon of sin in our lives. That's the beauty of it; our sin is covered and there is peace and calm:

> Marvelous grace of our loving Lord;
> Grace that exceeds our sin and our guilt
> Yonder on Calvary's mount out-poured,
> There where the blood of the Lamb was spilt.
> Grace, grace, God's grace,
> Grace that will pardon and cleanse within;
> Grace, grace, God's grace,
> Grace that is greater than all our sin.

Lest we forget, however, in this life believers continue to face Sin's treachery (1 Jn 2:15-16). When I first moved to Montgomery County, Texas in 1972, Lake Conroe was in the plans. Dam engineers thought it would take three years for the rain to fill it, but record rains day after day, week after week, filled all the ugliness beneath the surface in only one year. Some twenty years later we went water skiing in a perfectly calm cove at Lake Conroe. But when I gunned the motorboat to pull my son "out of the hole," I sensed some sluggishness before we could plane out on the water surface. As it turned out, the back of the boat had dropped down low enough to hit an old bridge trestle beneath the surface and ripped a big hole in the bottom of the boat, so we promptly sank. I never knew that nasty trestle was there. The rain had completely covered it. Likewise, when we "drop down in the hole" of our old identity in Adam we will still risk serious damage from our Sin Nature (Romans 6).

CHAPTER 5

"THE EMANCIPATION PROCLAMATION"
Romans 6:1-11

On January 1, 1863 our sixteenth President finished a document later called "The Emancipation Proclamation." Once ratified by Congress, this document had an especially devastating effect on the southern states. By the 1960s it would seem that some people in the southern states had still not gotten the message. I grew up during the civil rights movement in Nashville, where sit-down strikes first began. We had separate drinking fountains and restrooms for blacks. Blacks sat at the back of the bus; whites at the front. Blacks were not allowed at my high school. After the pastor of our church led a civil rights march in downtown Nashville he was "cordially invited" by his trustees to spend a year studying in Greece.

Surprisingly, however, when the Emancipation Proclamation was first issued, responses varied dramatically among the slaves who were freed. Some did not know what to do with their freedom and went out of control. Others seemed to ignore it and just kept on serving their old masters voluntarily, whether or not they were aware of their new freedom. But neither of these responses was true liberty. And it is just the same in the Christian life.

Paul has taught us that we were all born into this world as slaves to our Sin Nature; we had no option but to serve the Sin Nature (Rom 1:18–3:20). But Christ paid the price to buy us out of the slave market of Sin: we now belong to Him; we have been set free (3:21–4:25). Some take this new freedom as license to go hog wild: "Since we cannot out-sin God's grace [5:20], why not sin as much as we want?" Others seem unaware they have been set free and continue to live as slaves to Sin, not realizing they now have a choice. Still others know they have been set free but choose to keep on serving the same master, the Sin Nature. All these responses subvert God's ultimate intent in setting us free in Christ. Thus,

Romans 6:1-14 clarifies our New Identity in Christ, and 6:15-23 lays out God's New Intention for us in order to fulfill the agenda behind Paul's teaching in Romans 5–8: deliverance from the Power of Sin to reveal His Righteousness in us by faith (1:16-18; 3:21-22). Here is how 6:1-11 fits in the overall context:

I.	**SIN**	**(1:1–3:20)**
II.	**SALVATION**	**(3:21–4:25)**
III.	**SANCTIFICATION**	**(5–8)**
	A. **Freedom from Wrath**	**(5)**
	B. **Freedom from Sin**	**(6)**
	1. **Our New Position in Christ**	**(6:1-14)**
	a. **New Identity** *Explained*	**(6:1-11)**
	1) **Dead in Christ**	**1-4**
	2) **Risen in Christ**	**5-7**
	3) **Living in Christ**	**8-11**
	b. **New Identity** *Applied*	**(6:12-14)**
	2. **Our New Privilege in Christ**	**(6:15-23)**
	C. **Freedom from Law**	**(7)**
	D. **Freedom from Despair**	**(8)**

To be progressively sanctified we must *appropriate* our freedom from **sin** (Rom 6), **law** (Rom 7), and **despair** (Rom 8). Sin and law conspire to try to defeat God's purpose in and through us; this defeat is what Paul calls "death." But God does not want us to be miserable sinners bound for hell, so Christ died for our sins — He was our substitute in *death*. Neither does God want us to be miserable sinners bound for heaven, so Christ also wants to free us from the power of sin — He wants to be our substitute in *life* (4:25b), so that God may in fact bring out the righteous character He intended to develop in us through Christ's life (5:10b, 19b; see Gal 2:20).

I. Dead in Christ   6:1-4

1What shall we say then? Shall we continue in sin that grace may abound? 2Certainly not! How shall we who died to sin live any longer in it? 3Or do you not know that as many of us as were baptized into Christ Jesus were baptized into His death? 4Therefore we were buried with Him through baptism into death, that just as Christ was raised from the dead by the glory of the Father, even so we also should walk in newness of life.

As Paul reaches his conclusion in Romans 5, he anticipates an objection from at least some in his audience who follow the pattern of the Judaizers who opposed him throughout his ministry. Though there were three types of Judaizers who dogged Paul's steps, the one passion they had in common was the Law of Moses. They thought a Christian had to keep the Law of Moses for salvation, either from the penalty of sin or from the power of sin, or both. Paul makes a seemingly outlandish claim in 5:20: we cannot "out-sin" God's grace. The "math" might look like this: **Grace = (x)Sins + 1,** where x is any number (God's grace will always exceed any number of sins we may commit); or **God's Grace > My Sins** (God's grace is always greater than my sins). That sounds crazy and might well appeal to an opportunist.

When I first studied Romans in seminary, the head of the NT department, S. Lewis Johnson, said, "Men, if you are not accused of preaching 'easy believism' or 'cheap grace' when you present the gospel, then you are not preaching Paul's gospel. So, if you are accused of that, then you are in pretty good company." Is Paul's gospel cheap? Of course not — it was *free* for us, but *infinitely costly* for Him. So, Paul fully anticipates the concern and poses the claim of the hypothetical opportunist: "If we can sin all we want and still be accepted by God, why not *wallow* in it? [The word for "continue" is *epi + menōmen* = continuing on top of continuing = *to wallow.*] Since the greater the grace, the greater God's glory [compare Rom 3:7], we can simply wallow in sin; after all, it only *increases* His glory."

So, how would such an opportunist view Paul's theology to justify his claim?

1. Paul must have taught eternal security. There would be no way to come up with this objection unless Paul was teaching that we cannot lose our salvation.
2. The objector's claim was based on "remedial theology," with reasoning like this:
   a. Sin is *appealing* (compare Gen 3:5-6; 1 Jn 2:16);
   b. I can't lose my *salvation*;
   c. I can confess after I do it and still be forgiven by God's *grace* (Rom 5:17b; 6:1; compare 1 Jn 1:9);
   d. Therefore, I'll do it.

But this is like taking a defensive driving course where the professor pulls out a map of all the hospitals — assuming that we are such lousy drivers we are going to have a wreck — and then teaches First Aid and CPR. That would be a corrective or remedial theologian — what to do after you have messed up. Why not instead teach how to help *prevent* accidents by driving a safe distance behind the car in front of us, safely changing lanes, and braking in an emergency? Paul is more of a *preventive* theologian. We need both remedial theology (1 Jn 1:9) and preventive theology, but Paul focuses on preventive theology. He is interested in our sinning *less,* not more. The goal of the Christian life is not to go out like the proverbial "cat with nine lives" with the cross in one pocket and heaven in the other, having spiritual "accidents" all over the place. The idea is to sin *less,* not more, for we are called to *more life* in Christ's risen life (6:4), *not more death* (5:20a). And the ultimate purpose of more life in Christ is not self-serving: it equips us as God's image bearers to display His righteousness to the world, to represent Him honorably and reconcile others to Him through Christ (2 Cor 5:11-21).

So Paul immediately replies in v. 2, "Certainly not." Grace was never intended to be a license to sin, for we have "died to sin." By this he means we have died to that realm (Position) where Sin rules and have been transferred to a realm (Position) where Sin has no jurisdiction at all. It would be like a job transfer from France to America: France's government would have no further jurisdiction; we would no longer have any obligation to submit to France's government or be subject to its laws. We would be living in a new realm and subject to the laws of that realm.

Yet the idea is stronger than a job transfer. The word used is "died." It is more like being a Russian writer who wants to escape the communist regime during the Cold War, but his boat capsizes in the rough seas of the Bering Straights. He has only minutes to live, but an American sub pops up and saves his life. Russian newspapers report that he died at sea, but he is granted immediate asylum in America, given American papers and American citizenship, and enjoys full freedom in his new homeland. If in a moment of weakness he begins to miss his roots and asks the American authorities if he can return to Russia, they would reply, "Absolutely not; to them you are dead. You can only live here." So also, every Christian has a **New Position**: a new *citizenship* (heaven) with a new *identity* (in Christ). And he is also destined for a **New Condition:** new *privileges* (righteous character), and new *freedom* to pursue an abundant new *life*. To long for the old country or succumb to the false appeal of his old identity (in Adam) would only subvert his new freedom to enjoy productive citizenship in his new country.

This transfer occurs through *baptism* (Rom 6:3). But what does that mean? Some door-to-door evangelists once explained to me from Romans 6 that I had to be water baptized to go to heaven. When I looked at the text and asked where they found water, they were dumbfounded that I would even entertain the thought that baptism could occur without water. But there is no mention of water here, and baptism does not necessarily imply water (1 Cor 10:1-2). It means "to dip into, to immerse" and implies a new association, a change of identity: Jewish Baptism, John's Baptism, and Jesus' Baptism all included water. But the Holy Spirit's Baptism (1 Cor 12:13) does not include water. We are "dipped into" *Jesus*, not water.

Being dipped "into" Christ Jesus makes us like sugar in tea or paper in a book; wherever the book goes, the paper goes with it. Why? Because the paper is in the book. So when we are *in Christ* we go where he goes. We are buried with Him and raised with Him. This is why baptism by immersion is probably the best available illustration of baptism by the Holy Spirit. As we stand in the water, it illustrates our being on the cross with Jesus, "crucified with Christ" (Gal 2:20). As we submerge, it is a picture of being buried with Christ. As we emerge from the water, it depicts being resurrected with Christ. Finally, climbing out of the water pictures our ascension with Christ to sit at the right hand of the Father in heavenly places (Col 3:1; Eph 2:6). Wherever Christ went, we go via baptism of the Holy Spirit, so we are also joined to Him in resurrection, as Paul goes on to affirm in Rom 6:5. The water simply *illustrates* this truth.

With the concluding purpose clause (*hina*, "that . . .") in 6:4, Paul reminds us of the intended goal of our New Position through baptism into Christ: we are to "walk in newness of life." The Greek verb for "walk" (*peripatēsōmen*) is in the subjunctive mood, which implies that our walk *should* match our New Identity, but it *may not do so*. And this in turn becomes Paul's main concern in Romans 6:15-23: to "live out" our New Identity — to walk in newness of life — depends on our choice to present ourselves as slaves, not to Sin but to Righteousness (6:15-20), so that our "newness of life" (6:4) might produce the "fruit" of Righteousness with a view to holiness (6:21-23). Romans 6:5-14 thus stresses the urgency of making this choice lest we remain enslaved to our Sin Nature.

II. Risen in Christ   6:5-7

5For if we have been united together in the likeness of His death, certainly we also shall be in the likeness of His resurrection, 6knowing this, that our old man was crucified with Him, that the body of sin might be done away with, that we should no longer be slaves of sin. 7For he who has died has been freed from sin.

The Emancipation Proclamation was signed by Abraham Lincoln on January 1, 1863, but it didn't reach Texas until June 19th. For nearly six months, slaves in Texas had been legally free; they just didn't *know* it. These verses emphasize our freedom in Christ from the Power of Sin: we are no longer slaves of sin. But if a believer is not *aware of it* ("knowing this," 6:6), he cannot fully enjoy his freedom in Christ. And even though he may not *feel* it he can still *count on* ("reckon," 6:11) the truth in these verses. So, what does it mean to say "our old man was *crucified*" and in what way is "the body of sin . . . *done away* with"?

Some interpret the "old man" to be our Sin Nature. But my Sin Nature is hardly crucified and buried. I suggest that the "old man" or "old self" (NIV) is *all that we were* before we were born again: sinners "*in* Adam" (5:12, 19b; also "*in* the flesh," 7:5). When that identity was crucified with Christ we were *transferred* to a new realm with a New Position where He reigns (Eph 1:20; 2:6); and we *took on* a New Identity as brand new creatures (2 Cor 5:17): *righteous "in* Christ" (Rom 1:17b; 5:19b; 6:3, 11). However, we did not lose our old bodies or appearance or personalities.

Some press the new creature concept too far and hold that our "body of sin" (6:6, the Sin Nature residing in our flesh) *no longer exists*; when we "died" in or with Christ, our Sin Nature was eradicated. They get this idea from the word *katargeō*, which can be translated "destroyed" (NIV) or "done away with" (NKJV). The problem is that we run into the Sin Nature ("the Sin")[1] in quite a few verses in Romans 6 and 7 addressed to *believers*. It is still quite alive and quite powerful. So what does *katargeō* mean? Well, in many contexts the word means "to put out of business, to discharge or dethrone," and that meaning fits this context. The Sin Nature has not been destroyed but rather *discharged* or *dethroned*. It no longer has authority over us. So it is that every believer in Christ is freed from the *jurisdiction* of his Sin Nature in Adam. We can still serve it, but only by choosing to revert to the mindset and practices of "the old man."

That is why death is the perfect metaphor, not for the Sin Nature but for our *relationship* to it; Paul says that he who has died has been freed from sin (compare the "death" of marriage in Rom 7:2). Just as in physical death when hunger no longer has dominion over us, so also in our glorified bodies we can apparently eat as we wish but we no longer *have* to eat. Just as death will free us from the necessity of eating, so also we don't *have* to sin after we become believers — in our "death," crucified with Christ, we have been set free. Watchman Nee says:

> God's way of deliverance is altogether different from man's way. Man's way is to try to suppress sin by seeking to overcome it; God's way is to remove the sinner. . . . God's means of delivering us from sin is not by making us stronger and stronger but . . . weaker and weaker. That is . . . a peculiar way of victory, you say; but it is the divine way. God sets us free from the dominion of sin, not by strengthening our old man, but by crucifying him; not by helping him do anything but by removing him from the scene of the action.

> For years, maybe, you have tried fruitlessly to exercise control over yourself, and perhaps this is still our experience; but when once you see the truth you will recognize that you are indeed powerless to do anything, but that in setting you aside altogether God has done it all. Such a discovery brings human striving and self-effort to an end.[2]

Our New Identity is like escaping the force of gravity while hand-gliding or parachuting. I used to dream of flying whenever I saw Superman on TV or Peter Pan. My dream came true while on vacation in Switzerland. My wife and I were hiking on a beautiful ridge when a man suspended by a parachute suddenly

---

1 On Paul's terminology in Romans for the "Sin Nature," see note 1, Chapter 1, "Who You Gonna Call?"

2 Watchman Nee, *The Normal Christian Life* (Wheaton, IL: Tyndale, 1977), 53-54.

emerged out of one of the adjacent clouds about a hundred yards away. I was nearly in shock. As he disappeared back into the cloud, I said, "I've got to do that." So, at the bottom of the mountain I signed up and asked Betty if she would be waiting for me at the landing pad. She said she was going shopping. "You don't want to watch me *fly*?" "No," she replied, "I don't want to watch you *die*." It was the closest I will ever come to feeling like a bird, just gliding around, guiding myself by little ropes tied to the parachute.

Sin is like gravity. Our New Identity in Christ's death sets us free from the Sin Nature in this life, even before physical death: We were buried with Him in death to be raised with Him to new life. As long as we "hang on" and live according to our New Identity, Sin has no power over us, but that doesn't mean we can't choose to "let go" and yield to the appeal of Sin (Rom 6:1, 15); hence the high priority of appropriating ("reckoning") our "death" to Sin in Christ in order to live according to our New Identity (6:8-11). That is what this section of Romans is all about.

III. Living in Christ   6:8-11

8Now if we died with Christ, we believe that we shall also live with Him, 9knowing that Christ, having been raised from the dead, dies no more. Death no longer has dominion over Him. 10For the death that He died, He died to sin once for all; but the life that He lives, He lives to God. 11Likewise you also, reckon yourselves to be dead indeed to sin, but alive to God in Christ Jesus our Lord.

Paul now drives home the main implication of our "baptismal transfer" to our New Position as *risen* with Christ: that we are to *walk in newness of life* (6:4). Thus, he now mentions "live(s)," "life," or "alive" five times. As our substitute in *death* Christ freed us from the Penalty of sin; as our substitute in *life* He now frees us from the Power of sin so we might *live His life*. The word "reckon" in v. 11 (*logizomai*) is an accounting term in banking. When we say, "You can *bank on* it," it means you can *count on* it to be true for yourself. Both "believe" (6:8) and "reckon" (6:11) are in the present tense, so we *keep counting on* (appropriating) Christ's life in us by continuing to believe we will live in Him. As a "preventive" theologian, Paul wants us focused on our new Position and Identity in Christ so we might "live out" our New Condition. But this can't happen if we don't remain aware of what Christ accomplishes *for* us through the cross and resurrection.

"Knowing" (*being aware of*) Christ's resurrected ability to "live to God" (6:9-10) thus prepares us to fulfill our New Identity as "righteous in Christ" (5:19b): we reveal *His* righteousness only by continuing to appropriate *His* life in us (6:11) by faith (1:17; 3:21-22). Once we understand Christ's work on our behalf, the only way our Position can alter our Condition is to place full confidence in—*reckon* or *appropriate*—that New Identity as ours. Paul will show in 6:12-14 how that confidence then enables us to choose to serve Righteousness rather than Sin, and "newness of life" (6:4) will in turn depend on sustaining this choice (6:15-23).

Meanwhile, in vv. 1-11 he wants us to bask in the wonderful glory of our Position in Him. As we focus on our Position, these truths begin to transform our Condition (2 Cor 3:18). Our Condition can never affect our Position, but our Position can radically alter our Condition. It is a matter of focus (Col 3:2-3). As we focus on our miserable Condition, our Condition gets worse; as we focus on our marvelous Position, our Condition will slowly but surely conform to our Position. We will become what we think about all day long.

This truth is illustrated in Nathaniel Hawthorne's story, "The Great Stone Face." In a beautiful Appalachian Valley there was a strange legend about a wise and beneficent man who would someday come to the valley and do much good for all who learned from his wisdom. They would recognize him by his strong resemblance to a configuration known as the "Great Stone Face" high in the hills above the valley. A little boy named Ernest was determined to be the first one to spot the wise man that would look like the Great Stone Face, so he would walk the valley on the way home after school and sit below the Great Stone Face to study every feature in detail.

The first man to come to the valley was a wealthy shopkeeper named Gathergold. But his face lacked the beneficence of the Great Stone Face, and he was miserly. The next candidate was a great general dubbed Old Blood-and-Thunder. This man had a strong will and a hard face, but not the wisdom and love of the Great Stone Face. Another man had left the valley to run for president and came back to campaign. They called him Old Stoney Phiz. Ernest had high hopes for Old Stoney Phiz, but he had a "weary gloom in the deep caverns of his eyes" like a child who had grown weary of his toys. He was a man of no lofty ideas or purpose in life.

Finally, years later a well-known poet came to the valley to meet Ernest, who was now old but known far and wide for his wisdom and sagacity. On meeting the poet and admiring his poems, Ernest studied his features, only to find that his likeness did not match the Great Stone Face; but at least he had a new friend. One evening they walked to the foot of the Great Stone Face, where Ernest often enjoyed sharing his wisdom with many admirers who gathered to listen.

> Ernest began to speak, giving to the people of what was in his heart and mind. His words had power, because they accorded with his thoughts; and his thoughts had reality and depth, because they harmonized with his life which he had always lived. It was not mere breath that this preacher uttered; they were the words of life,

because a life of good deeds and holy love was melted into them. Pearls, pure and rich, had been dissolved into this precious draught. The poet, as he listened, felt that the being and character of Ernest were a nobler strain of poetry than he had ever written. His eyes glistening with tears, he gazed reverentially at the venerable man, and said within himself that never was there an aspect so worthy of a prophet and a sage as that mild, sweet, thoughtful countenance, with the glory of white hair diffused about it. At a distance, but distinctly to be seen, high up in the golden light of the setting sun, appeared the Great Stone Face, with hoary mists around it, like the white hairs around the brow of Ernest. Its look of grand beneficence seemed to embrace the world.

At that moment, in sympathy with a thought which he was about to utter, the face of Ernest assumed a grandeur of expression, so imbued with benevolence, that the poet, by an irresistible impulse, threw his arms aloft, and shouted, "Behold! Behold! Ernest is himself the likeness of the Great Stone Face!"

Then all the people looked, and saw that what the deep-sighted poet said was true. The prophecy was fulfilled. But Ernest, having finished what he had to say, took the poet's arm, and walked slowly homeward, still hoping that some wiser and better man than himself would by and by appear, bearing a resemblance to the GREAT STONE FACE.[3]

As we behold the Lord, we become like the Lord (2 Cor 3:18).[4]

Now as we proceed to develop the practical implications for us of this intended conformity to Christ (Rom 6:12-14) we will first retrace the logical basis in 6:6-11 for "reckoning" our New Identity in Him ("righteous in Christ") as the critical foundation for "presenting" ourselves to God.

---

3   Nathaniel Hawthorne, *The Great Stone Face and other Tales from the White Mountains* (San Diego, CA: ICON Group International, 2000), 23-24.

4   We are *not* promoting the power of positive thinking. Merely *thinking about* Jesus could not transform us without the supernatural power of the Holy Spirit (2 Cor 3:18), as we will see in Romans 8.

CHAPTER 6

"DEDICATION before EMANCIPATION = INCARCERATION"

Romans 6:12-14

One of my favorite stories on dedication to Christ comes from the lips of a missionary to Africa named Clark. As he was leaving his mission station with his associates to visit some of the native villages one afternoon, they heard a scream in the underbrush. Taking his rifle, the missionary began plunging his way through the underbrush until he came to a small clearing. There a young African boy was bleeding badly after being mauled by a lion, which was about to pounce on the boy and finish him off. Clark raised his rife and shot the lion dead. They took the boy back to the mission infirmary and cared for him until the boy was strong enough to return to his village.

Some months later as Clark was sitting on the open veranda, he looked down the path and saw a procession approaching, with the same young boy at the head of the procession. The little boy came up to Clark and said, "Sir, I have come to give myself to you this day to become your servant for the rest of my life." Clark replied, "This is not required; you don't need to do that." But the boy insisted, "Sir, you do not understand the law of the forest. If anyone has saved us from certain death, our life belongs to the one who saved us. So according to the law of the forest, my life belongs to you. I come to give myself to you. My friends are carrying all of my possessions." His friends came and laid all the boy's possessions at the feet of the missionary. As Clark recounted his experience he said, "There for the first time I think I began to realize what it must mean to Jesus Christ for a person to present himself and all that he has to God."

So, what motivated the little boy? Certainly, the missionary saved his life, for which the boy was deeply grateful, but that is not why he presented himself as his life servant. Did the boy love the missionary? It is highly unlikely that he would have more love for the missionary than for his own parents, people, and friends. Perhaps he just wanted to come to live at the mission station rather than in the bush. But as another man's servant? Doubtful. No, the basis for his life dedication was the Law of the Forest. It was a matter of obligation. According to this law, the boy's fitting position was to become the property of the man who saved his life, and he gained a new identity as the man's child. Regardless of his longing for home, parents, friends, or the bush, he belonged at the side of the missionary. His dedication was based on reckoning himself subject to the rules of ownership stipulated by the Law of the Forest. With his transfer of ownership, the child dedicated himself to his new master only because of full confidence in his new position, his new identity, and the obligations pertaining thereto.

Paul now tells us to *apply* what we know about our New Identity in Christ: we are to present (dedicate) ourselves as alive and our "members" as instruments of righteousness (Rom 6:13b). Some traditions motivate a Christian's dedication with an appeal to gratitude — "He gave His all for you; the least you can do is give your all to Him." Some even fold this "give your life to Jesus" appeal into a "He Gives/You Give" gospel: "God gives Jesus to you, *if* you give your life to God. Do that and you are in." Not so. Christianity is the only religion in the world with a One Way gospel — the giving goes one way: "God . . . gave His only begotten Son" (Jn 3:16), period. In my tradition, the appeal comes just after a touching emotional story about Christ's love and sacrifice for us. As the choir lifts the melodious strain of "I Surrender All," we are invited to the front to dedicate or *re*dedicate or *re*-rededicate our lives to Him.

So why don't these dedications stick? Often they are built on the wrong foundation. A born-again Christian may have a deep appreciation for what Christ has done for him and be moved in an emotional moment to dedicate his entire life to Christ. After telling himself and others that he is sold out to Christ and has given his all, he finds himself yielding to the same old sins that have beset him for years. Alas, the newly dedicated Christian soon discovers that sin still dwells in his "members" (Rom 7:23) and he begins to feel like a hypocrite. He realizes that his love and gratitude for Christ — lofty though they may be — are not enough to rescue him from the sea of sin in which he drowns daily. At best he is tempted to give up, at worst to doubt his salvation. Unfortunately, *dedication* before *emancipation* only leads to *incarceration*.

Longstanding churchgoers frequently hear teaching on *salvation* and *dedication*, but not nearly enough about *emancipation*. And the failure all too often lies in the pulpit. After painting the ugly picture of Sin in Romans 1–3, we open the gates of heaven in Romans 4 for brand new believers to look at the wonderful promises of justification and salvation by faith alone in Christ alone. But if we then hop to dedication in Romans 12 without teaching how God intends to free them from the Power of Sin to live out their adopted identity (Rom 5–8) as people of God who reveal His righteousness by faith (Rom 9–11), we only oblige them to present themselves with no power to fulfill that calling. They are left incarcerated by Sin, not realizing that the cell was unlocked; so we have an army of believers marching out to serve while still in bondage to the Sin Nature, often questioning their salvation after repeated failure. Sin will squeeze the love of Christ right out of us. Why? Because we love sin more (at least at the moment we choose to sin). That may seem shocking to some of us, but it is true. At the moment of temptation, sin makes an offer of counterfeit life; it is like *fools gold* — momentarily we feel rich but we are eventually left utterly destitute. Those of us who have ever been caught in the headlock of sin know whereof I speak. No matter how much we feel we love Christ, there are times when we love sin more.

Even sincere believers may not realize they are dedicating the *flesh* — the self-life from Adam (Rom 7) — thinking that their love for Christ will sustain them in service and lead to sanctification. It will not. No matter how much we feel we love Christ, we love Sin *more* when we present ourselves in the self-reliant flesh.

What, then, can ever carry us through a life of dedication? Where do we get a solid basis for consecration? Unless we grasp and appropriate the steps to freedom laid out in Romans 6:6-11, dedication will only lead to hypocrisy and defeat. So let's review these steps:

1. *Know* 6:6

Knowing this, that our old man was crucified with Him, that the body of sin might be done away with, that we should no longer be slaves of sin.

I used to attend a church where a listener could easily conclude that freedom from sin came from just stuffing more Bible doctrine into our heads. And it is true that Christianity is not a head trip. On the other hand, I went to another church where the preacher repeatedly railed against Bible doctrine. Say what we want about Bible doctrine, we certainly cannot apply it until we know it. We find the word "doctrine" (or "teaching") twenty-one times in the NT — fifteen in the Pastoral Epistles alone (1 & 2 Timothy and Titus), which were written specifically that we might know how to conduct ourselves in the house of God (1 Tim 3:15).

Miles Stanford aptly said, "Only the believer who knows, grows."[1] We are less interested in Bible doctrine than we were thirty years ago; we prefer hearing (music) or watching (movies, TV, video games). Yet the Bible was written to be

---

1   Miles J. Stanford, *The Principle of Position* (Colorado Springs, CO: n.p., 1967), 4.

read by God's people. Unless we read it or hear it we can't know it. But *what kind of knowledge?* There is a Christian reaction in our postmodern culture to what is pejoratively called *head knowledge*:

> There is a crippling tendency today to deprecate head-knowledge of the truth and even doctrine itself. Emphasis is being put on so-called heart-knowledge gained by means of experience. This, however, is to place condition before position, which is the opposite of the biblical pattern. . . . Head knowledge gives us the facts upon which we exercise faith or reckon. In time, through deeper understanding and quiet assimilation of the truth, there is both head-knowledge and heart-knowledge. . . . Some people belittle head-knowledge because they see so many Christians who seem to know so much Scripture yet whose lives fail to "adorn the doctrine" (Tit 2:10). Doubtless there is some justification for this reaction, but it should be realized that one's knowledge of the truth is always in advance of his growth in that truth. . . . Ideally, head-knowledge precedes heart-knowledge. However, neither one is preeminent above the other — both are necessary for healthy growth and effective ministry. Heart-knowledge alone cannot progress beyond babyhood. It can exhort, emotionalize, and share experiences and blessings, but it cannot lead others to establishment in the truth. In order to share effectively, we must be brought to maturity of both head-knowledge and heart-knowledge.[2]

I love Watchman Nee's little illustration of Fact, Faith, and Feeling walking along the top of a wall.[3] Fact led steadily on, turning neither to the left or right, and never looked behind. All went well as long as Faith kept his eyes focused on Fact; but as soon as he got concerned about Feeling and turned his head to see how Feeling was doing, he lost his balance and tumbled off the wall, and poor old Feeling fell down after him. The Facts always stand as the Statue of Liberty, welcoming Christians to the land of freedom and independence from our Sin Nature in Adam. Only the believer who knows, grows (Eph 4:21); yet this growth[4] also requires *faith.*

2. *Believe*   6:8

Now if we died with Christ, we believe that we shall also live with Him.

---

2   Miles J. Stanford, *The Complete Green Letters* (Grand Rapids, MI: Zondervan, 1983), 191.

3   Watchman Nee, *The Normal Christian Faith* (Anaheim, CA: Living Stream Ministry, 1994), 144-5.

4   This is *not* to say that truth can only be known *verbally* and *propositionally*; the emotions, conscience, and intuitive knowledge (1 Jn 3:16-24; Rom 2:14-15; Eccl 3:11) all help us respond to the Spirit (1 Cor 2:10-12) to integrate what Stanford calls "heart knowledge." *Head* and *heart* knowledge are mutually informing requisites of spiritual growth.

The word translated "believe" is *pisteuō* — the noun form of this word means "faith." Right after Fact comes Faith. We cannot leap from facts to feelings. Many believers try to do this, but it amounts to equating faith and head-knowledge. We could liken it to becoming a Christian. I have said many times that a person can know all the facts about Christ and never have Christ in his heart until he puts his *trust* in those facts. That is faith. It can come as a rather passive persuasion without any conscious choice, or it can include a conscious decision to trust that certain promises are facts even though there is no objective, discernible evidence (Heb 11:1).

This is reminiscent of Blondin, the famous tight-rope walker who pushed a wheelbarrow over Niagara Falls while walking on a cable. When he got back, he asked a little boy if he thought Blondin could push someone across in the wheelbarrow. The little boy assured Blondin that he knew it could be done. But when Blondin asked the little boy to jump in, he disappeared. The little boy was persuaded or convinced that Blondin could push the barrel across and back. After all, he had seen him do it. But the great feat could not be performed on the basis of the little boy's knowledge alone. He lacked faith.

Some will argue that the little boy did have faith since he was persuaded that Blondin could accomplish the feat. Nevertheless, something happens inside the person when he has a strong personal interest at stake. If the little boy got into the wheelbarrow, he would have a strong personal interest at stake. Would he have to get into the wheelbarrow to have faith? No, getting in would be *evidence* of his faith; faith is something internal. But the moment he decides to get in, a settled trust germinates in his heart. *Then* he could act, but not before.

The same is true of trusting Christ as Savior. If I am swimming in the ocean and someone comes by in a lifeboat and offers to take me ashore, I might say, "No thanks." The people rowing the lifeboat might ask me if I question the ability of their boat to get me to shore. I could say that I have complete confidence in the boat's ability to get me to shore; in fact, I might be persuaded that this boat is the best lifeboat on the ocean. But I need to see that I have something personal at stake. Once I see that my life is at stake in some way and I have run out of human strength, then I am ready for the lifeboat. At that point, if an offer is made to take me ashore, I would quickly make my decision to get in the boat; only then will the boat do me any personal good.

So we can *know* all the facts about our death to sin from Romans 6:1-10, but our Condition will not change significantly until we decide to *trust* in these facts. That is the moment our head-knowledge becomes heart-knowledge. The same is true of trusting Christ for life every day — remember, eternal life is not just a *destiny* but also a *quality* of life to be lived in the present. This verse affirms that if we died with him we can also *live* with him *now*, which is precisely what is "at stake" in this passage if we are to incarnate God's righteousness within us (Rom 6:13b; see 1:17; 3:21).

3. *Reckon*   6:11

Likewise you also, reckon yourselves to be dead indeed to sin, but alive to God in Christ Jesus our Lord.

The word translated "reckon" (NKJV) or "count" (NIV) is *logizōmai*. It has three basic senses: 1) to credit to one's account; 2) to add up the evidence; 3) to meditate, consider facts. Of thirty-five uses in the NT, nineteen are right here in Romans. Obviously, Paul considers it an important word for Christians to grasp. The first meaning fits most of the uses in Romans, especially in chapter 4. It is an accounting term meaning "to credit/charge to one's account," usually either righteousness (4:3) or sin (4:8). Here it has the sense of crediting to our account both death to sin and life to God in Christ (5:9-10).

To *reckon* thus entails progress beyond initial faith. If it meant just to examine the evidence or facts and count them as true, then this is done before faith. We do not trust something we do not believe to be true. But to count it up and put it on our ledger — that is a progression of faith.

In Romans 6:11 Paul has gone beyond asking us to reckon on *Christ's* death and resurrection; he is asking us to appropriate *our own* death and resurrection *in* Christ. We are absolved of sin through Christ's death (Rom 4:25a), but a brand new person has also been raised with Him (4:25b) in order to walk in newness of life (6:4). Yet not until we know, believe, and *appropriate* this Identity will it help our Condition—to *actually walk* in newness of life.

Perhaps I can illustrate *reckon* this way. If you came up to me and said, "Dave, I've just come into a lot of money, and I've decided to give a million to you." I would probably say, "You're kidding." But you show me your bank account with its millions. You show me how a million had just been withdrawn that day. Then you produce a deposit slip with my account number on it. These are the facts I see, and I am convinced. I know it must be true, and I believe it. How do I reckon on it? I open up my check book and I credit a million to my account. And then I start writing checks. You see, I can know the facts and believe the facts, but not until I credit my account with a million and start writing checks have I reckoned on the facts.

In the case of the little boy and Blondin, the boy knew Blondin could do it and he would have faith if he decided to get in the wheelbarrow. But to *count on* Blondin's ability is to actually take the master tightrope artist's hand with a view to getting in the wheelbarrow. If Blondin had stopped him at that point, the boy would still have had faith; this was the point of Abraham's willingness to sacrifice Isaac without actually completing the act (Heb 11:17-19).

My illustration of the million dollars is not so far-fetched. It just so happens that after the Civil War a man came to Texas, discovered oil and became a millionaire, but died without a wife or children, leaving thirty million. The lawyer discovered his only sister had died and left a single grandson who had lived for years as a beggar in Philadelphia. The lawyer went to Philadelphia and found the beggar was still alive. He opened an account in the beggar's name with a million dollars from the deceased man's estate. He told him, "You are a millionaire. I just deposited a million in your name at the local bank, and there are twenty-nine million more to come." The beggar just scoffed, refusing to concede, believe, or reckon on the facts; he just kept on sleeping in the gutter and eating out of garbage cans. That was his condition, even though by his legal position, he had a New Identity as a millionaire.

This is very much how God's sees us. In our Condition we are beggars and have been living in moral and mental filth for years. But in Romans 6 He announces, "Look at your New Identity; you're millionaires. I've deposited the righteousness of Christ to your account. You are free from sin, for you have died and been raised with Him." We can either continue living as beggars in spite of the facts or we can *concede* that we are dead to sin and alive in Christ, then *believe* and *count on* (appropriate) it. We reckon ourselves spiritual millionaires by taking off the clothes of the Old Man that we were, the rags of anger, wrath, malice, blasphemy, and filthy communication that spring out of our mouths from the Sin Nature and we put on the clothes of the New Man that we are (Eph 4:22-24). As spiritual millionaires, we can *appropriate* the fact that we have all this spiritual wealth — we can confidently draw on our heavenly account to clothe ourselves in a lavish wardrobe: shirts of kindness and humility, suits of meekness and longsuffering, blouses of forbearance and forgiveness, slacks made out of love. This is what it means to *reckon*.

In laying a foundation for dedication (Rom 6:1-11), Paul says nothing about love or gratitude for what Christ has done; these are noble motives but not sufficient for dedication. This passage affirms that the only sound, lasting basis for Christian service is our new Position and Identity in Christ (2 Cor 5:17). The believer who presents himself for service on any other basis is begging for trouble, for he is still under bondage to the Sin Nature in his own efforts to serve he finds himself in a prison of hypocrisy, frustrated by his inability to deal with his own life, let alone help others with theirs. *Dedication* before *Emancipation = Incarceration*. Only when we *admit, believe,* and *count on* the reality of emancipation are we then equipped to *appropriate* this reality (apply it to ourselves) in dedication. And this is just where Paul's argument is headed:

B.	**Freedom from Sin**		**(6)**
	1.	**Our New Position in Christ**	**(6:1-14)**
		a. **New Identity** *Explained*	**(6:1-11)**
		b. **New Identity** *Applied*	**(6:12-14)**
	2.	**Our New Privilege in Christ**	**(6:15-23)**

4. *Present* 6:12-14

12Therefore do not let sin reign in your mortal body, that you should obey it in its lusts. 13And do not present your members as instruments of unrighteousness to sin, but present yourselves to God as being alive from the dead, and your members as instruments of righteousness to God. 14For sin shall not have dominion over you, for you are not under law but under grace.

Notice that v. 12 starts with "Therefore." We are urged to *present* ourselves based on the truth provided in 6:1-11. It is in realizing our Position in Christ as *dead* to the Sin Nature and our New Identity as *alive* in Christ — *reckoning* this to be true, *appropriating* that Identity — that we finally have warrant to present (dedicate) ourselves to the righteousness of God. Verses 12 and 13 present, respectively, two negative and two positive commands.

a. Two Negative Commands 12-13a

The First Negative (12). We are told not to let "sin" reign. The Greek here is helpful because "sin" is preceded by the definite article which makes the noun very specific, just as in vv. 1, 2, 6, 10, and 11. The "sin" Paul has been discussing for eleven verses is now further qualified as dwelling within us: it is not a specific *personal* sin but precisely what we have been calling the Sin Nature (or Sin).[5]

The believer needs to be very clear about the fact that his New Identity in Christ did not eradicate his Sin Nature. He carries it forward from the Old Man (all he was in Adam *before* Christ) to reside within the unredeemed flesh of the New Man (all that he is *in* Christ). Becoming a believer changed his standing (Position) before God, but it did not change his personality or eliminate his physicality or the Sin Nature from what Paul calls the "flesh" (6:19). That is the bad news. But the good news is that we no longer have to obey Sin.

The word "reign" (*basileuō*) is the same verb as we saw in 5:17, 21, from which we get the noun "kingdom." So Paul pictures our bodies as a kingdom in which there is a throne. It is our choice as to who will sit on the throne of our lives, our Sin Nature or Jesus Christ. Since Sin has been is deposed and no longer has

---

5   See note 1, Chapter 1, "Who You Gonna Call?"

authority over us, we are free to serve someone else, though we can still choose to serve Sin. The appeal here is to serve God. Sin is no longer king in our lives by virtue of our new Position, so how absurd to obey it!

How can we tell who is on the throne of our lives? By the results — the word "that" in v. 12b has the force of "so that" and denotes "results." When we sense the lusts of our bodies controlling us then we can be pretty sure that our Sin Nature is on the throne of our lives. The word for lust, *epithumia*, can simply mean "desire." The desires of our body for food, rest, drink, and sex are not evil in and of themselves. Without them we could not live or propagate the human race (Gen 1:28). However, the Sin Nature can take any one of these and pervert it for evil until it dominates our life as an addiction. A good marker of this domination is the characteristic presence of works of the flesh (Gal 5:19). Since these are rooted in the Sin Nature, they tell us when Sin — and thus death — is reigning in us (Rom 5:17a, 21a).

But again, we do not have to let our Sin Nature take control. Someone aptly said, "There is no known sin in the Christian life which isn't voluntary sin." If I were to reply, "Oh, no, I just couldn't help it," maybe so, but *Jesus* could help it. As one little girl said, "When Sin knocks on your door, send Jesus to answer." This recalls the substitutionary life of Christ — the Christ-life for the self-life ("flesh"). If I obey an evil lust, either it is serving as a counterfeit source of life or I am trying to fight it with self-reliance, rather than Christ in me. Christ in me is really the only worthwhile and enduring source of righteousness leading to life (Rom 5:17b, 21b), even though at times it may seem like an offer of death.

The Second Negative (13a). Paul now "fleshes out" the first negative by commanding us not to present our members to Sin as instruments of unrighteousness. Again, "Sin" is the Sin Nature. The word for "instruments" (*hopla*) refers to weapons of warfare, so Paul is clearly portraying the Christian life as a battle. We can use our "weapons" to fight on the side of Sin or the side of God. It is our choice. The Greek word for *unrighteousness* (*adikia*) is the same as in Romans 1:18; Paul is simply emphasizing how absurd it is for those being saved as agents of God's righteousness to serve *un*righteousness instead, which only incurs God's wrath (1:16-18).

The Greek word (*paristēmi*) for "present" (NKJV) or "offer" (NIV) is a religious term, meaning to present an offering at the altar — it literally means "to stand beside." It is as though God and Sin are each asking for volunteers to step forward. If we choose God, then we go stand alongside Christ. When a church has an altar call, sometimes the pastor is asking us to come up front and say, "I will be on the Lord's side. I present my body for His service in His battle." We place ourselves at the disposal of another, just like the old hymn: "Who is on the Lord's side? Who will serve the king? Who will be His helpers, others' lives to bring? Who will leave the world's side? Who will face the foe? Who is on the Lord's side? Who for Him will go?"

In this battle it is sobering to realize that our bodies, which God created and called good, can instead be used as weapons of destruction when offered to an evil king like Sin. The stomach can serve as a garbage dump for all sorts of refuse. The eye can be used as a spy satellite to scan and invade territory that is off-limits. The hand can be a thief to rob or a club to beat, even to kill. The tongue — ah, the tongue — can be used as a bayonet to stab and wound innocent victims (Jas 3:5-12). And how about our sexual "members" (1 Cor 6:12-20)?

b. Two Positive Commands   13b-c

After the two things we are *not* to do, there are now two things we *should* do. The "but" (*alla*) that divides Rom 6:13a from 13b-c makes the strongest possible contrast in the Greek. With this word Paul moves decisively from the negatives to the positives.

The First Positive (13b). In contrast to "letting Sin reign" (v. 12) we can opt to present ourselves to God. Why should we do this? By now we should realize that it is stupid to serve an evil king who has been deposed. If Hitler or Stalin or Jim Jones had been deposed but was still alive, you would have to be insane to volunteer to serve them. It's just as insane to serve an evil king who only brings misery to our lives when we don't have to. We have another word for this kind of craziness: co-dependency. It is like the wife who keeps going back to the husband who beats her. Why should we volunteer for God's army? Because we are *dead* to Sin but *alive* in Jesus (6:1-11). Can't we just be neutral? No. We serve in one army or the other.

Is this a *one-time* dedication or something that is repeated? Can I rededicate my life after I dedicate my life? Here the tenses involved might be helpful. Although the command "to present" occurs twice, the tenses are different: The first (negative) is in the *present* tense, while the second (positive) is in the *aorist*. The present tense is appropriate if someone needs to stop doing what they have been doing habitually. But if they need to *begin* a new habit — start doing something new — the aorist tense is used ("ingressive aorist"). Since the ingressive aorist is used here after Paul has exhorted his readers to *stop* the old habit of serving Sin, he wants them to *start* a new habit: Serve God. It assumes that at some point in time a decision is made to follow Him, to join His army, to serve the King, but it is meant to continue.

Jesus also tells us to deny ourselves, take up the cross daily and follow Him if we want to be His disciples, on His side (Lk 9:23). Every day. Each morning I wake up with my default setting on the flesh. I must make a conscious choice to hit the C+S keys: Control + Spirit. I need to start my day with a conscious choice to walk by the Spirit in order not to "fulfill the lusts of the flesh" (see Gal 5:16). I have talked with some Christians who claim they don't wake up with their default setting on the flesh. God bless 'em, but they still have to deal with Jesus' command to deny themselves, take up their cross *daily* and follow Him (Lk 9:23). The aorist tense signifies a *conscious, daily choice,* whether the moment I wake up or at some other time that day. Every day after that initial commitment I can still defect; it is a daily commitment.

The Second Positive (13c). Paul narrows down to the specifics of the generality affirmed in v. 13b. Present your body — specifically, the *members* of your body — as instruments of war with the goal of righteousness rather than unrighteousness (v. 13a). Just as these body parts can be used for *evil,* so they can be used for *good* when controlled by the Spirit in submission to the reign of God. This completes Paul's explanation of the "mechanics" by which those in Christ who *accept* the free gift of grace are released from subjection to the rule of Sin and death so that they might reign in Righteousness to life (5:17b, 18b, 21b).

The presentation of "members" is illustrated by the Greek philosopher Xanthus, who sent his servant to market for the very best food to prepare for some important guests. When they were seated, Xanthus called for the first course. His servant brought in an appetizer of boiled tongue cocktail. Delicious. For the next course the servant brought in a wonderful tongue Caesar salad. But the third course was baked tongue. Fourth? Skewered tongue. Dessert? Tongue sundae. Greatly agitated, Xanthus called his servant aside and said, "I told you to buy the very best food you could find." His servant replied, "But master, what could be better than the tongue? It is the organ of eulogies, the organ of encouragement, the organ of inspiration, the organ of eloquence, the organ of worship, the organ of truth, the organ of . . ."

Xanthus cut him off. "Fine," he said sternly, "Tomorrow you are to go to market and buy the very worst food you can find." The servant complied. When the guests were seated, Xanthus called for the first course. An appetizer of boiled tongue cocktail. The second course: tongue Caesar salad. The third course: baked tongue. Fourth? Skewered tongue. Dessert? Tongue sundae. Greatly agitated, Xanthus again called his servant aside and said, "I told you to go to the market and buy the very worst food you could find." His servant replied, "But master, what could be worse than the tongue? It is the organ of deceit, the organ of discouragement, the organ of blasphemy, the organ of dirty jokes, the organ of slander, and the organ of gossip."

The tongue, just like other members of our bodies, can serve positive or negative purposes (Jas 3:8-12). It can be used by God or by Satan (contrast Matt 16:16-17 with 16:23). Paul wants us to present our members to God as weapons of warfare through our Lord Jesus to produce righteous behavior.

And why should we do this? *"For* you are not under law but under grace" (Rom 6:14).

c. Free to Obey under Grace 14

There is no emotional appeal here to dedicate oneself. Paul simply notes a change in governance. Just as we have received a new king (from King Sin to King Jesus), we live under a new principle for life: grace instead of law. When we choose self-reliance through our flesh in Adam (6:19) we subject ourselves again to the standard of Law which only convicts us through our consciences and sentences us back to incarceration under the "dominion" or reign of sin (6:14; see 2:14-15; 3:20; 5:20a, 21a). In this state of "dominion," we can only indulge the Sin Nature, as we shall see in Romans 7. Just so, when we choose to rely on Christ in us, He subjects us to Grace, not Law, through dependency on His Spirit, as we shall see in Romans 8.

Again, the appeal here is to Positional truth. Imagine a ship at sea that was found to have a crook for a captain. The captain is thrown into the brig and replaced by the first mate until they reach port. Now, to whom should the crew members present themselves — the crooked captain who keeps appealing for their loyalty, or the first mate, the acting captain? The crew may very well have built up a tremendous loyalty and love for the old captain. He pays well, feeds them well, and can hold his liquor well. Why should the crew present themselves to the new captain and ruling principle? Because by Position, they are under the employ of the ship owners, and by Position they should be loyal to whoever is acting in the interests of the owners. The old captain was not doing this. The crew members should present themselves as loyal members to the new captain, not because they love the new captain more than the old, not because the new captain will pay them better, not out of gratitude, but because in their position as employees of the ship owners, they should serve the agent who is *faithful* to the owners.

Andrew Murray states:

> A superficial acquaintance with God's plan leads to the view that while justification is God's work by faith in Christ, sanctification (growth) is our work, to be performed under the influence of the gratitude we feel for the deliverance we have experienced, and by

the aid of the Holy Spirit. But the earnest Christian soon learns how little gratitude can supply the power.[6]

And by virtue of our position, we should identify with our owner through the faithful Son (Heb 2:10; 3:6; 12:2). Sanctification, like justification, is by grace through faith in Christ who is our substitute in death but also in life. Receiving Christ's substitutionary death apart from His substitutionary life is like leaving a newborn baby to grow up on its own.

A good illustration of this truth is the hand and the gardening glove. When I pick up the glove, it is incapable of accomplishing anything. I can urge, encourage, cajole, manipulate . . . but the glove will do nothing. But when I put my hand in the glove, it is capable of all sorts of things. In the same way, we are incapable of accomplishing anything of eternal significance on our own; but by appropriating our New Identity — the substitutionary life of Christ — His "hands" of grace use us like gloves to bear much fruit (Jn 15:6-8).

Conclusion: Dedication *before* Emancipation = Incarceration

So far we have covered four of the five steps in the stairway to our emancipation from the Sin Nature. Know → Believe → Reckon → Present/Dedicate. Knowing our Position/Identity in Christ equips us to be released from domination by our Sin Nature in Adam. Our death, burial, and resurrection with Christ are among the very first facts a new Christian should learn. If he does not he may lose years, never knowing that although the Sin Nature is still present in the flesh, he is free from its rule and does not have to obey it. When he realizes this and appropriates it then he is ready to present or dedicate his life and his members to the Lord, but not before.

And what is the basis for our dedication? Again, it is not our *love* for Christ — at times we get more counterfeit "life" from sin. And it is not our *gratitude* to Christ — too often we are ingrates towards God's grace and even "despise the riches of His goodness" (Rom 2:4). The basis for dedication, to risk life and limb, is our New Position and Identity in Him — it is the basis for all spiritual growth.

How can we overstate the importance of the truth of Romans 6? Some think these truths about our New Identity in Christ are too deep for the new Christian to understand, just like some think prophecy is too deep to understand. Yet Paul spent only three weeks with the Thessalonians, and during those three weeks he grounded them in the details of prophecy. Why? Because our blessed hope in Christ's imminent return is half the answer to solving our misery in our Condition

---

6   Andrew Murray, *Abide in Christ* (London: James Nisbet & Co., 1888), 65.

on earth. But the other half is Positional truth. If Paul grounded new Christians in prophetic truth, you can be sure he grounded them in Positional truth.

This is preventive theology. It tells us how we can be free from the domination of the Sin Nature. It all hinges on our death, burial, and resurrection with Christ, our Position in Christ. These are some of the first facts a new Christian should learn. If he does not, he may lose years never knowing that although the Sin Nature is still in his life, he is free from its rule and does not have to obey it. When he realizes this and reckons it to be true, he is ready to present or dedicate life and limb to the Lord, but not before.

The movie "Anastasia" well illustrates the intended connection between our Position and our Condition. It is the story of the one child of Nikolas and Alexandra Romanoff to escape the slaughter of the Tsar and his family by the Bolsheviks in 1918 — the only living heir to the throne of Russia. For her own protection, when Anastasia was sent into hiding somewhere in Austria, she was never told who she was. So she was not raised to be a princess, but instead she lived the life of a commoner and behaved like a commoner. A Russian discovers her and must convince Anastasia's aunt that she was the real princess, and much of the movie is teaching Anastasia how to walk and talk like royalty. She had to work on her bearing, her table manners, her accent, her appearance — practically everything in her lifestyle had to change.

But even harder than convincing the aunt was convincing Anastasia herself that she really belonged to the royal family. At times she thought she was playing the role of an imposter. The Russian finally convinced her through a birth mark that she was really a princess. But that was when the *real* work began. He taught Anastasia to walk and talk like a queen so she could live out her *identity* as a queen. After months of focusing on how she as a queen was called to behave and speak, Anastasia's Condition began to reflect her royal Identity.

Anastasia's experience is exactly how the believer finds freedom from Sin to conform his behavior to his true identity. Christians are adopted into God's royal family, but our destiny is to be kings and queens who rule forever with the King of Kings in a way we do not yet fully see (Rom 5:17b, 21b; 8:15-17). As new creatures in Christ our birth mark (baptism into His death, 6:1-4a) identifies us as members of this royal family. But only by fully understanding, believing, and appropriating our Righteous Identity can we then present ourselves to God as instruments of Righteousness, so our earthly Condition might conform to our heavenly Position and bring life (6:4b-14). This is being preoccupied with Christ, as the familiar hymn urges us:

> Turn your eyes upon Jesus;
> Look full in His wonderful face,

> And the things of earth will grow strangely dim
> In the light of His glory and grace.

To summarize Paul's argument in Romans 6:1-14, the imagined objector (6:1) asked why we should not wallow in sin if we can't out-sin God's grace; after all, the more grace from God, the more glory for God. The answer? That's insane! Why keep serving a tyrant if we have new citizenship in the land of the free? Why keep going back to a husband who beats you? That is a sick co-dependency.

But Paul now anticipates a modified objection (6:15). If it doesn't make sense to wallow in sin, what could be so bad about just indulging sin from time to time for a "taste" of the old life? After all, a little bit of sin never hurt anyone. Oh yes it does. This is a subtle but deadly error, for our intended destiny of freedom and life as kings and queens — to rule forever with the King of Kings — is soon subverted as we quickly revert to our prior enslavement to Sin and death under Law (Rom 6:15-23). As Jesus put it, "He who commits sin is a slave of sin" (Jn 8:34).

CHAPTER 7

"FREEDOM THROUGH SLAVERY"
Romans 6:15-23

One of the items on my "bucket list" was to go salmon fishing in Alaska. I finally did it, but I got more than I bargained for: I was not prepared for Nature's beauty in that part of the world. The combination of water, forests, mountains, and mists made for a unique journey through God's glorious creation. One particular cove I will never forget. We had already maxed out for the day in king salmon, so we decided to try a little fly fishing for silver salmon. We took our boat where a stream broke into two branches just before entering a pristine cove. As we entered the cove its stunning beauty took our breath away. The cove was rimmed by spruce and pine trees as old as Alaska itself. The water was cold but clear, and salmon were jumping all over the place. And the *birds* — I counted twenty-three American eagles perched around the cove. It looked like man had never been there. But as I put on my waders to get in the water, another visitor showed up — a big brown bear with a sense of entitlement to the cove. Only twenty yards separated us, so I decided the better part of wisdom was to get back in the boat while he fished. But while I watched him, I watched the eagles soar and the salmon jump. It occurred to me that this fishing hole was for the eagles as well as the bears and salmon — I had never seen so many in one place.

Maybe I was a bit giddy from the whole experience but I began to imagine the eagles trying to swim and the salmon trying to fly. From one of my other bucket list items (remember the sky-diving?) I knew that God has designed the bird quite uniquely to use the air for soaring and gliding. Humans just fall. A bird is at its best in the air. Take it out of the air, put it under water, and it would quickly die. Conversely for the salmon: They may have been jumping for joy, but their joy would be short-lived if they stayed in the air very long. God designed them for water. In their proper domains, the salmon and eagles enjoy tremendous freedom. But whenever one of God's creatures seeks freedom outside its proper domain and contrary to its design, death soon follows. So too for those who are in Christ. We enjoy true freedom only within our proper domain and in conformity with our unique design. When we seek freedom outside that domain, death comes quickly. Not *physical* death (though that is possible) or *spiritual* death (which is impossible for the child of God). I mean the death of spiritual *defeat* and *despair* that inevitably follows slavery to Sin.

Goethe said, "None are more hopelessly enslaved than those who falsely believe they are free." Only the Creator enjoys infinite, absolute freedom. True freedom for a created being is not absolute — our freedom is limited by our design and domain. Ironically, the first step toward true freedom is to recognize that everyone is someone's slave. That is why Jesus wants us to know the truth — "you shall know the truth, and the truth will make you free" (Jn 8:32). What truth? Paradoxically, *freedom comes through slavery*. Let's see how, in Romans 6:15-23.

B.	**Freedom from Sin**	**(6)**
1.	**Our New Position in Christ**	**(6:1-14)**
2.	**Our New Privilege in Christ**	**(6:15-23)**
	a. Two *Principles*	15-16
	b. Two *Positions*	17-18
	c. Two *Practices*	19
	d. Two *Products*	20-23

As we move to the second half of Romans 6, we build on our Position in Christ as we look at our Privilege in Christ. After assuring us that we cannot out-sin God's grace (Rom 5:20b), Paul had anticipated the risk of promoting licentious living by emphasizing how utterly contrary it would be to the entire prospect of our freedom in Christ — it keeps us enslaved to a tyrant that has no spiritual jurisdiction over us (6:2-14)! But as Paul concludes his argument with another statement about grace (6:14), he anticipates another loophole: "OK, I'll grant you that wallowing in sin is not healthy. But since we are under grace and not the law, why can't we sin just a little?" This is a typical scenario: "It's wonderful to be eternally secure, knowing I can't lose my salvation no matter what I do. God knows I'm not perfect, life is tough, and I need a "little taste" of the old life now and then. Since I can always confess right after I sin, what's a little sin? I'm under *grace*, and He'll forgive me; at least I'm not as bad as . . . ."

In a nutshell Paul replies that he who sins is the slave of sin, right then and there. It's like the recovering alcoholic who asks why he can't have just one little drink. I suspect we all know the answer, and it's just the same for the recovering *sinaholic*: we quickly revert to the slavery of our addiction. So what's the solution? Ironically, the final step of our full emancipation from the power of Sin is *obedience*. It is in voluntarily submitting to God's righteous design for us (Rom 5:17-21) that we are delivered from Sin's slavery *to* full freedom in Christ:

FREEDOM

5. Obey (6:16) ↑

4. Present (6:13) ↑

3. Reckon (6:11) ↑

2. Believe (6:8) ↑

1. Know (6:6) ↑

SLAVERY ↑

Therefore, in this half of the chapter Paul will show us that the fullest life possible — full freedom from our Sin Nature — comes by obeying one master rather than the other.

A. Two *Principles*   6:15-16

15*What then? Shall we sin because we are not under law but under grace? Certainly not!* 16*Do you not know that to whom you present yourselves slaves to obey, you are that one's slaves whom you obey, whether of sin leading to death, or of obedience leading to righteousness?*

Paul goes out of his way to underscore the absurdity of the prospect of reverting to sin, replying as in 6:1 with emphatic negation (6:15). We might say, "No way!" or "Not!" Why? There are two principles: 1) We are still slaves of whichever master we obey; and 2) the choice we make leads to inevitable consequences. Whoever would raise the possibility of sinning even a little has already lost sight of God's main goal in Romans for our "presentation": *righteousness revealed.*[1] William James put it this way: "Sow a thought, reap an action; sow an action, reap a habit; sow a habit, reap a destiny."

To illustrate the **first** principle, a blacksmith during the Middle Ages prided himself that he had never made a flawed link for a chain. But after committing a crime, he was imprisoned and chained. As he began looking over the chains, link by link, searching for a flaw that might give him his means of escape, he finally came to a link that bore his own insignia. Defeated by his discovery, he dropped the chain — he had been bound by a chain of his own making. While it is true that we have been delivered from the eternal Penalty of sin by Jesus, it is also true that we can be bound by our own chains when we presume on God's grace

---

1   Here, as generally in Romans 5–8, *righteousness is behavioral conformity* to our new righteous Position and Identity in Christ (1:17; 5:16, 19).

by submitting to Sin's Power. "Is that what you want — to be slaves to sin?" Paul reasons. *Of course not*, we reply. "Then don't choose to sin," says Paul, "for then you also choose to be a slave of sin."

We are deceived if we think we are free to go back to sin because we have moved from the law "principle" to grace. The moment we commit a sinful act the first time, it becomes progressively easier to repeat, until we are trapped in a web of our own making that leads to slavery. Christian psychologist Jay Adams explains the process:

> The downward cycle of sin moves from a problem to a faulty, sinful response, thereby causing an additional complicating problem which is met by an additional sinful response. . . . The downward cycle enslaves one in hopelessness and guilt, thus bringing on a slowing down or cessation of activity, called depression. . . . Sinful habits are hard to break, but if they are not broken they will bind the client ever more tightly. He finds that as sin spirals in a downward helix, pulling him along, he is captured and tied up by sin's ever-tightening cords. He is held fast by the ropes of his own sin.[2]

The same truth is echoed in Proverbs 5:21-22, "For the ways of man are before the eyes of the Lord, and He ponders all his paths. His own iniquities entrap the wicked man, and he is caught in the cords of his sin." Peter sees the same in false teachers: "While they promise them liberty, they themselves are slaves of corruption; for by whom a person is overcome, by him also he is brought into bondage" (2 Pet 2:19). This last verb in the perfect tense suggests an existing state of slavery. Finally, Jesus Himself said, "Most assuredly, I say to you, whoever commits sin is a slave of sin" (Jn 8:34).

The **second** principle is depicted in the contrasting destinies of Dave and Drew, two boys enrolled at excellent prep schools in Tennessee in the early 1960s. Dave went to the McCallie School in Chattanooga which had strict rules and required that each student take a Bible course. Drew attended Sewanee Military Academy. Both boys were a bit on the wild side and loved the rush of getting away with breaking school rules. Nothing really serious — just a little parking with a girlfriend or sneaking off campus to hustle up a deck of cards.

One day Dave was caught parking on campus with his girlfriend. School authorities sent him home for three days to think about it. With plenty of time to reflect on the Greyhound Bus, Dave remembered what the Bible said about his being a sinner, but until now he was convinced he could stop sinning whenever he wanted. Not so. The Bible also said Jesus died for his sins and rose from the

---

2 Jay E. Adams, *The Christian Counselor's Manual* (Grand Rapids, MI: Baker, 1973), 376-7.

grave. So Dave said, "OK, Jesus, if you really rose from the grave, then you must be on this bus somewhere. I am going to trust you to save me from my sinfulness. Please forgive me for all that I have done." From that moment Dave knew he was a different person. When he graduated and went off to college, he got involved with Campus Crusade for Christ. His love for the Bible just continued to grow and he became a preacher devoted to God.

Drew was a true Kentucky blueblood, wealthy by inheritance. The only thing he really loved was the adrenaline rush of getting away with things he shouldn't be doing. Where would he get his kicks after high school? He did not want to go to college, so he took a different route[3] and joined the military. He thought he would enjoy the danger of fighting and served his country in Grenada and other risky missions. When he got out of the military, he thought a good place to continue guns and fighting would be in the police department so he joined the PD in Lexington, KY. Drew was put on drug detail but could not resist the temptations that came with pursuing drug dealers. Soon he himself was dealing drugs, even though he was still a policeman. He set up a drug ring with some cronies from prep school, one of whom was a Kentucky congressman. Soon they were running one of the largest drug rings in the South and repeatedly evaded the law with their deep political connections. Each thrill escalated to a new level, and Drew began flying cocaine in from Columbia.

On Drew's last trip, with 250 million dollars worth of cocaine on board, the police were tracking him by radar. An accomplished paratrooper, he first threw most of the backpacks full of cocaine out the window, hoping he could recover them later; then he then jumped out with the plane on autopilot and fifteen million in cocaine strapped to his back. No one knows why his chute didn't open, but Drew plunged to his death on someone's driveway in Tennessee with the cocaine still strapped to his back. He was wearing night goggles, a bulletproof vest, and Gucci loafers. He had $4,500 in cash, a knife, and two revolvers. Sadly, a dead black bear was found in the forest where Drew had dumped the rest of the cocaine. The bear had overdosed on the drug. Ironically, Drew landed not far from Sewanee where his rule breaking began, as if to underscore the inevitable outcome of his earlier choices.

"Sow a thought, reap an action; sow an action, reap a habit; sow a habit, reap a destiny." Two masters, two destinies. It is logically absurd to revert to sin as a Christian. It is like a man who burns down his house to collect the insurance money. He takes advantage of his insurance company but loses his home in the process. Most of us would say we would not stoop that low. But I assure you, we

---

3   Andrew L. Thornton II and his Kentucky cadre of friends ran a lucrative drug operation until he parachuted to his death. See Dominique Dunn, "Power, Privilege, & Justice," *Freefall* (Feb 8, 2004).

stoop far lower when we revert to sin because we are under grace and not law. It is flagrant presumption on God's grace (Rom 2:4). Something is terribly wrong when we indulge Sin and embrace death by taking advantage of a principle meant to release us from Sin's power under the law so that we might reign in righteousness with a view to experiencing a full and meaningful life (5:17, 21; 6:22-23).

So, how should we convince ourselves not to commit deliberate sin? The threat of God's discipline? . . . loss of rewards? . . . tarnished witness? Paul knows that many of us are too self-centered to be deterred by the argument that our sins grieve God. But if we understand Romans 6:16, every intentional sin drags with it the chains of slavery, and with that slavery come *deathly* consequences. So he argues by appealing to self-interest: To commit willful sin triggers a "law" of moral slavery in our lives — the law of sin and death (see 8:2).

Each of us is guilty of deliberate sins. Only after our imprisonment by sin do we discover that the chains are of our own making. Is there no hope of breaking these chains that bind us? Of course there is, says Paul, so in 6:17-18 he reminds us of our present Position in Christ, which is governed by the "law" of grace, and not the law of sin and death.

B. Two *Positions*   6:17-18

17But God be thanked that though you were slaves of sin, yet you obeyed from the heart that form of doctrine to which you were delivered. 18And having been set free from sin, you became slaves of righteousness.

The word for "form" in v. 17b is *tupos*, from which we get the word "type." Paul is directing his readers' attention to the new "type" of teaching which their salvation brought them — their new privilege as believers baptized in Christ (6:1-4): Formerly, we were under the *law* principle with all its demands (performance-for-acceptance); in our *new* realm we are under a different governing principle, the principle of *grace*. In our former Position in Adam we were "slaves of sin" ("the Sin," *hē hamartia*),[4] which ruled over us through *law*. When we heard the gospel of grace in Christ's death on the cross, we obeyed[5] and were set free from the old realm — where we had *no choice* but to sin — to become "slaves of righteousness," a statement related to our New Position in Christ.

The implication carried over from the question in 6:15 is that even though we were set free to become slaves of righteousness we are free to choose which

---

4   See note 1, Chapter 1, "Who You Gonna Call?"

5   The obedience in view here is responding to the gospel by *believing*. Paul did not mean "the commitment to obey every command of Jesus for the rest of our lives" — this requirement has been *added* by some Reformed theologies.

realm to live in. Paul's gratitude here for the transfer from sin to righteousness is thus expressed with a subtle sense of leverage: "Given your new freedom, why on earth would you want to live in slavery to sin again? You were set free to live righteously, so why would you contradict your new righteous identity in Christ by reverting to Sin?" In the following verses, he will immediately clarify why he even needs to address this possibility in light of the obvious contradiction in identity — it all has to do with the unredeemed flesh that all believers retain, even with their New Identity. By virtue of their New Position in Christ, they now have the privilege in Christ to choose freely between two ways of life, only one of which leads to public exaltation of His holy name.

C. Two *Practices*   6:19

I speak in human terms because of the weakness of your flesh. For just as you presented your members as slaves of uncleanness, and of lawlessness leading to more lawlessness, so now present your members as slaves of righteousness for holiness.

Before identifying with Christ, we were *involuntary* slaves because of the flesh and could only use our members to serve uncleanness and habitual lawbreaking (see 7:5). But a new choice is available to us in Christ. We are now *voluntary* slaves to Sin or to Righteousness. By virtue of our Position as slaves of Righteousness, God intends for us to *live out* that Identity in Christ — to present our members as instruments of righteousness leading to (*eis*) holiness (*hagiasmon*, "sanctification"). As such we are *set apart* as display cases of His grace, mercy, love and truth to reveal His righteousness by faith (1:17; 3:21-22) to a darkened world. In fact, as we shall see in Romans 8, God's goal for our lives is to make us as righteous as His Son Jesus.

But Paul still has to "speak in human terms because of the weakness of your flesh." He means that we are still incapable of living out our righteous identity *in our own ability* — all that we inherited from Adam (5:12-21). Our frail human design necessitates our dependence: just as we depend on air, water, and food in the physical realm we are also dependent agents in the moral arena, incapable of carrying out righteous or moral choices on our own. So Paul is warning his readers: if you choose Righteousness, don't fall prey to trying to do it on your own. If we try to meet His righteous standards through Law-keeping, Romans 7 will show how this "weakness of your flesh" only subverts God's intent. Thus, the whole point of "presenting" members is that it is God through Christ who actually *does* the righteousness in our "members."

The intent to display righteousness is like a single woman who wants to fulfill her life through marriage. In our culture the girl doesn't ask to be married. She can't even rightly ask for a date. So she just sits around waiting for the phone to ring. Finally, some guy comes along and she thinks, "Oh, that's the guy," but he doesn't ask her out. So she just goes on waiting. She's involuntarily single. Then, all of a sudden, he comes in, just like Prince Charming. And they marry. Now she is free to be faithful . . . but she doesn't have to be. She should be. Why? Because she loves him so much? No. She, like Scarlet in *Gone with the Wind*, may be secretly holding on to an Ashley Wilkes, who commands her affections even after she is married to another man. But she should be faithful because of her Position as the wife of her present husband. Nevertheless, she must be voluntarily faithful. It's best that she be faithful, but she doesn't have to be, does she? It's voluntary.

That's exactly what Paul is saying. When I was lost ("unmarried") I was involuntarily committed to my Sin Nature in Adam. Even if I hated this slavery I had no choice. However, when Jesus saved me from the penalty of sin, I discovered that I had new options. I could say Yes or No to my still-present Sin Nature and it was now my *privilege* to be faithful or unfaithful. Freedom from Sin does not mean it is dead. So if the Sin Nature is still present in me, how am I free? I'm free from its *mastery*. I have the privilege of choosing what manner of life I shall live in my flesh. Two Principles; two Positions, and now I must choose between two different Practices — *sin* or *righteousness*. To help motivate us to choose righteousness Paul will close out this section by highlighting the radically different outcomes of the two choices.

D. Two *Products* 6:20-23

20*For when you were slaves of sin, you were free in regard to righteousness. 21What fruit did you have then in the things of which you are now ashamed? For the end of those things is death. 22But now having been set free from sin, and having become slaves of God, you have your fruit to holiness, and the end, everlasting life. 23For the wages of sin is death, but the gift of God is eternal life in Christ Jesus our Lord.*

Using a transparent play on the word "free,"[6] Paul rhetorically asks his readers, "When you were 'free' of righteousness [*incapable* of living a righteous life] what fruit did you have? The rotten fruit of shameful deeds that lead to death. But now you are 'free' from your previous master, your Sin Nature in Adam. Now as *God's* slaves, the righteous fruit you produce leads to holiness [a people *set apart* to display His righteousness].[7] And the result of *this* kind of living is eternal life."

---

6 Compare Paul's similar use of "alive" in Romans 7:9-10; see note 3, Chapter 9, "Satan's Beachhead."

7 It is essential to understand what Paul means by *hagiasmon*—"holiness" or "sanctification" (NASB)—in both 6:19 and 22. Many evangelicals have inherited a legacy of revivalism and pietism in which holiness or sanctification is identified with *private* and often *deeply introspective* piety or devotion. However, Paul's emphasis is rooted squarely in the OT notion of a people of God called to publicly uphold the

Thus, reverting to slavery to Sin only bears "fruit" to death; but living out our New Identity as slaves to Righteousness sanctifies us with a view to eternal life, understood as *abundant living now* (6:22-23).

Romans 6:23 is often used to evangelize, so we often assume Paul uses *eternal life* here to denote salvation from the Penalty of sin to a future destiny in heaven. And that is just what eternal life means in some contexts, but here it includes more. "Eternal life" can also refer to a *quality* of life. While both believers and unbelievers will exist forever (Jn 5:28-29), the quality of their existence will differ vastly; moreover, believers can begin to enjoy that quality life in their new realm now by choosing to serve righteousness. Thus, Paul is speaking here to believers and building on his prior introduction of the notion of a present "reign through righteousness to eternal life" (Rom 5:17b, 21b) as implied by his broader term "Gospel of God" (1:1), used to introduce the Book of Romans.

That is why former Dallas Seminary professor S. Lewis Johnson called Rom 6:23 "the gospel to the saints." Thus, Psalm 16:11 also depicts eternal "fullness of joy" in God's presence, and six of the seven instances of eternal life in John 17 are to be enjoyed on earth — this is the abundant life Christ came to give (10:10). This life is not something we must wait for: it fulfills the OT notions of *shabbat* (the seventh day Creation "rest") and *shalôm* (the "wholeness" and "order" of Creation restored) entailed in the righteousness that God always intended his people to display in this life in response to His "broad" Gospel (Rom 1:16-17).

Similarly, "death" does not always refer to physical or spiritual death. As for physical death, we all know people who lived sinful lives yet survived to be eighty or more. No, "death" here refers to a state of being. It refers to a life of corruption in which everything is in a state of decay. Children languish as their families disintegrate; marriage decays as two people live totally separate lives in the same house; one's labor in life as a man or woman only wears them out. They are the living dead (1 Tim 5:6).

The radical difference in outcome between the two choices presented by Paul can be seen here in by his use of the term "wages" (6:23, Gk: *hopsōnia*), the daily ration of salt and fish distributed to mercenary soldiers. John the Baptist used this word when the soldiers came to him and asked what they should do. He said, "Be content with your *hopsōnia*," or daily ration (Lk 3:14). The Latin Vulgate

---

character ("name") of God among the nations (see 1:4-5, 8, 15): "Holy [*qōdesh*] to the Lord" (see, e.g., Zech 14:20-21). The overriding goal for his readers is that the "substance" of God's righteousness be made visible (Rom 1:17) in their sanctification, which (as we have argued throughout) entails a new Position, Identity, and Condition. But all this is designed by "the gospel of God" (1:1) to have an impact on the nations. The church was not designed to be a "holy huddle." Believers were called to be positive image bearers to the rest of the world.

translation of *hopsōnia* was *stipendia*, from which we get the word "stipend." So, Paul imagines two generals or commanders: the Sin Nature and God. If we choose to sin (Rom 6:15), we choose to be ruled by our Sin Nature, and our daily ration will be *death*. Neither physical death in battle nor old age nor spiritual death in final judgment could be described as a "daily ration." No, this is the same death we have seen over and over in this section on sanctification. It is the daily death of defeat, disillusionment, and despair. In short, it is a life of misery.

Thankfully, we have another option. The blessed privilege of those in Christ is to serve on the side of Jesus. If we do this, our daily "ration" is actually a *free gift*. It is a quality of life no unbeliever can ever know, because it can come only to those who are connected to God. Separation between a person and God (spiritual death) ends when he trusts Christ as Savior and receives the free gift of eternal life — the quality of life that comes from being connected to God. Now, this quality of life can get better and better in the life of a believer, but only as he freely receives the "abundance of grace" needed to serve in the King's army and "reign in righteousness to eternal life" (5:17, 21).

The word for the *gift* of God in 6:23 is *charisma*, just as in 5:15-16. Unlike Roman soldiers, we cannot claim that God owes us a full and meaningful life when we serve in His army. God graciously gifts us with this life (5:15), and we choose daily whether to continue receiving the gift and "reign in life" as a quality of existence. That's why Paul urged us to present ourselves as slaves to righteousness (6:19): God wants us to dedicate ourselves and continue (aorist ingressive) to serve righteousness with a view to *holiness* —sanctified (set apart) as His people to "make Him look good." It is precisely because we can never put God in our debt (the delusion of legalism in Romans 7) that we are urged to continue as *voluntary* slaves; for only then can we possibly bear the fruit of righteousness to set us apart as His true "agents" in the world (6:21-22, see 1:17; 3:21).

We have already seen how the universal slavery principle in 6:16 works: whether we know it or not we are all slaves to whoever we yield our "members." There are only two masters to choose from, and we cannot serve both (Matt 6:24): Our *former* Position was as slaves to our Sin Nature with a corresponding Condition as "sinful" in Adam (5:19a); our *new* Position is as slaves to God (6:22), and the matching Condition is intended to be "righteous" in Christ (5:19b). But due to the "weak" flesh (6:19), our Condition often does not conform to our Position. We can assume our old Identity and resume living as slaves to our old master, just like many of the freed slaves after the Civil War. One act of sin initiates a chain that binds us as slaves. But if we live out of our New Position as slaves of God, we are ironically set free to a full liberty in the Holy Spirit that bursts out in life (2 Cor 3:17).

As I have talked with a number of mature Christians, each said his or her real growth began after the kind of dedication Paul urges in v. 19. It is not based on an emotional appeal but rather on our Position in Christ as free from the mastery of the Sin Nature. This dedication is essential for God to harness our service (or "agency") for His righteous purposes, but we must also take up our cross daily and follow Him. If we have never made an "all out" dedication of life and limb to our new master then we have *already* opted for slavery to the old master. But why settle for *that*? We don't have to. It is our privilege as believers in Christ to choose *Him* as our master daily. The outcome of this choice is twofold: a holiness that displays His righteousness; and the ripe, rich fruit of abundant life right here on earth.

We enjoy this life in true freedom only by operating according to our *design* (joined spiritually to God through Christ) and within our proper *domain* (dead to the reign of Sin and alive to the reign of Christ). To obey the old master only produces the fruit of a decaying life, like a fish out of water or a bird in an oil slick: though it lives, it would be dead. But Jesus said, "I have come that they may have life, and that they may have it more abundantly" (Jn 10:10b). To obey our new master sets us apart as agents of His righteousness and yields an abundant life right here and now.

Digging Deeper: What is the Basis for the Abundant Life in Romans 6:23?

While most would agree that faith in Christ secures our future destiny in heaven, different groups today offer various suggestions as to the basis for the abundant life in this life. We will see why each of these is self-defeating, and then reaffirm the biblical basis for the abundant Christian life.

1. Confession (1 Jn 1:9)

a. The Claim. If the abundant Christian life is rooted in fellowship with Christ and fellowship is restored by confessing known sins, then confession is the key to abundant life. Confession also removes the barrier to filling by the Holy Spirit, who gives the victory in the Christian life. Some who teach this approach would even say that confession trips a switch that opens the door to the Holy Spirit who fills us automatically at the moment of confession.

b. The Correction. While there is much truth in these claims, confession cannot be the basis for abundant life in Christ, for 1 John 1:9 is remedial, not preventive. Confession deals only with the symptoms, not the disease (our Sin Nature inherited from Adam). As Watchman Nee illustrates,

> Suppose . . . that the government of your country should wish to deal drastically with the question of strong drink and . . . decide that the whole country should go dry. . . . If we were to search every shop and house throughout the land and smash all the bottles of wine or beer or brandy we came across, would that meet the case? Surely not. We might thereby rid the land of every drop of alcoholic liquor it contains, but behind those bottles . . . are the factories that produced them, and if we only deal with the bottles . . . , production will still continue [with] no permanent solution to the problem. No, the drink-producing factories . . . throughout the land must be closed down if the drink question is ever to be effectively and permanently settled.[8]

First John 1:9 deals only with the existing "bottles" that are causing problems, not the "factory" that produces the bottles. Ask any Christian who is enslaved to a particular sin — and knows all about 1 Jn 1:9 — whether he has abundant life. You will hear either self-justification or confusion and frustration over his failure. No, confession is not the basis for abundant life in Christ.

2. Sinless Perfection (Rom 6:6)

a. The Claim. Some read Romans 6:6 to affirm that the Sin Nature is actually *abolished* so they never sin again. Such "sinless perfection" comes with a second work of grace after initial justification when the Holy Spirit does a sanctifying work in the life of the believer that sounds like regeneration; they call it the making of a new life. Others think the Sin Nature stays with us in this life but is rendered so weak that a believer can still have plenty of unknown sin in his life yet live the rest of his life without deliberately sinning; the compulsion is removed.

To be fair, many who advocate this approach to abundant life call their experience "entire sanctification," not a life without sin. This means their heart is entirely inclined to adoration and devotion to God — they live on a higher plane where deliberate sin is no longer a viable option. However, this smacks of some serious self-delusion. It certainly contradicts the experience of the Apostle Paul, who called himself "chief of sinners" (1 Tim 1:15)[9] shortly before his death.

b. The Correction. So what do the sinless perfection people call outbursts of anger or the penchant toward lying or gratification of the flesh? These, they claim, are minor defects of character or weaknesses that need strengthening

---

8 Watchman Nee, *The Normal Christian Life* (Wheaton, IL: Tyndale, 1977), 59-60.

9 Some believe this is an allusion to Paul's pre-Christian experience, expressed in the "historical present"— putting the past into the present for the sake of vividness. However, the historical present almost always occurs in *narrative* literature (such as the Gospels) and never in the first person or with the verb "to be"; yet Paul says "I am . . ."

— any convenient term to avoid the sin label. However, if the Sin Nature were abolished after we are baptized into Christ, why would Paul tell us in Romans 6:12 to *stop* presenting our members as instruments to Sin? In our exposition of 6:6 we showed that the word *katargeō* can also mean "to dethrone, depose, put out of authority." When we are transferred in Christ from death to life, God removes us from the realm where Sin has jurisdiction, like moving from California to Ohio — the California authorities no longer have jurisdiction over us. But Sin is *not* eradicated and will reassert its former authority whenever it is given the chance; the text says we become its slaves merely by obeying its temptations (6:12-23). Again, we could not *choose* to serve Sin if it were dead or eradicated, so this take on the abundant Christian life also fails to deal in a credible way with the "factory" of Sin.

3. The "Second Blessing" (Acts 2:2-4)

a. The Claim. There are many variations of this explanation for the abundant life, but most of them hinge on a charismatic "baptism of the Holy Ghost," stemming from 19th century American Wesleyanism and revivalism. These all distinguish between Holy Spirit baptism into the Body of Christ (the universal church) that occurs *at* initial faith in Christ as Savior (1 Cor 12:13) and a baptism by the Holy Spirit sometime *after* initial faith. Evidence of this "second blessing" is often considered to include at least one experience of speaking in tongues. Not until then does the believer have the power necessary for a consistent, victorious Christian life. Once the Holy Spirit is received for power, the believer will be as different as Peter after Pentecost.

b. The Correction. The majority of Second Blessing advocates are sincere, dedicated, and humble, but they are very likely misled. Efforts to show two different Holy Spirit baptism experiences in the Bible are suspect: Paul says there is only one (Eph 4:5). Peter says that every believer has faith of equal value and quality, as well as all the resources needed for godliness and abundant Christian life the moment he believes (2 Pet 1:1-3). The NT emphasis is not on getting more power for deliverance but on becoming aware of *how much power we were already given* through the Holy Spirit when we first believed (Eph 1:19).

Moreover, the second blessing approach also fails to deal with the "factory." Years ago I had a friend who claimed that if he did not speak in tongues for twenty or thirty minutes every morning he was unable to live victoriously that day. Ten years later he admitted that for many of those years he had been fighting an addiction to indecent exposure and did not know how to tell his wife. Twenty-five years later his wife called to tell me their marriage was in deep trouble — the man was defeated, completely captive to internet pornography; hardly an abundant life. This is just one case, but it is clear that his "second blessing" was not the key to deliverance.

4. Surrender (Rom 12:1)

a. The Claim. "Surrender" is basically a plea for *discipleship*: the rich rewards of the spiritual life cannot be ours until we are completely sold out to the Lord. Not until we let go of this world completely and give our all to Him can He give His all to us. There is certainly much truth to these words: both Romans 6:12-14 and 12:1 clearly appeal to surrender.

b. The Correction. Unfortunately, an all out "surrender" *à la* Romans 12:1 *before* being grounded in the truth of Romans 5–11 can easily lead to a *less* than abundant life. Recalling our prior discussion of Rom 6:12-14, surrender is the fourth step on the Romans 6 ladder to Freedom from Sin (Know, Believe, Reckon, Present, Obey). If I try to leap from the ground to the fourth rung of a ladder, I almost certainly will fall. To present my whole life to the Lord before the first three steps merely presents the *flesh*, the self-life, the "here-I-am-to-do-my-best" life. It would be like a Ford salesman going to General Motors to present his services to sell Chevy's while still on Ford's payroll. The GM manager would have to say, "As long as you're on the Ford payroll, you're still serving Ford. You have a conflict of interest. But if you want to quit Ford you can gladly join us." In the same way, surrender by itself without taking stock of our death in Christ to the Old Self cannot guarantee the abundant Christian life. This does not mean a new Christian has to have a full understanding of being "in Christ" before serving Christ; after all, how many believers fully understand our New Identity as "baptized into Christ's death" (6:3-4)?

5. Filling of the Holy Spirit (Eph 5:18)

a. The Claim. In tandem with confession ("1" above), "filling" may well be the most popular approach to the abundant Christian life. Ephesians 5:18 is understood as a command that every believer is to be filled by the Holy Spirit. The five participles that modify the verb "be filled" are usually explained as *results* of being filled: *speaking* to yourselves in psalms, hymns, and spiritual songs; *singing* and *making melody* in your heart; *giving thanks*; and *submitting* one to another. Many formulas for filling have been suggested, but this one is a widely disseminated:

1. Scrutinize yourself for any areas of known sin.
2. Confess all known sins.
3. Submit completely to God to reverse any rebellion against Him.
4. Ask to be filled with/by the Holy Spirit.
5. Believe you are filled by the Holy Spirit and thank God for it by faith.

b. The Correction. There are many good and godly men who teach this approach; however, it is not without difficulties:

1. Eph 5:18-33 is addressed to groups, not to individuals. In context Paul moves from the world (5:1-17) to the church (5:18-21) to the home (6:1ff). A good parallel would be 1 Corinthians 14 where we see an extended example of the group worship described in Ephesians 5:18-21.

2. If the participles describe the results of being filled, they do not match the fruit of the Holy Spirit in Galatians 5.

3. When we fail to see results after applying the formula we assume that some unconfessed or undetected sin is blocking our filling. This is a set-up for defeat, disillusionment, self-doubt, and despair: there is no evidence that filling stopped because of known sin.

4. In every NT example of filling by the Holy Spirit (preaching, speaking in tongues, kicking in the womb), those who were filled never had to ask for it. The obvious evidence in their lives made it clear something unusual was happening.

5. And once again, this method still does nothing to deal with our Sin in Adam.

Therefore, the filling of the Holy Spirit in Ephesians 5 may well be a *corporate* filling that follows our mutual submission in the Body of Christ, as epitomized by the activities listed (5:18-21).

6. Legalism (Gal 3:1-3)

Historian Arnold Toynbee once said, "All religion gravitates toward legalism." Like a creeping vine it crawls unnoticed right into the house of God. It is by far the most widespread yet least recognized approach to a full and meaningful Christian life.

a. The Claim. It is said that legalism just refers to man-made rules people try to live by. But for believers, legalism also implies that by living according to a given standard, we think we can earn God's favor, whether in this life or the next — we hold God in our debt. The sure-fire sign of a legalist is anger at God when life isn't going well, justified by the foolish presumption that He *owes* us (Gal 3:1-3). Even devoted believers have said "no" to this world yet succumbed to legalism in the name of "doing right for God"; it only leads to slavery (Rom 7:14-25).

b. The Correction. As noted in our exposition of Romans 6:23, the "wages" of 23a are paralleled by the "gift" of 23b: if we serve Sin, our daily wages (ration) are "death" (defeat, disillusionment, and despair), but if we serve Jesus, God "gifts" us with eternal life (supernatural quality of life in this life and the next). Paul uses "gift" precisely because we cannot hold God in our debt: "You promised to bless me if I would do good things for You, and I've been faithful. You owe me, so give it up." Legalism is just a form of magic. It puts man in control of God: "I do; You bless."

Living by high standards is commendable, as Jesus taught in the Sermon on the Mount, but it *can* be totally selfish. The disciples had an ongoing debate as to which of them would be the greatest in Christ's kingdom (e.g., Mk 10:35-45), even during the Last Supper (Lk 22:24). Even though they had given up businesses, money, time, and even family relationships to follow Him, all they did was transfer self-interest to Christ's kingdom. Jesus promised great rewards for sacrificing in this life to gain an inheritance in the next, but that doesn't mean we appear at the Judgment Seat and tell Jesus, "You owe me." The problem was exposed by the parable of the vineyard (Matt 20:1-16): Those who worked longer hours were angry that those who had worked less got the same wage; they thought they deserved more and held God in debt. This is legalism.

The standard used by legalists can be man-made or God-made, self-imposed or God-imposed. The standard is not the issue. There is nothing wrong with the Law *per se* (Rom 7:12): Jews were under the Law of Moses; Christians are under the Law of Christ (Gal 6:2). But it is used by the legalist to try to hold God in his debt. Every good and perfect gift comes down from the Father of lights in whom there is no variation or shadow from turning (Jas 1:17). A gift is not a salary; He never owes us. We earn neither Justification (Rom 3:21–4:25) nor Sanctification-Glorification (Rom 5–8). We are justified and sanctified by receiving His abundant grace (5:15-21).

7. The Biblical View: A New Identity *Lived Out* by Faith

So, what is the basis for the abundant life? In Ephesians 1:3-14 there are ten references to our Position, including "in Christ," "in Him," "in whom," or "in the Beloved." And that's what we find in Romans 6:23: "life in Christ Jesus our Lord." We were baptized into Christ by the Holy Spirit. Like paper in a book, we were in Christ on the cross, in the tomb, and now in heaven. We go where Christ goes because we are "in Christ." The basis for the abundant Christian life is our New Position and Identity in Christ. It is the theme of Romans 5–6: Freedom from Sin in Adam to reign in life through the Righteousness of Christ (5:17, 21).

We are slaves by design, whether physically (to air, food, water) or spiritually (to God or Sin). With the deceitful beast of Sin as our master, we are mired in defeat and disillusionment; there can be no abundant life. Even if we confess our sin and climb out of the pit for awhile, life is like walking on a tightrope over the pit of "death." One slip and down we go. The moment we get back on the rope, Sin is still there waiting to jiggle the rope so we fall again. Obviously, if we spend more time in the pit than on the rope, we will not "reign in life through righteousness."

So, do we choose to live according to our New Identity or succumb to the false promise of life through the flesh and revert to slavery to Sin (6:15-23)?

No, if some sin has me in its clutches, I will not overcome that sin through the Second Blessing or Confession. Sinless Perfection is self-delusion. Surrender only presents the self-reliant flesh. Praying to be filled by the Holy Spirit does not diminish Sin's stranglehold. More self-effort in Bible study, prayer, fellowship, and witnessing only breeds more hypocrisy. If we know we are "in Christ" we are free from Sin's rule, so we can focus on our Position, not our Condition, to live out our New Identity: *believe* it, *bank* on it, then *present* ourselves *by choice* as slaves to God (6:12-14). When we choose to serve God then we are free from Sin's rule in both Position *and* Condition, even though Sin still remains dormant in our unredeemed flesh.

So how do we get rid of Sin to enjoy abundant life? We *don't*! Isn't that a relief? If we constantly dwell on our sin we only become more sinful. Besides the restoration of confession, we should forget about our sin; stop dwelling on it; commit it to the Lord — we can't get rid of it. We are to focus on our new Position and Identity; set our hearts on the things above where we are now "seated with Christ in heavenly places" (Eph 2:6). Only the Holy Spirit can do the transforming as we live in Jesus (2 Cor 3:18). We are the glove. The Holy Spirit is the hand that empowers the glove. Every godly man or woman I have ever known is preoccupied with Christ, which produces abundant life. Preoccupation with self reaps death.

[END OF EXCURSUS]

"Turn your eyes upon Jesus, look full in his wonderful face, and the things of earth will grow strangely dim, in the light of His glory and grace." This is Romans 6 and Colossians 3 put to music. If we focus on our heavenly Position and Identity in Christ we won't obsess over our earthly Condition. The key to Christian growth, maturity, progressive sanctification, and the fruit of abundant life can all be summed up in one word: Source (Jn 15:4-5). Our Position is *in Him*, the Vine, the Source of life. To abide in Him means to rest in our Position in order to live out our righteous Identity — to trust our source to provide what we need for life, growth, and fruit. This takes the striving out of our daily walk. Salvation is God's work, and so is sanctification. Labor, therefore, to *enter* (to "appropriate") that rest (Heb 4:11). When we focus on our heavenly Position instead of our earthly Condition, then one day the weight of sin that so easily besets us will be lifted and we will be free to enjoy the abundant life that Christ promised.

C. S. Lewis wrote:

> Our Lord finds our desires not too strong, but too weak. We are half-hearted creatures, fooling about with drink and sex and ambition, when infinite joy is offered to us, like an ignorant child who wants to go on making mud pies in the slum because he cannot imagine what is meant by the offer of a holiday at the sea. We are far too easily pleased.[10]

On a recent trip to Nicaragua I was taken to the largest "dump" in Managua. It reminded me of a scene from the movie, "Wall-E": trash stacked ten feet high, stretching in both directions for hundreds of yards. And in the midst of this trash? Children . . . and rats . . . and stench. Little children — starving, filthy, looking for food. Later at the airport I saw a very different group of kids from California who had come down to Nicaragua to surf that time of year. But I couldn't get the dump kids out of my mind. What would *they* give for a day at the sea? They had nothing. But if I could take them to freedom of the sea, why would they want to return to the dump?

All too many of us stay in the dump or even return there because we think it is our only choice. But why dig for life in the dump when we can enjoy our freedom where we are? In Christ, and He in us! I do not for a minute dismiss the reality of pain that comes from adversity on earth. But isn't that the test of an abundant life? If we can enjoy the fruit of the Spirit in the midst of suffering, then that is free, abundant living, indeed.

Did Jesus have an abundant Christian life? He was certainly free from Sin. But on the outside, it was not a very attractive life: single, rejected at home, blamed for others' mistakes, a victim of false rumors, innocent yet on death row, taunted and mocked, betrayed by friends, and finally crucified. Yet He lived the most meaningful life any human has ever lived. He enjoyed unbroken fellowship with the Father until the cross. And He could endure the cross, despising the shame, because of the joy set before Him (Heb 12:2). So also the abundant life — a life free to display God's righteousness from the inside out — can only be lived out of our New Identity, based on our New Position, rooted in Christ.

---

10   C. S. Lewis, *The Weight of Glory and Other Addresses* (Grand Rapids, MI: Eerdmans, 1965), 1-2.

CHAPTER 8

"AN HONORABLE DISCHARGE"

Romans 7:1-6

Charles Trumbull once received an unfavorable response to his teaching that the victorious Christian life is the outright, supernatural gift of God. Here is an excerpt from the letter:

> Under the heading, "Victory Christ's Work, Not Ours," you state: "Christ is living the victorious life today; and Christ is your life. Therefore, stop trying. Let Him do it all. Your effort or trying had nothing to do with the salvation which you have in Christ; in exactly the same way your effort and trying can having nothing to do with the complete victory which Christ alone has achieved for you and can steadily achieve in you . . . " I have no hesitancy in saying I do not believe in your position. My entire experience refutes it. . . . I believe that the victorious life . . . is brought about by the continuous desire and effort to gain it, and that it will not come without that desire and effort. I realize, of course, that no man can save himself, but I believe that God expects every man to do his part toward that salvation.[1]

If the most difficult teaching in the world for the unbeliever to accept is that *salvation* is a free gift of God apart from works of the law, then the most difficult teaching in the world for the believer to accept is that *sanctification* is a free gift of God apart from works of the law. A prevalent religious philosophy of our age is that God helps those who help themselves; but that is a false, law-based philosophy for salvation and sanctification alike. As Miles Stanford puts it:

> When we beg God for help in the Christian life, we are saying, "God I'll do my part and You do Your part. Together we'll get the job done."

---

1   Charles G. Trumbull, *Victory in Christ* (Fort Washington, PA: Christian Literature Crusade, 1972), 46.

> But . . . that portion of our Christian lives which we consider "our part" . . . hinders Christ in living out His life through us. And it's this very philosophy that we must do our part to help God . . . perform the work of sanctification in our lives . . . which keeps so many Christians under the heavy yoke of bondage to the law principle, which ultimately only stirs up a hornets' nest of sin in their lives which drives them into continual defeat and discouragement.[2]

Such views are not confined to "lay people." One day after playing tennis with a minister in one of our local churches, we engaged in a theological discussion in which he said, "Yes, we believe that salvation is a gift from Christ. But we also believe that after receiving that gift we must do something to keep it." Such convictions justify the words of C. I. Scofield:

> Most of us have been reared and now live under the influence of Galatianism. Protestant theology is for the most part thoroughly Galatianized, in that neither the law nor grace is given its distinct and separate place . . . but they are mingled together in one incoherent system.[3]

Our full freedom in Christ includes our freedom from *law*. While Romans 6 explains our freedom from the Sin Nature, Romans 7 explains our freedom from the Law. Paul had mentioned a link between Law and Sin in 6:14-15 as if these two tyrants were closely related, so we might well ask, "What does the Law have to do with my Sin Nature?" Paul had planted the seed in 2:14-16 and further developed this connection in 3:20 and 5:13-14, 20a: *the Law increases our awareness of and accountability for sin through the normal function of conscience.* So if it was foolish to pursue *Sin* for abundant life in Romans 6 because it only leads to more condemnation by the conviction of Law working through conscience, how absurd now to seek that same life by going *straight to* the Law in Romans 7! Thus, while it may have seemed out of context to mention law in 6:14, it is the idea of *slavery* introduced there—"For sin shall not *have dominion over you*, for you are not under law . . ."—that establishes the continuity with Romans 7, "Or do you not know that the law *has dominion over a man* as long as he lives?" (7:1).[4]

---

2 Miles J. Stanford, *The Complete Green Letters* (Grand Rapids, MI: Zondervan, 1983), 87.

3 C. I. Scofield, quoted by Stanford, *Abide Above* (Hong Kong: Living Spring Press, 1970), 26.

4 The word "dominion" here recalls that the Law was given so that our Sin Nature inherited from Adam might "abound" to *reign* in death (5:17a, 19a, 20a, 21a). "Abound" connotes *full personal accountability for sin* just like Adam, through the normal function of *conscience* (see note 16 and associated text, Chapter 4, "Humanity, We Have a Problem"). Since *Sin* cannot bring abundant life "because of the weakness of your flesh" (6:19), why would the same flesh afford any more life by pursuing the *Law* (7:5)? They both result in condemnation (incarceration by Sin, leading to "death"). And it is precisely this condemnation from which Paul anticipates his (and our) release through Jesus Christ (7:24-25).

Paul's introduction to our freedom from the Law (7:1-6) thus explains how and why Christ secured our Discharge from the Law. He follows this with an explanation of the Design of the Law (7:7-12) and concludes the chapter by depicting our Despair should we choose to return to the Law (7:13-25). So in discussing our Discharge from the Law, he first lays out the *principle* (v. 1) of Discharge, then *illustrates* (vv. 2-3) and *applies* it (vv. 4-6).[5]

I.	**SIN**	**(1:1–3:20)**
II.	**SALVATION**	**(3:21–4:25)**
III.	**SANCTIFICATION**	**(5–8)**
	A. **Freedom from Wrath**	**(5)**
	B. **Freedom from Sin**	**(6)**
	C. **Freedom from Law**	**(7)**
	1. **Discharge from the Law**	**(7:1-6)**
	a. **The *Principle***	**1**
	b. **The *Illustration***	**2-3**
	c. **The *Application***	**4-6**
	2. **Design of the Law**	**(7:7-12)**
	3. **Despair under the Law**	**(7:13-25)**
	D. **Freedom from Despair**	**(8)**

For Christians to believe salvation is God's work but sanctification is *man's work* is to live under law and not under grace; as Paul says, we have "fallen" from grace (Gal 5:4; compare Heb 12:15). He does not mean we have lost our salvation but that we were saved by the heavenly principle of grace (unearned favor from God), and once saved, we turn back from that superior heavenly foundation to the earthly principle of law, thinking we can earn our sanctification from God by our own efforts. This is the "Law Principle" (Rom 6:14) that Paul now explains.

A. The *Principle*   7:1

Or do you not know, brethren (for I speak to those who know the law), that the law has dominion over a man as long as he lives?

Here, Paul recalls the law's intended effect of convicting us through conscience (Rom 1:19-20; 2:14-15, 3:20, 5:20a). His rhetorical question is addressed to "those who know the law" — those in Christ who try to meet God's righteous expectations out of *self-sufficiency*: As long as "I" am alive, the law has dominion over me. It rules over me to my own demise. Stanford says,

> All through the years of defeat, we have been slowly learning that
> the harder we tried to live the Christian life, the deeper we came

---

5   Outline of 7:1-6 according to William R. Newell, *Romans: Verse by Verse* (Grand Rapids, MI: Kregel, 1994), 252.

under the dominion of the law of sin. We tried to 'be,' we tried to 'do,' and there was nothing but failure year in and year out.[6]

Unfortunately, many Bible teachers have taught that we are capable of obeying God's law and achieving holiness or sanctification through such obedience. Listen to the words of Charles Finney, a former popular revivalist Bible expositor (d. 1875):

> It is self-evident that the entire obedience to God's law is possible on the ground of natural ability. To deny this, is to deny that man is able to do as well as he can . . . [I]t is plain that all the law demands, is the exercise of whatever strength we have, in the service of God. Now, as entire sanctification consists in perfect obedience to the law of God, and as the law requires nothing more than the right use of whatever strength we have, it is, of course, forever settled, that a state of entire sanctification is attainable in this life, on the ground of natural ability.[7]

The teaching on "entire sanctification" is a Wesleyan doctrine that deals more with complete dedication of the heart than sinless perfection. Nevertheless, when "entire sanctification" is understood as a goal, the *means*, according to Finney, is human strength. Even if Finney believed salvation is *God's* work, he clearly held that sanctification is *man's* work.

This is modern-day *judaizing*. In Paul's day the Judaizers infiltrated the Body of Christ with a message antithetical to the gospel of grace: some taught that to be saved one must also keep the Law of Moses and either be of Jewish lineage or convert to Judaism; others conceded that Gentiles need not become Jews but still insisted they also had to keep the Law of Moses and be circumcised. The question was settled in Acts 15 (see also Galatians 2), using Titus, a Gentile, as a test case: the Jerusalem Council decided in favor of Paul's gospel of free grace for Gentile salvation. However, the Judaizers then began to insist on law-keeping for *sanctification*, and it spread through the local churches like a cancer. Romans 7 corrects this latter error: it is deadly to believe one is still alive under

---

6   Miles Stanford, *The Reckoning that Counts,* "Romans Seven Reckoning," available at http://www.bibleteacher.org/stanfordrek04.htm. Accessed October 26, 2010.

7   Charles Finney, quoted in Miles Stanford, *Abide Above*, 24. Note also J. C. Ryle: "Genuine sanctification will show itself in habitual respect for God's law, and habitual effort to live in obedience to it as a rule of life" (*Holiness* [Lafayette, LA: Sovereign Grace Publishers, 2001], 17; or H. Bonar, "Redemption forms a new obligation to law-keeping as well as puts us in a position for it. Yes, Christ 'hath redeemed us from the curse of the law,' but certainly not from the law itself" (*God's Way of Holiness* [London: James Nisbet & Co., 1864], 74); or Arthur Pink, "Is the disciple to be above his Master, the servant superior to His Lord? Christ was made under the law (Gal 4:4), and lived in perfect submission thereto, and has left us an example that we should 'follow His steps' (1 Pet 2:21). Only by loving, fearing, and obeying the law shall we be kept from sinning" (*The Doctrine of Sanctification* [Granbury, TX: Providence Baptist Ministries, 2010], 71).

the jurisdiction of the law and must therefore obey it to grow more righteous in Condition (be sanctified) and gain God's favor. Until we reckon that we have died with Christ to the Law we only grow more *self-righteous* (deluded that we are keeping the law as we understand it) or more *guilt-ridden* and *hopeless* (realizing we cannot bear this heavy yoke).

This then is the crux of the issue. As long as we believe that we have life within us and can do righteousness on our own ("according to the flesh") we will only find "death": defeat, disillusionment, and despair. If we think we can fulfill God's commandments and rules on our own we are doomed to a life of *slavery to law*, a life of floundering and failure. The principle is that law reigns over us only as long as we are alive — we have no choice but to obey its dictates; but when we *die* in the realm of the law we are no longer under its jurisdiction. And of course, this is exactly what Paul boldly proclaims in Romans 7:1: when one is no longer alive in the realm where law is king, the law has no more jurisdiction over him.

This is not so hard for us to understand. Suppose a patrol car spots a driver who has just run a red light and then side-swipes a car, but does not stop. The patrolman says, "That driver is guilty of running a stop light and leaving the scene of an accident." As he begins following the escaping car, the policeman notes that the hit and run driver is going 85 mph. The policeman says, "Now he's guilty of breaking the speed limit." Continuing the chase, the escaping car swerves from one side of the road to the other, and the policeman is prepared to charge him with careless driving. He puts on his red flashing light and his siren begins to whine. The car ahead starts to go even faster. Here is a man to be charged with resisting arrest as well. He pursues the speeding automobile into a sharp curve, a curve which the speeding car is unable to negotiate. It swerves and smashes into the barricade on the side of the road. The policeman hears an explosion and watches the flames. As he stands beside that smashed automobile and sees the ruined body of the driver, he sees a man who, because he has first died, has moved out of the jurisdiction of the law. He can no longer be charged with running a red light, leaving the scene of an accident, speeding, reckless driving, and resisting arrest. Death ended the jurisdiction of the law over that individual.

Our freedom in Christ is so crucial that Paul now goes on to illustrate this principle with an even more graphic analogy (7:2-3).

B. The *Illustration* 7:2-3

²For the woman who has a husband is bound by the law to her husband as long as he lives. But if the husband dies, she is released from the law of her husband. ³So then if, while her husband lives, she marries another man, she will be called an adulteress; but if her husband dies, she is free from that law, so that she is no adulteress, though she has married another man.

A contemporary allegory may help shed light on Paul's analogy:[8] Once upon a time a lovely, gentle woman found herself married to a tyrannical perfectionist. All he did from the day they were married was to lay down the law about his wife's behavior. No matter how hard she tried to please him, nothing was ever good enough and never once did he offer to help her become the kind of woman he wanted her to be. Year after year went by like this, and the relationship was severely strained. Most of her time she spent worrying over whether she had upset him, then feeling guilty, then resentful. But her husband was a good man in the truest sense; in fact, he was *perfect*. And that was the very problem in their relationship: she was *not* perfect.

Unable to live with her sense of personal failure, she began to secretly wish that he would leave her or even die, if that's what it took. But alas, he was in perfect health and so very moral that divorce would be out of the question under the law. To make matters worse, she met another man every bit as perfect as her husband but with a gentleness and love about him she had never enjoyed. As he began to woo her, she felt herself falling deeply in love with this wonderful man. And then he popped the question. "Will you become mine?" He knew she was already married so he came to her with a plan: Since her husband would not leave her or die, the only other solution would be for *her* to die and be free from the law. The present marriage would be legally terminated, and she would be free to marry the new man. What an ingenious plan!

But wait . . . If she were dead, how could she marry anyone, let alone this wonderful man? Of course! She would have to be *raised* from the dead. Believers are analogous to the wife in the allegory. The law is the perfectionist husband who filled us with relentless guilt, reminding us of all our failures and inadequacy (Rom 2:14-16; 3:20; 5:20a). Only by dying could we break his bond to us; so we died with Christ; crucified with Him, we were set free from the dominion of both Sin and law. But it does not end in a grave. We were raised from the dead with Christ; and that, really, is the whole point of our identification with Christ (Rom 6:4-7). Romans 7:4-6 now explains this intended result of our new marriage to Christ.

C. The *Application*   7:4-6

4Therefore, my brethren, you also have become dead to the law through the body of Christ, that you may be married to another — to Him who was raised from

---

8   Adapted from Hal Lindsey, *The Late Great Planet Earth* (Grand Rapids, MI: Zondervan, 1974), 179-80.

the dead, that we should bear fruit to God. 5For when we were in the flesh, the sinful passions which were aroused by the law were at work in our members to bear fruit to death. 6But now we have been delivered from the law, having died to what we were held by, so that we should serve in the newness of the Spirit and not in the oldness of the letter.

No longer alive in the realm of our old husband, the law, we are alive in a realm where the law has no jurisdiction over us. By death we were set free from the law to marry Christ, but for what purpose? It is that we might bear fruit to God (7:4). As long as we were married to the law we were weak in our flesh, slaves to Sin, and could not bear the fruit of righteousness to holiness (6:19-22). As long as we ourselves are alive, the law has jurisdiction — we must keep the standard of righteousness through our own effort to be sanctified, to please God. But this is doomed to failure. "Unless a grain of wheat falls into the earth and dies, it remains alone; but if it dies, it bears much fruit" (Jn 12:24 NASB). Such "fruit" can only be produced by the Spirit and not the inadequate, mortal flesh of our former life in Adam. The rotten fruit we produced *then* only led to death, for the law served only to stir up the passions of our sinfulness in Adam: "The sting of death is sin, and the strength of sin is the law" (1 Cor 15:56).

This is well illustrated by the children's story, Ferdinand the Bull. Ferdinand was not like the other bulls who liked to fight. He preferred to sit under the chestnut trees and sniff flowers. But one day bull inspectors from Mexico City came to select brave bulls for the bull fights. The other bulls showed off their snorts and their fierce charging ability. But not Ferdinand. He just walked over to the chestnut trees to sniff the flowers and sat down . . . right on a bumblebee! Suddenly, they saw a new Ferdinand: he bellowed louder than all the other bulls put together and began charging anything in his way. The bumblebee had instantly transformed Ferdinand into the most ferocious bull on the farm. In the same way, the Sin Nature may *seem* quite placid and calm and even produce much "good," but let it sit on a bumblebee — the *law* — and watch out.

This is precisely the thrust of Romans 7:5. While the verse refers to our former life as non-believers, Paul's point is that the *same provocation* can be seen in the Christian who attempts to follow the law in his own ability, as depicted so graphically in 7:14-25. Thus, the word "flesh" or "fleshly" reoccurs in 7:14, 18, and 25. Whenever we try *in our flesh* to live up to a prescribed standard of behavior to gain God's favor, we are controlled by Sin.[9] Recall Paul's words to the Galatians

---

9 "Flesh" is therefore distinct from Sin (*hē harmatia*) throughout Romans 6–8. See note 1, Chapter 1, "Who You Gonna Call?" "'Flesh' . . . is not part of the person, nor even exactly an impulse or 'nature' within the person—for this reason the NIV translation 'sinful nature' for *sarx* throughout Rom. 7-8 is very misleading . . . [it is] a 'power-sphere' in which a person lives" (Douglas J. Moo, *The Epistle to the*

in 3:1, 3: "Oh, foolish Galatians, who has bewitched you . . . ? Having begun in the Spirit are you now made perfect by the flesh?" After gaining new life by regeneration of the Holy Spirit, why try to bear fruit by the works of the flesh? Whenever a Christian seeks to measure up to a standard set by other men, that very standard will only work like a bumblebee to spur his dormant, docile Sin Nature into action like a charging bull. Instead of enjoying the fruit of the Spirit, he will explode like an erupting volcano in works of the flesh.

Being "in the flesh" (Rom 7:5; also 8:9) is therefore a statement of Position ("realm," "power sphere") in Adam; one who is *not* "in Christ." But *according to the flesh* in Romans 8 refers to the Condition of unrighteous behavior when believers *revert* to that realm, which is rooted in our still unredeemed flesh (7:5).[10] Romans 7:7-13 will thus describe Paul's pre-conversion state, "in the flesh" or "in Adam,"[11] as a transition to 7:14-25, where the same convicting effect of the Law is seen to govern his *post*-conversion experience.[12] When we work to "do righteousness" out of fleshly self-reliance, Satan uses the Law to stir up and expose the Sin Nature (see 5:20a). This self-reliance is doomed to "death" throughout Romans 7 (note esp. 7:24) but in 8:5-13 it is contrasted — just as in 7:5-6 — with the life-giving "mind of the Spirit."

Just as "discharge" was the best translation of *katergeomai* in our slavery to Sin in 6:6, so also for *katergeomai* in 7:6: in Christ's death we have also been "discharged" from the Law. Our new Position in Christ is the basis for our freedom from both the Sin Nature (Romans 6) and the Law (Romans 7). We have been moved out of the realm where Sin is "master" — and the Law its "instigator" — and into the realm where we are released (as in 6:7) to serve in newness of the Spirit and not oldness of the letter (7:6). The chart below thus shows the absurdity of continuing to rely on the flesh to fulfill the Law.

"HUSBAND"	REALM	FRUIT	RESULT
Law	Flesh	Rotten	Death
Christ	Spirit	Good	Life

Romans NICNT [Grand Rapids, MI: Eerdmans, 1996], 418). Note how this use of "the flesh" differs from that of Galatians 5:16-21 where Paul does not use *hē hamartia* ("Sin") but rather *hē sarx* ("the flesh") as a metonymy for the Sin Nature.

10   Such "reversion" in believers explains why "flesh" reappears 14 times in Romans 8:1-13 (Majority Text).

11   This is indicated in 7:7-13 by the past tense, although it is also possible to see this section as addressed to Paul's early Christian experience.

12   This is marked by the conspicuous shift to the present tense, which never signifies past events when narrated in the first person singular (Daniel B. Wallace, *Greek Grammar Beyond the Basics* [Grand Rapids, MI: Zondervan, 1996], 528-32).

In Romans 6 our death in Christ deposed our Sin Nature from its throne and ended the Law's grip on us through sin. Now in Romans 7 we see that we have been "discharged" from the Law that we might serve in newness of the Spirit, not in oldness of the letter. So, as with Sin, by knowing, believing, and reckoning on this fact, our Condition can conform to our new Position. Stanford says it well:

> If believers knew more fully the deliverance of the first part of Romans 7, they would experience less of the defeat of the latter part! . . . Positionally, in Christ, no believer is under the law. . . . Conditionally, almost all believers are to some extent under . . . law "as a rule of life." The all too general attitude is: I must love the Lord and others; I must maintain my testimony; I must witness and work for Him; I must resist self; I must stop this sinning. The feeling of constraint expressed in "I must" makes for Romans 7 defeat . . . . Anything we seek to do or keep from doing in our own strength brings us under legal bondage. Any promises or vows we make to the Lord, any code of ethics or rules of conduct that we set up for ourselves or have placed upon us, are on the basis of law and therefore result in failure and ever-deepening enslavement.[13]

I always hated school during my younger years, with all the books and studying. Now I spend most of my time studying and in books. Why the change? I was discharged from the law. As I grew up I set for myself a certain standard of performance in order to please myself and my parents. So even though I hated studying I did it to meet that standard ("law") through sheer willpower and pride. When I entered seminary I again set up my little performance standard, but after a semester I knew something was wrong. I was studying God's truth eight hours a day and I hated it. I had put myself under the law, and it became a "ministration of death."

That realization, plus the resulting conviction that it was wrong for me to compete for spiritual knowledge, brought me out from under the law. For my last three years of seminary I never looked at a returned test or grade. As Howard Hendricks told us in class, "No one is going to look at your transcript when you get out of here, so don't study for a grade . . . study for a lifetime of ministry." Suddenly, the oldness of the letter was gone. I hit the books with a newness of spirit. I loved it. I craved it. I found I could study twelve to fourteen hours a day and still be hungry for more. I had been *discharged* from the law — an *honorable* discharge.

---

13   Stanford, *Green Letters*, 207.

It works the same in "ordinary" Christian life. All those things we have heard that good Christians ought to do? They take on a new light when you realize we do not *have* to do them. Now we *want* to do them because we reckon on having died to our old husband, the law. It is our new husband that empowers us, not *duty* or *obligation*; so the "things Christians do" end up as "fruit of righteousness" to set us apart as *His* and give us abundant life (6:19-23).

Then what about all the commands and rules in the NT? A command is a command, right? William McRae elucidates:

> One under the law sees the commands of Scripture and thinks he must do these to get God's blessings. So he seeks God's help. One not under the law sees commands as areas for dependency on God. I ask God to enable me or to do it through me. I don't ask Him to help me. You say, "That's hairsplitting." But that kind of hairsplitting will change your Christian life, my friend. Law says, "God helps them who help themselves." One not under the law says, "God, I can't do that. . . . If it's going to be done, you'll have to do it."[14]

Accordingly, William Newell adds this apt exhortation:

> Refuse to make "resolutions" and "vows," for that is to trust in the flesh. . . . To be disappointed with yourself is to have trusted in yourself . . . To preach devotion first, and blessing second, is to reverse God's order, and preach law, not grace. The law made man's blessing depend on devotion; grace confers undeserved, unconditional blessing: our devotion may follow, but does not always do so — in proper measure.[15]

So, where does divine power stop and human responsibility take over? Please hear us clearly: *Our human responsibility is to trust in and accept divine power,* which never runs out. I can do all things through Christ who strengthens me (Phil 4:13). Charles Trumbull explains:

> The effortless life is not the will-less life. We use our will to believe, to receive, but not to exert effort in trying to accomplish what only God can do. Our hope for victory over sin is not "Christ plus my efforts," but Christ plus my receiving . . . [T]o believe on Him in this way is to recognize that He is doing for us what we cannot do for ourselves.[16]

---

14 William J. McRae, "Release from the Law," from Romans Sermon Series, Grace Bible Fellowship Online, available at www.gbfc-tx.org/Pages/BillMcrae.html. Accessed October 26, 2010.

15 Newell, *Romans*, 247-48.

16 Trumbull, *Victory in Christ*, 51.

Yes, *salvation* is by grace through faith apart from works of the law, but *sanctification* is also by grace through faith, apart from works of the law. So, abide in the vine. We conclude with this well-crafted comment by Norman Douty:

> If I am to be like Him, then God in His grace must do it, and the sooner I come to recognize it the sooner I will be delivered from another form of bondage. Throw down every endeavor and say, "I cannot do it; the more I try the farther I get from His likeness." What shall I do? Ah, the Holy Spirit says, "You cannot do it; just withdraw; come out of it. You have been in the arena, you have been endeavoring, you are a failure; come out, and sit down . . . Don't try to believe Him, just look at Him. Just be occupied with Him. Forget about trying to be like Him. Instead of letting that fill your mind and heart, let Him fill it. Just behold Him; look upon Him through the Word. Come to the Word for one purpose and that is to meet the Lord. Not to get your mind crammed full of things about the sacred Word, but come to it to meet the Lord. Make it to be a medium, not of biblical scholarship, but of fellowship with Christ. Behold the Lord.[17]

Paul put it more succinctly when he wrote, "May the very God of peace sanctify you wholly. . . . Faithful is He that called you, who also will do it" (1 Thess 5:23). And we would add that to shift our focus from our Condition to our Position is to be less preoccupied with self and more preoccupied with Christ. And don't forget, you will *become* what you think about, all day long!

---

17 Norman Douty, quoted by Miles Stanford, *Green Letters*, 28.

CHAPTER 9

"SATAN'S BEACHHEAD"
Romans 7:7-12

As George Philips of Meridian, MS was about to go to bed, his wife saw that he had left the light on in the garage. But as George went out the back door to turn off the light, he noticed burglars in his garage stealing things. Being an older man, he did not want to confront them himself so he went back inside, called the police, and reported the robbery. The dispatcher asked if they were inside his house. He said "no" and was told to stay in his house and lock the doors; all officers were busy at that time, but one would arrive as soon as they were available. George said "OK," hung up the phone, waited thirty seconds, then called the police again. "Hello, I'm the man who just called in about a burglary at his home. Don't bother sending an officer because I just shot the robbers." Then he hung up. Within five minutes six police cars, a SWAT team, an EMS vehicle, and a helicopter descended on his house, caught the burglars red-handed, and then went over to talk to George. "I thought you said you shot these robbers," said the officer in charge. George looked the policeman right in the eye and said, "I thought you said no one was available." This kind of experience might lead George to think something was wrong with the law. And that is the same concern Paul anticipates in Romans 7: "Maybe there is something wrong with the law."

Just as we learned how to be free from the Sin Nature in Romans 6, we must now learn to be free from the Law in Romans 7. Whenever Paul mentions "the law," it can refer to one of several possibilities: the Ten Commandments; the first five books of the Bible (the Torah); or sometimes the "law principle," that is, legalism — the notion that we must perform in order to earn God's blessings, whether in this life or the next. The legalist tries to live up to (perform) the Law of Moses (OT) or the Law of Christ (NT, e.g., Gal 6:2) or some other self-imposed set of rules. While it is true that we are no longer under the Law of Moses but under the Law of Christ,[1] the key issue is not the particular standard used — we can fall into this same trap in our approach to any of the commands in the NT, especially in the epistles. The key issue is the delusion of thinking we can pursue any righteous standard to earn God's favor. Focus on the word "earn." The legalist thinks God owes him for his good behavior (his performance). He believes God is indebted to him, whether in this life or the next. That is why he gets mad at God when he "gets dealt a bad hand" in life.

This is an important issue because it raises implications about God's character. As we saw in Romans 7:5, Paul introduced an apparently illogical cause-and-effect: the Law actually *stirs up* the Sin Nature — it is the "bumblebee" that brings the bull (our Sin Nature) to life. It is the burr under the saddle of the Sin Nature. If I believe God gave us the law as a way to please Him, but instead He uses the law to stir up my Sin Nature, then not only must the law be evil, but God himself must be the cause of evil in my life. Just like Adam who blamed God for giving the woman to him, we might be tempted to blame God for our sin since He gave us the very law that incites my Sin Nature. If we can follow this potential concern on the part of the reader then we are well on the way to recognizing how Satan gains his subversive Beachhead in our lives and how it (the Law) can still be good.

Paul therefore begins this section with the obvious question in the mind of the reader: "Isn't the law sinful if it stirs up the Sin Nature?" Paul answers this question carefully as he wends his way down to 7:12. In so doing, he will expand on his prior explanation of God's good purpose in giving the Law (2:14-16; 3:20; 5:20a): to bring us under the conviction that we cannot fulfill God's righteous standard through the self-effort epitomized "in the flesh" (7:5).

C.	**Freedom from Law**		**(7)**
	1.	**Discharge from the Law**	**7:1-6**
	2.	**Design of the Law**	**7:7-12**
		a. The *Enquiry*	**7a**
		b. The *Example*	**7b**
		c. The *Explanation*	**8-10**
		d. The *Exploitation*	**11-12**
	3.	**Despair under the Law**	**7:13-25**

As we follow Paul's logic we will see how Satan gains a beachhead in our lives. Think of it this way: Dwight Eisenhower was head of Allied Forces in charge of invading Europe to stop Hitler's army. What was the first thing he had to do?

---

1 It is a new divine administration during the Church Age (post-Pentecost). Some of the laws from the old administration (the Law of Moses) have been carried over into the new administration, some have been done away with, and there are some newly minted laws contained in the Law of Christ.

Establish a beachhead, right? Romans 7:7-12 shows how Satan uses the Law to gain a beachhead in our flesh, from which He can attack us both individually (to subvert one Christian at a time) and on a broad scale (to subvert Christianity as a viable faith). However, God turns Satan's strategy to His own advantage: the Law made us aware of our Sin and death in Adam so that *personal* sin might be imputed and we might be held accountable (5:13-14). But the Law also made Sin "abound" to show us our slavery to Sin and death (5:20a, 21a) and thus our dire need of life in the Spirit (8:1-14). Paul illustrates and explains this role of law by recapitulating these events in his own past experience, just as with Adam in the Garden (7:7-12).

A. The *Enquiry* 7:7a

What shall we say then? Is the law sin? Certainly not! On the contrary, I would not have known sin except through the law.

The word "known" here is from the verb *ginōskō* and refers to *experiential* rather than *intuitive* knowledge. And since the word for "sin" has a Greek article in front of it (*hē hamartia*, "the" sin) throughout Romans 7, it is referring to our Sin Nature,[2] not just "sin" in general. So, since the Law and Sin seem to work in tandem (7:5), is the law then sinful? "No way!" exclaims Paul. The law made us *aware* of our Sin and death in Adam and held us *accountable* (3:20b; 5:13-14).

My three sisters and I recently had to put my mother into assisted living. She was living by herself in a big old house in Louisville, Ky, and was quite lonely. She still got out, visited her friends, and drove thirty miles to play bridge twice a week, but her driving was getting shaky, so after she drove off the road into a snow bank, we decided it was time to lay down the law: NO MORE DRIVING! Taking the keys away from an old person is like dragging Sasquatch to the zoo — you'd have thought we told her she could not *eat* any longer. She said, "If you take those keys away from me, I'm gonna steal somebody's car and drive it into the Ohio River. Then you'll feel guilty for the rest of your lives." She was a nice old lady until we laid down the law. The law was for her own good and that of others. But Satan exploited the Law through her Sin Nature to make her angry and despairing.

The Law is to my Sin Nature as a flashlight is to a dirty closet. I may be surrounded by dirt in a closet but totally unaware of the filth until it is illuminated. The Holy Spirit uses the Law like a flashlight so we can see our sinfulness more clearly. When the light exposes the dirt, does that mean the light is dirty? How absurd. In just the same way the Law is not evil. It simply exposes the evil Sin Nature.

---

2 See note 1, Chapter 1, "Who You Gonna Call?"

That is the bold principle that Paul needed to underscore. We can follow his logic when we notice the three uses of "for" in 7b, 8b, and 11 that point, respectively, to the *example*, the *explanation*, and finally the *exploitation* of the principle in Paul's own experience.

B. The *Example* 7:7b

For I would not have known covetousness unless the law had said, "You shall not covet."

Here Paul cites the tenth commandment, using the verb *epithumēseis* ("you shall covet") and the related noun *epithumia* ("covetousness"), the same word found in 1 Jn 2:16, which speaks of the *lust* of the flesh, the *lust* of the eyes, and the pride of life. This lust is a craving that consumes the thought and energy God intended for us to invest in righteousness (5:17, 21). Paul would not have felt the conviction of that unrighteous craving had the Law not said, "You shall not have a craving desire." Thus, God permitted Satan to exploit the Law in Paul's experience in order to *magnify* the craving and thus expose Satan's partner in crime, our Sin Nature.

I experienced this kind of craving as a young pastor. I *love* chocolate covered caramels. I can pluck the caramels out of a Russell Stover box of assorted chocolates with my eyes closed (they are always square.) You can imagine my delight when I discovered this long, chocolate covered caramel bar called the Marathon candy bar because it was so long . . . and *soooo* good. And since I tend to get on food kicks, thus began my Marathon candy bar kick. For months I ate two bars for a pick-me-up at ten AM, four for lunch, and two for a snack at three in the afternoon.

Then someone, fearing for my life, gave me a copy of the book *Sugar Blues*. I read about the evils of sucrose, refined sugar. Awrggff. I was convicted. I went off sugar cold turkey. Up went the sign: NO SUGAR. But that meant no Marathon candy bars. Suddenly my desire for chocolate covered caramel candy bars transformed into a craving that thoroughly consumed me. I thought about them when I should have been studying the Bible or praying at ten AM. I thought about them at lunch. By three in the afternoon I was in flagrant withdrawal. On the way home it was all I could do to keep my steering wheel from turning into the convenience store that supplied my little habit. What was going on here?

When God's law is "posted" to restrict our freedom, we are incited to rebel against the law and judge the lawgiver (Jas 4:11-12) in order magnify our transgression and bring us under conviction. This effect of magnifying sin to expose the Sin Nature is just what Paul described in 3:20b, "by the law is the knowledge of sin," and expanded in 5:20a, "the law entered that sin might *abound*." Paul will thus elaborate on his own experience to explain how Satan exploits this "beachhead."

C. The *Explanation*   7:8-10

8But sin, taking opportunity by the commandment, produced in me all manner of evil desire. For apart from the law sin was dead. 9I was alive once without the law, but when the commandment came, sin revived and I died. 10And the commandment, which was to bring life, I found to bring death.

The word "opportunity" (*aphormēn*) means "place of origin, starting point." It is the "beachhead" Satan uses to make us doubt God, to lose our faith in God, to cause us to be disillusioned with God. We also need to understand the meaning of "dead." "Dead" in this context does not mean non-existent. The Sin Nature ("sin") is like an internal Geiger counter; when removed from a source of radioactivity, it is virtually inactive. But bring some radioactive material near the Geiger counter, and it comes to life — bring the law near the Sin Nature, and it "comes to life." Thus *dead* means "inactive" and *alive* means "active."

Paul exemplifies this process in his own self-sufficient attempt to fulfill the righteousness epitomized in 6:16-23: "I was once *alive* [not bound by the constraints of righteous requirements, compare 6:20] without the law, but when the commandment came, sin revived and I *died* [was unable to bear righteous fruit, compare 6:21]. And the commandment, which was to *bring life* [the fruit of righteous living, compare 6:22, 23b], actually *brought death* [inability to bear righteous fruit, compare 6:23a]."[3]

I experienced this effect of the law firsthand through one road sign that I grew to hate intensely. The problem was, it was placed on a stretch of road I had driven for years with no posted speed limit. It was a lonely road, which led into the golf course where I played. I believe I always drove that road at a safe, reasonable speed. Suddenly, a sign appeared out of nowhere. There were no houses, just the golf course on one side and woods on the other. This stretch of road was about a mile long. Sixty would have been a safe speed, but it had not been previously

---

3 While Romans 7:7-12 seems to describe the preconversion state "in the flesh" in 7:5, Paul's first person account could apply as well to his *early Christian experience*. It is hard to see how a "blameless" Pharisee (Phil 3:4-6) could have been "caught" by the Law after his conversion. However, after Paul found Christ and was freed from the Law (Rom 6:14), he could have reverted to it *"after the flesh"* and thus "rediscovered the commandment." In this case "alive" would mean "active as a Christian": "I was once *alive* [active as a Christian] without the Law, but when I reverted to law, my Sin revived, and I *died* [became *inactive*]. And the commandment, which was to *bring life* [stir up a more active Christian life], instead *brought death* [caused me to become *inactive*]" (7:9-10). "Life" and "death" in v. 10 could also mean "victory" and "defeat": "The commandment, which was meant to bring me *life* [full *quality* of life], actually brought *death* [defeat and despair as a Christian]." However, if in fact 7:7-12 is describing Paul's preconversion experience, then 7:13-25 depicts how a *Christian* who *then* reverts to the Law at *any time* of his walk in Christ (not only his early experience) can be just as "dead" as in his preconversion state.

PORTRAITS OF RIGHTEOUSNESS

posted. Forty-five was reasonable but would have been difficult. But it was not forty-five, thirty-five, or even twenty-five . . . it was *twenty*. TWENTY. Now I was mad. Not only did I not want to go twenty, I wanted to go a *hundred*! The law stirred up the latent rebellion bound up in my heart. But not only that, I discovered I was hypercritical of the idiots who made that law. Of course the rebellion was sinful, the judging was sinful, and if I ever *did* speed on that road after that (far be it from me!), that would be sinful too. The potential for such sin was inside me all along; it was just not *activated* until the law was posted.[4]

There are transparent parallels in these verses between Paul's account and Satan's agenda in the Garden (Gen 3:1-6). Satan uses the law to gain a beachhead or base of operations in the flesh to prevent God's people from fulfilling their commission to reflect His image by revealing His righteousness on earth (1:17). Thus, Paul's argument here is designed to show why it is such a bad idea to return to the law after having been released (6:7, 14; 7:1): by trapping us in sin (7:5), the law prevents us from displaying righteousness in Christ as slaves of God and thus experiencing the life he has offered us (6:16-23).

D. The *Exploitation* 7:11-12

11*For sin, taking occasion by the commandment, deceived me, and by it killed me.* 12*Therefore the law is holy, and the commandment holy and just and good.*

Here is the word *aphormēn* again. In v. 8 it was translated "opportunity," whereas here it reads "occasion." But it is the same word. *Aphormē* is the place in the body where a disease starts; in a war, it is the *beachhead* or *base of operations*. Thus, surprisingly, Satan gains a beachhead in his war against the saints through God's Word — he uses Scripture to defeat those who try to please God by law-keeping (those who "know the law," 7:1). You would think Satan would worm his way into our lives through the lust of the eye, the lust of the flesh, or the pride of life (the "world system" of 1 Jn 2:16) or through our lusts which war in our members (as described in Jas 4:1). The world and our Sin Nature are the devil's *accomplices*, but they are not his beachhead in the flesh. Thus the Sin Nature exploits the [otherwise good] law to secure Satan's base of operations in the flesh and thereby deceive us and kill us.[5]

---

4 William Newell uses a similar illustration (*Romans: Verse by Verse* [Grand Rapids, MI: Kregel, 1994], 265).

5 Although the text says it is the Sin Nature that uses the Law to gain its "opportunity" in the flesh, Satan and the Sin Nature work *together* to gain this beachhead. Whereas Satan succeeded with the first Adam (Gen 3, see below), he *failed* with the Second Adam (Rom 5:14c), whose own model for fulfilling the Law (= "according to the Spirit," Matt 4; Lk 4) ends up providing the entire foundation for Paul's argument in Rom 8:1-14.

The words Paul uses for "deceive" (*exapateō*) in 7:11 and "revive" (*anazaō*) in 7:9 give us a good clue as to what Paul has in mind in the background of the larger passage, 7:7-12. The intensive form of *exapateō* is used only five times in the NT, but one of these sheds great light on Romans 7:11. The same word in 2 Corinthians 11:3 signifies how the serpent "beguiled" Eve. In Romans 7:9 *anazaō* means "spring to life." So in tandem with "beguiled," Paul's use of terms in 7:7-12 suggests an analogy between the Sin Nature and a serpent.

One fall I was on a father/son hunt for quail with my son and some friends in S. Texas. Suddenly, a twelve year old yelled, "Snake!" When we got to the kid, the biggest rattler I have ever seen was coiled and ready to strike. The boy was one step away, three feet max. This snake was over six feet with a head as big as my fist, and they can strike to a length and a half (= nine feet). A bite from that monster could have killed that boy, and the only reason it did not strike is that it had just swallowed a large rabbit. But the ground tremors of the approaching boy had revived the deadly snake, and it "sprang to life." As one person said, "Nothing resembles a dead serpent more than a living serpent, so long as it doesn't move." Sin is just like a snake lying dormant in the flesh until it is aroused. It may be lying there still . . . until the law comes along to "revive" it, and it *springs to life*, poised and ready to strike. And it is just as deadly.

Even Paul's choice of the tenth commandment — the commandment against coveting — fits well with Genesis 3. Adam and Eve, of course, coveted God's knowledge, and Paul's use of the word "commandment" instead of "law" recalls the single command in the Garden ("Do not eat . . ."). God told Adam and Eve that they would die if they ate the fruit. The command was to preserve their lives, but Satan used it as his opportunity or tool to secure a "base of operations" in their flesh by arousing their desire to be self-sufficient.

Paul's use of "death" here also parallels Genesis 3. After eating the fruit, Adam and Eve didn't physically die right away. But the death sentence had been passed. Although they continued to live physically for years, the consequences of the curse also continued. We can thus confidently conclude that Genesis 3:1-6 is the backdrop for Rom 7:7-12, so let's take a closer look at what happened in the Garden before proceeding in Romans 7.

Digging Deeper: Satan's Exploitation of Law to Incite Sin in the Garden

In Genesis 3 the serpent defeated Eve in a two round "boxing match." And it was "tag team" at that: the serpent and the world partner up to knock Eve out. Only the serpent is boxing in the first round. Once he weakens Eve with a left hook, a punch to the stomach, and an uppercut (as described below), he has done his job; he slithers (or hops) out of the ring and leaves round two to his partner, the world. Three more blows from the world (the lust of the eye, the lust of the flesh, and the pride of life, 1 Jn 2:16), and Eve is knocked out cold. The serpent did all his work in round one. That is where he weakened Eve and set her up for the knockout blows from the world with his own three punches, all of which exploited God's Word to achieve the knockout:

1. He **doubted** God's Word ("Did He really say . . . ?").
2. He **denied** God's Word ("You will not surely die").
3. He **distorted** God's Word ("It will make you wise like God").

Satan follows this same strategy against both society in general and individuals in particular. His attack against Christianity in the last three hundred years has caused Western Civilization to doubt, deny, or distort God's Word. By 1880 there was not a seminary on the continent of Europe that believed in the inerrancy of Scripture. By 1900 there was not a seminary in the British Isles that believed in the inerrancy of Scripture. By 1910 the same was true for America. Thankfully, in the last hundred years many have formed in reaction to the liberalism that swept through Western Christianity. But the damage had been done. Round One had done its work. Finally, the world (lust of the eye, lust of the flesh, the pride of life) has fulfilled the strategy to alienate humanity from the true God.

We now live in what many call post-Christian America. Satan's beachhead in the lives of individuals today is the same as it was in the Garden and in the temptation of Jesus. Satan and his accomplice the Sin Nature use God's Word to worm their way into the believer's flesh and weaken him enough so the world can knock him out of the battle.. Here are some ways they cause us to *doubt, deny,* or *distort* God's Word:

1. **Truth** — You can't out-sin God's grace.
   Lie — Go for it; He will always forgive you (Rom 6:1).
   Lie — It won't hurt to go back and sin a little (Rom 6:15).
2. **Truth** — God loves you unconditionally.
   Lie — He will bless me with good health, lots of money, good kids, and an ideal mate.
3. **Truth** — You should not commit adultery.
   Lie — Anything short of adultery is OK, including fornication.
4. **Truth** — Giving 10% is a good principle.
   Lie — If I give 10%, God will bless my business and I can spend the rest on myself.
5. **Truth** — God will provide all your needs in Christ (Phil 4:19).
   Lie — Since my [perceived] needs aren't being met, I can't really trust God.
6. **Truth** — You are fearfully and wonderfully made by God (Ps 139).

Lie — He did a lousy job in the womb, so I can't trust Him in this life.

Just as with the Tree in the Garden, there is nothing wrong with the Law. It is the Sin Nature and our enemy the devil that take advantage of God's law to incite personal sin, "after the likeness of the transgression of Adam" (5:14c).[6]

[END OF EXCURSUS]

Paul thus concludes his argument in reply to the logically anticipated question in 7:7. Is the Law evil because it stirs up our Sin Nature to cause us to want to sin more? — of course not (7:12): even though it causes sin to abound, God's law is holy (*hagios* means pure, set apart, sacred), just (*dikaios* means righteous), and good (*agathos* means intrinsically good). The law that was meant to bring life by reflecting God's standard for righteous behavior is also the light that penetrates our consciences to expose how sinful we are (7:7). It brings "death" (defeat, disillusionment, and despair) so that we might be made fully aware of how sinful we are (7:13). Law can never bring life in the unredeemed flesh, because that is the realm where Satan uses the law to arouse Sin and produce death (7:5) rather than bear fruit to God (7:4).

Yes, it seems shocking, even scandalous to suggest that Satan uses God's Word to gain his beachhead in the flesh to defeat us in our walk with God, but it should not surprise us too much. After all, the serpent was more cunning than any beast of the field.

So how do we defeat the devil? Beat him at his own game. Know the Bible well enough that he cannot use it against us. That is what Jesus did: "It is written . . . It is written . . . It is written" (Matt 4:4-7). As the psalmist wrote, "Oh, how I love your law" (Ps 119:97). And again, "Blessed is the man who fears the Lord, who delights greatly in his commandments" (Ps 112:1). And again, "Your Word have I hidden in my heart that I might not sin against You" (Ps 119:11).

No, there is nothing wrong with the Law. It is not evil. It is our Sin Nature and our enemy the devil who take advantage of God's law to work in us all manner of evil.

This takes us to the turning point in Paul's argument. He now anticipates how the same dilemma of law-induced slavery to sin that he had observed in the

---

6 God thus allows Satan to implement His sovereign plan, in that the law fulfills God's intent to impute sin *personally* (3:20; 5:13) and make it "abound," enslaving us to Sin and death (5:20a, 21a). This in turn makes humans even more desperate to receive the "abundance of grace" through God's gift in Christ (5:17; 20b), so that we may *reign in righteousness by faith,* as the "gospel of God" originally intended (5:21b; see 1:1, 16-17).

unbeliever (6:14; 7:1) will also arise in the *believer* who remains focused on law-keeping (7:13-25). However, Paul will harness this logical concern to show how the very thing that Satan intended for evil is used by God for good (7:13), in that it unmasks the *real* problem in such a believer (Rom 7:14-17) — our still unredeemed flesh!

CHAPTER 10

"THE DO-IT-YOUSELF KIT"
Romans 7:13-17

How would you like to have a Do-It-Yourself kit for the Christian life? I once saw a cartoon that reminded me very much of Romans 7. It showed a man standing at the counter of a Do-It-Yourself shop. Apparently, he had bought a Do-It-Yourself TV kit, but his attempt blew up on him. As he stood before the counter with a broken picture tube in one hand, another tube sticking out of his ear, and a bent-up TV antenna under his arm, he asked the clerk, "Do you have an 'Undo-It-Yourself' kit?" This is essentially what Paul will be asking by the end of Romans 7.

Recall that Paul introduced this entire section by identifying his readers as "those who know the law" (7:1). The Law once appealed to Paul like a Do-It-Yourself kit for righteousness, and he now shares the results of that kind of thinking with those in Christ who might be tempted to revert to the Law to bear righteous fruit (6:19, 22). The kit came packaged with "ten simple steps to spiritual maturity." But when Paul tried to follow the instructions, he couldn't get the formula to work. Everything blew up on him. When the smoke cleared, Paul was looking for an Undo-It-Yourself kit: ". . . who will deliver me from this body of death?" (7:24).

The problem is, there *are* no successful Do-It-Yourself kits for the Christian life. The Law *appears* to be such a kit, but our Sin Nature in Adam only exploits the Law to deceive us into thinking we can or must do it ourselves. This is the false appeal of our inadequate flesh, but the self-reliant pursuit of the law only leads to "death." This sense of "death" in Romans 5–8 is captured by the progression: *defeat, disillusionment,* and *despair.* Just as when we allow *sin* to be our "commander" through the weakness of the flesh (6:15-23), this "death" is also the daily ration meted out by the Sin Nature when we try in our own ability to submit to *the Law* as our "commander" (7:13-25). The harder I try, the harder I fall into defeat, disillusionment, and despair.

So Paul deliberately moves us into this Arena of Despair by anticipating a second logical illusion on the part of his readers: if I died when the Law came (7:7-12), it must have been the Law that killed me; after all, it only made me even more sinful and miserable. If true, the implied solution would be to avoid God's Word altogether, since it only reveals the Law — ignorance is bliss. "God forbid," Paul replies. That is like claiming that since so many marriages wind up in divorce and unhappiness, people should not get married. "Absurd," Paul would say, "there's nothing wrong with marriage; there's something wrong with *us*." Our "death" comes from Sin in us, and the Law is essential to show us the utter failure of the Do-It-Yourself-Kit (relying on our flesh) to free us from that Sin. To this end, Paul provides a sequential three-step argument in 7:13-25. Each step follows the same cycle of a Statement, followed by Logical Support, and concluding with a Summary.

B.	**Freedom from Law**		**(7)**
	1.	**Discharge from the Law**	7:1-6
	2.	**Design of the Law**	7:7-12
	3.	**Despair under the Law**	7:13-25
		a. **Arena** of Despair	13-17
		b. **Agent** of Despair	18-20
		c. **Admission** of Despair	21-25

In the first cycle, "Arena of Despair" (7:13-17), the Statement appears in v. 13, the logical Support in vv. 14-16, and the Summary in v. 17. The last two cycles are tightly argued and will be dealt with together in the following chapter.

A. ARENA of Despair   7:13-17

1. The *Statement*   13

Has then what is good become death to me? Certainly not! But sin, that it might appear sin, was producing death in me through what is good, so that sin through the commandment might become exceedingly sinful.

Is the law the cause of death? No, says Paul, the cause of death is our Sin Nature. But law plays a key role in making us fully aware that the death we experience is in fact due to the Sin Nature. The same law Satan uses to provoke sin (7:7-12), God also uses to our *advantage* — that we might recognize our sin, be held fully accountable for it, and see our death as the just consequence.[1] Again, by

---

1   Paul counters the imagined objector's negative insinuation by explaining the *positive* role played by the
    law ("the commandment") in exposing sin as he had demonstrated in 7:7-11. His logic in these verses
    is rooted in his prior explanation of the purpose of the Law in 2:14-16 and 5:13-14, 20-21. The key is to

"death" Paul is not referring to spiritual death or necessarily even to physical death, although that may be a final consequence of the struggle in Romans 7. Rather, "death" refers to the agony of defeat — disillusionment and despair — that robs us of anything we might call life and keeps us from bearing righteous fruit (see 6:19-22). Indeed, the person in this arena sometimes wishes he *were* literally dead.

Paul identifies the culprit which leads to such death: the Sin Nature uses the Law or the Word of God — which is *good* — to bring defeat and despair, but ultimately even this is meant by God for good. It may seem counterintuitive, but let's explore how it works.

Before conversion, we are naturally prone to self-reliance (we are "in the "flesh," 7:5). At the moment of conversion we are happy and positive about our new life in Christ and look to the Word for growth in our spiritual life. But with life's inevitable challenges and adversity, we are distracted from our purpose in Christ: to bear righteous fruit to holiness (6:19, 22). So we reach for our "mountain climbing equipment" (our "flesh" = *natural ability* in Adam) and set out to climb the "Mt. Everest" of our dreams. And "those of us who know the law" (7:1) may approach the Bible as a Do-It-Yourself kit to be more like Jesus, have a happy home, be a success, or gain financial freedom. But before we get half way up we find ourselves slipping and falling. Time after time we get up, only to fall again; it becomes such a struggle, we finally lose hope and give up, defeated. "What's the use?" "I have no impact in my world." "I can't be a docile, submissive wife." "I can't control my anger or my tongue." Eventually, we fall into total disillusionment and despair. Our vision and passion are dead, and so is our spiritual life.

This is the "death" Paul describes. We can't blame it on the Bible; we can't say, as many of us do, that it just "doesn't work." So how can this utter failure be seen as "good" (7:12)?

2. The *Support*

¹⁴*For we know that the law is spiritual, but I am carnal, sold under sin. ¹⁵For what I am doing, I do not understand. For what I will to do, that I do not practice;*

---

recognize that the two purpose clauses in 7:13 parallel Paul's logic about the role of the law in 5:13 and 5:20a. The purpose clause "that it might *appear* sin" is better translated "that it might be *exposed* as sin." The premise that sin is not at first evident recalls Paul's claim that *sin is not imputed when there is no law* (5:13). This was a problem, for without law there was no way to warrant death as a just condemnation or sentence for sin. The second purpose clause "so that sin through the commandment might become exceedingly sinful" can be read ". . . *more abundantly* sinful" and seems to echo 5:20a, "the law entered that the offense might abound." Since the latter clause resolves the problem raised in 5:13, Paul's parallel conclusion in 7:13 is now clear: The law is *good* (7:12) because it makes us aware of our own sin and holds us *fully accountable* for that sin, so that death will be seen as the just consequence of that sin.

but what I hate, that I do. [16]*If, then, I do what I will not to do, I agree with the law that it is good.*

The key to Paul's explanation for the dilemma of law-induced "slavery to sin" is the Greek word *sarkinos*, translated here as *carnal*. This is simply the adjective form ("fleshly") of the noun *sarx*, translated "flesh" in Romans 6:19; 7:5, 18, and 25. As we discovered in our discussion of Romans 7:1-6, "the flesh" in Romans 7 is Paul's label for our bent toward self-sufficiency inherited from Adam. So one who is "fleshly" tries to function autonomously and thus — for "those who know the law," (7:1) — to keep the law by *self-effort*. When Paul says "the law is spiritual," he is saying that the ultimate goal of the righteous behavior required by the law goes *beyond* "the letter" (7:6).[2] Unlike the law, self-reliance is not "spiritual," and herein is our hope in disillusionment and despair: law can *drive us to the Spirit* to fulfill the law's "righteous requirement," as Paul first suggested in 7:6 and will conclude in 8:4.

The problem emerges when we use the law's standard (the Word of God) as a blueprint or recipe for righteous behavior to *earn God's favor,* whether in this life or the next. This is like trying to ride a ten-speed bike in tenth gear up a steep hill. We will not get very far. We soon run out of strength. Our chances greatly improve when we use the principle of "gear-ratio" ("abundance of grace," 5:17b) to get us up the hill, as Paul will elaborate in Romans 8. Does that mean we are free of obligation? One housewife asked, "Does what you're teaching on the law mean I don't have to do it? Guess what. I don't feel like doing my housework today." If we don't feel like doing things that seem burdensome, does grace mean we don't have to? The answer is yes and no. No, we do not *have* to do these things to "buy" God's continued favor. But yes, God *does* ask us to be his "agent" in specific circumstances to display His righteousness *out of love* and bring life (6:22-23). The key to avoiding the mere "letter" of the law is to recognize when it is *God* who is asking, and that our "obligation" is to His Spirit's lead and not to our flesh (8:12-14).

The problem in Romans 7:7-25 is that the Spirit (7:6) is nowhere in sight. The entire struggle going on here is to bring Paul, or any self-reliant believer, to the point that he realizes he cannot fulfill what God asks of him out of his own power. Even though the believer is no longer "in Adam" via his new position "in Christ," he can still revert to living a self-reliant life through the flesh. God wants us to come to the point where we realize we can't pedal up that hill in tenth gear. He is waiting for our strength to run out so He can fill us with His — it is God who

---

2   This is precisely Jesus' point in the Sermon on the Mount about the righteousness of God. If we are to be perfect ("spiritual") like our Father in heaven (Matt 5:48), our righteousness must *transcend* the "letter" (5:21-47).

gives us the basic desire and power to do them (Phil 2:13). "And whatever you do, do it heartily, as to the Lord and not to men" (Col 3:23); we may actually find the joy of the Lord bubbling forth as we work for Him — not for our earthly boss or parents or husband or wife, but for the Lord.

So we see that there are some things mentioned in the Bible which are a total delight. We will put them into one circle, the Circle of Delight. Other things may be drudgery to us. Obviously these things which are drudgery are not things which I desire to do in and of themselves. However, the secret to doing these things without putting ourselves under the law principle is to broaden our perspective in order to realize that God has asked us to do these things, and He has given us the basic desire and power to do them (Phil 2:13).

Therefore, both the Circle of Delight and the Circle of Drudgery fit into a larger Circle of Desire to do His will, whatever that may be. So, if he asks me to clean commodes, or dig ditches or any of many other distasteful tasks, I can do them heartily with a song on my lips because he asked me to, and I desire to please Him. "Whatsoever you do, do heartily as unto the Lord, not unto men" (Col 3:23). And as we do this we may actually find the joy of the Lord bubbling forth. He can transfer tasks out of the Circle of Drudgery right into the Circle of Delight as I do them for Him, not for my boss on earth or my parents or my husband or my wife.

The result of this kind of life — empowered by the desire to fulfill God's righteous goals in us — will be a life of discipline with integrity: nothing less than conforming our Condition (behavior that reflects His righteousness) to our Position (in Christ), whether it is fun or not. But this is not the same as what we usually think of as self-discipline. Before I believed in Jesus and for some time after that, I equated discipline with willpower — a Do-It-Yourself system doomed to the failure of Romans 7:7-25. Remember, *He* gives us the power to do His good pleasure, His will (Phil 2:13). As Charles Trumbull said, "The effortless life is not the will-less life. We must exercise our will to submit to His. Not my will but thine be done."[3] The key here is to be aware of what His will is, as we are led by the Spirit (Rom 8:14). We maintain our integrity as His people when the power source is the Holy Spirit, not "fleshly" self-effort.

Thus, Paul's contrasting assertion in v. 14, "The law is spiritual, but I am carnal, sold under sin," is reminiscent of Galatians 3:3, "Having begun in the Spirit, are you now being made perfect by the flesh?" A "fleshly" person cannot fulfill a "spiritual" law, for such a person is "sold under sin." The verb "sold" recalls the slave trade, and its perfect tense implies a state of being — as long as this person insists on self-reliance he continues in a state of slavery to sin and cannot possibly

---

3   Charles G. Trumbull, *Victory in Christ* (Fort Washington, PA: Christian Literature Crusade, 1972), 51.

fulfill a spiritual law (Rom 7:15). Thus Paul agrees from his own experience (7:16), both that the Law *is* good and that he is "sold under sin" (compare 7:13-14).

In verse 15 we stand in the middle of the Arena of Despair. Paul finds that as he does his best to live the Christian life on his own, he is completely stymied. In self-reliance he is a slave to his Sin Nature (v. 14), kept from doing what he wants to do: "I just can't figure myself out. I really *want* to do what is right but I keep doing what is wrong. What gives?" This is the man who desperately wants to stop lying but as soon as he opens his mouth, out pops another lie. It is the wife who desperately seeks some peace and love in her home, yet before her husband has been home five minutes she opens her mouth and starts in on him again. It is all who want to break addictive behaviors but succumb again before the day is over. It results in the cry of despair, "Sometimes I just hate myself," a groan which echoes out of the arena of Romans 7:15. It is proof positive of a defeated Christian sold to the Sin Nature as its slave.

So, how does Paul know that the Law is spiritual (7:14a)? Because when he really wants to do what God asks of him (7:15) he finds that in his fleshly self-reliance (7:14b) he does things he really does not want to do (7:16a) and thus agrees that the Law has spiritually convicted him, so it must be good (7:16b; compare 7:12, "holy, just, good"): it exposes our inadequacy (7:17).

3. The *Summary*   17

But now, it is no longer I who do it, but sin that dwells in me.

Paul summarizes the whole situation by saying in v. 17, "It must be the Sin Nature dwelling in me which causes me to do these things I hate." His main point in v. 13 — realizing that it was *not* the Law that caused his death-like state of despair — is now completed with the discovery that the culprit is his Sin Nature and the arena ("in me") is his flesh (see 7:18). In v. 17 Paul has thus come full circle around the Arena of Despair: Statement (13b), Support (14-16), and Summary (17).

As depressing as this Arena of Death can be, there is some encouragement to be found in light of this "spiritual schizophrenia": the "I" here is the one who has died with Christ (7:4), but when we choose to operate in our flesh ("me"), the Sin Nature within us brings us down. As we grow in Christ we become more aware of the heinous depth of depravity that takes refuge in our flesh. We are shocked by our thoughts: "How can we be Christian and still feel such anger, bitterness, lust, envy?" This is when we can take hope in knowing that these sinful dispositions or actions arise not from our New Identity but from the Sin Nature that dwells "in us," in our unredeemed flesh (7:14, 18). That's why they are called "works of the flesh" (Gal 5:19).

Most first person references in the NT outside of Romans 7 are to our New Identity in Christ. Once we believe in Jesus as our Savior, we are new creatures in Christ (2 Cor 5:17). We are no longer children of wrath; we are children of the King of kings. With Christ, the Father, and the Spirit living inside of us we are no longer the Old Man (all that we were before Christ). We are held to account for our sinful deeds and attitudes, but they do not express who we really are in Christ. We can admit that our Sin Nature will not disappear this side of eternity yet still resist the devil's appeal to our flesh — we simply acknowledge the source (our Sin Nature acting through our flesh) and denounce it: "That evil thought came from the wicked factory within me, but I don't have to obey it, and I flatly deny it is an expression of who I really am in Christ."

The Arena of Despair is a place of disillusionment for the believer who submits to the law principle where the Sin Nature uses law as a whip to keep us enslaved and defeat us, rather than bring the life Christ came to offer: freedom from slavery to Sin. Where is this arena? It is internal. It is that place of struggle where I choose to do good, but find myself doing evil. It is Romans 7:15. We imagine ourselves to be spiritual schizophrenics: split personalities. We cannot figure ourselves out. We are confused when we see how easily Satan deceives us by using something *good* (the Law, 7:12) to enslave us again, just as when we were "in the flesh" (7:5). So why do we believe the lie?

Digging Deeper: How Satan Appeals to the Flesh

The devil whispers two great lies in our ears to appeal to our flesh and keep us defeated. The first great lie is that we must meet a certain *standard of performance* in order to feel good about ourselves and be accepted by God. However, Romans 7:7-12 dealt with the inevitable failure of our self-sufficient attempts to fulfill righteousness. That is legalism in its purest form. Other people are not necessarily involved. But a second lie works in tandem to bring even more misery and despair: I must have the *approval of others* in order to feel good about myself. This lie brings to bear all the added power of peer pressure in assessing my performance, my person, my personality, and my appearance.

The Sin Nature then exploits these lies to enslave us: From birth the human soul cries out with pain rooted in two giant voids — *insecurity* and *insignificance*. The first void makes us feel un*loved*; the second makes us feel un*worthy*. Moreover, we feel outer (physical) and inner (emotional) pain and instinctively want to avoid pain. If I put my hand on a hot stove, I remove it quickly; the same goes for the inner emotional pain of insecurity and/or insignificance. As the pain continues, I develop a coping system to forestall or relieve the pain. The remedy may work at first, but the quicker the relief, the sooner I am addicted; the more I use, the more I need. In time I am physically and/or psychologically enslaved. These addictions become strongholds in my life, and before I know it, "I am carnal ['fleshly'], sold [a slave] under sin" (Rom 7:14).

There are many addictive pain killers besides alcohol and drugs: making money; abuse of power; eating disorders; sex; falling in love with love; emotional religious experiences; indulging negative emotions like anger, bitterness, and hatred; and many more. But the most widespread strongholds may well be *performance* and the *approval* of others. RAPHA teaches how these two lies are related: Self-Worth = Performance + Approval.[4] In other words, I feel good about myself to the degree I am pleased with my performance and others are pleased with me. In both cases, the false metric of legalism is at work: I can measure myself by my own performance according to some self-imposed standard or by the approval of others according to their standard.

In both cases the Sin Nature uses external standards as a coping mechanism to relieve the pain of feeling insecure and insignificant. If I perform, I feel significant. If I am approved, I feel secure (loved). Some of us may feel we have never been deceived by these lies. But wait: am I ever driven by the fear of failure? Have I ever held back in a relationship because of fear of rejection? Many people are driven to very high performance levels, not so much by their love of winning but by a deep-seated fear of failure. Often they are running from a deep psychic pain, usually coming out of their childhood in which their parents had them under a *performance* system, especially one in which they never won. They become performance addicts. Performance is their coping mechanism to deal with their pain. Still others get enmeshed in superficial relationships or shut down to their own spouses due to intense fear of rejection — they are *approval* addicts. Many of us suffer from both.

[END OF EXCURSUS]

Fortunately Romans 7 is not the "end of the story." In Romans 8 God offers a way out of our pain that does not hurt us or others, especially those we love. But this reassurance in turn raises a nagging question. If the Sin Nature causes so much defeat, disillusionment, and despair for the Christian, yet God still loves us and wants us to have an abundant life, why didn't He just eradicate our Sin Nature when we died with Christ? Why does he allow Sin to drag us like gory gladiators into the Arena of Despair day after day to battle against it until Christ returns?

---

4   Robert S. McGee, *The Search for Significance* (Houston, TX: Rapha Printing, 1990), 43-116.

We find the answer in the stated purpose of the Book of Romans, the heart of the gospel (1:16-17): The primary goal of our salvation in Christ is that we display the righteousness of God by faith as our Condition conforms to our New Identity in Him. If there were no Sin Nature, we would not need Christ's power within us to reveal the righteousness of God in our behavior. We could "pedal up the steep hill in tenth gear" out of self-effort, thus obviating the need to depend on God to deliver us. Since all pride and sin is rooted in the demand for independence — "God, I don't need you. I can do it myself" (Gen 3:5) — God left the Sin Nature in us and let us use our Do-It-Yourself kit to show us the gross inadequacy of self-reliance and our need to depend on God by abiding in Christ and walking by the Spirit (Rom 8:1-13). We cannot really understand our need for Romans 8 until we have experienced the failure of Romans 7 — out of death issues life, out of despair comes dependence. God waits until we have exhausted our own strength so that He can work in us and we can share His glory as sons (8:14-39).

Watchman Nee illustrates this beautifully. While swimming one day on a retreat with some other Christian brothers, one of them got a cramp in his leg and was sinking fast. When Watchman motioned for another brother who was an excellent swimmer to save the drowning man, to his great dismay, the fine swimmer did not budge. In desperation, Nee cried out, "Don't you see the man is drowning?" But the good swimmer just sat there on the bank. Watchman said to himself, "I hate that brother. How can he claim to be a Christian and just let his brother die?" But when the victim was at the point of exhaustion, the apparently complacent swimmer jumped in, took a few swift stokes, and brought the man to shore, safe and sound. Watchman could not hide his disgust, but the swimmer put brother Nee in his place: "Had I gone in earlier, he would have held me so tight, we both would have drowned. You can't save a drowning man until he is utterly exhausted and ceases to make the slightest effort to save himself." So Nee concludes,

> When we give up the case, then God will take it up. He is waiting
> until we are at an end of our resources and can do nothing more for
> ourselves . . . The flesh profits nothing! God has declared it to be fit
> only for death. If we truly believe that, then we shall confirm God's
> verdict by abandoning all fleshly efforts to please Him. For our
> every effort to do His will is a denial of His declaration in the cross
> that we are utterly powerless to do so. It is a misunderstanding on
> the one hand of God's demands and on the other hand of the source
> of supply.[5]

---

5 Watchman Nee, *The Normal Christian Life* (Wheaton, IL: Tyndale, 1977), 167-69.

As C. I. Scofield says, the Arena of Despair (Romans 7) is the stepping stone to Romans 8.

> Not everyone, by any means, has had the experience of the seventh of Romans, that agony of conflict, of desire to do what we cannot do, of longing to do the right we find we cannot do. It is a great blessing when one gets into the seventh of Romans and begins to realize the awful conflict of its struggle and defeat; because *the first step* to get out of the seventh chapter and into the victory of the eighth, *is to get into the seventh.* Of all the needy classes of people, the neediest of this earth are not those who are having a heart-breaking, agonizing struggle for victory, but those who are having no struggle at all, and no victory, and who do not know it, and who are satisfied and jogging along in a pitiable existence of ignorance of almost all the possessions that belong to them in Christ.[6]

It is better to have tried a Do-It-Yourself Kit in the Christian life than never to have tried at all. We can be assured when we enter the Arena of Despair in Romans 7 that our defeats are but stepping stones to the full deliverance of Romans 8. When our Do-It-Yourself Kit has finally blown up on us, we can come humbly to God and ask for His "Undo-It-Yourself Kit."

---

6 C. I. Scofield, quoted by Miles J. Stanford, *The Complete Green Letters* (Grand Rapids, MI: Zondervan, 1983), 56-57 (emphasis added).

CHAPTER 11

"THE RAT"
Romans 7:18-25

The story is told of two Houston parents and their five year old daughter, walking on the beach at Galveston. When the little girl wandered off by herself to collect shells, she came upon a little dog lying on the beach that had apparently drowned. But when she touched the dog she could tell it had a faint heartbeat. She picked it up and asked her parents if she could take it home so their toy poodle could have a friend, and they agreed. When the family returned home that evening, the little girl gave the "dead" dog a bath. Then she blew its hair dry and combed it out. She found some old doll clothes, dressed it up, and put it in the cage with their toy poodle for the night with some food and water. But when she got up in the morning and went to the cage, she found that the dog food had not been touched; nor the water. But their toy poodle was dead and half eaten.

It turns out that the "drowned" animal that had come back to life was not a dog at all, but rather a large Australian rat that had come over on a boat into the Houston ship channel. In trying to leave the ship and swim to shore it had taken in too much salt water and almost died. But alas, it lived only to ravage its hunger on the family poodle. The moral of the story should be obvious. You can give a rat a bath, comb out its hair and blow it dry; you can even dress it up. But a rat . . . is a rat . . . is a rat. And that rat lives inside of each of us: it is our Sin Nature and it will never improve. We can try to wash it, clean it up, dress it up, but it is still a rat.

Every day we wake up we are faced with the Rat inside us. And often the inner pain caused by our own losing struggles with the rat leaves us looking for someone else to blame for our troubles: our parents, our company, our church, maybe even our God. After all, He is the One who made this mess of a person. We may finally decide everything is hopeless: "We cannot change. There is no way out. We are just victims of circumstances beyond our control."

Behind the law-keeping mindset of Romans 7 there are four lies that our Sin Nature (the Rat) uses to trap us in a life of disillusionment and despair. We covered how Satan uses the first two lies in the "Digging Deeper" section of the last chapter. These four lies are listed by RAPHA ministries:[1]

1. **Performance**. I must perform up to a certain standard in order to feel good about myself.

2. **Approval**. Certain people must approve of me in order for me to feel good about myself.

3. **Blame**. Someone or something outside myself is the cause of my failures and rejections.

4. **Shame**. There is something wrong with me that cannot be repaired. I am what I am. I was born this way. I cannot change.

All four lies feed the choice of *self-reliance* in order to meet righteous expectations yet they only culminate in the abject despair expressed by Paul at the end of Romans 7. Like Paul, a lot of believers find themselves in utter despair. Recall the three cycles of Despair under the Law in Romans 7:13-25: each is comprised of a Statement, Support for the Statement, and a Summary. Here we cover the last two cycles:

3. Despair under the Law	**7:13-25**
a. *Arena* of Despair	13-17
b. *Agent* of Despair	18-20
c. *Admission* of Despair	21-25

There is a way out, but first we have to understand how we get stuck in this "death spiral." Paul identifies the critical relationship between the Sin Nature and our flesh in Adam.

B. AGENT of Despair   7:18-20

1. The *Statement*   7:18a

For I know that in me (that is, in my flesh) nothing good dwells.

Paul's reason for failure in pursuing law ("I am *fleshly*," 7:14) parallels his previous explanation for our failure in pursuing sin ("because of the weakness of your *flesh*," 6:19). Again, the "flesh" here is not identical to our Sin Nature, which Paul designates in near context (7:17, 20) with the term *hē hamartia* ("the" sin);

---

1 Robert S. McGee, *The Search for Significance* (Houston, TX: Rapha, Printing 1990), 43-116.

"flesh" is the Greek word *sarx*, and it signifies all we inherited from Adam (body, soul, spirit) that remains *unredeemed*.[2]

This does *not* mean that an unbeliever can do *nothing* good. In declaring all our righteous deeds are like filthy rags, Isaiah concedes (64:6) that we do righteous deeds in our fallen state. Paul's point is that if we could do nothing while we were **in Adam** to bear the fruit of God's righteousness in the flesh (Rom 7:5), then we can do nothing *by that same flesh* now that we are **in Christ** to produce righteous deeds that bear fruit to holiness ("visibly set apart to God," 6:19-22). Remember, we carry our flesh from Adam forward into our new life in Christ, and it will tarnish that "visibility" whenever we trust it to produce righteous deeds in our lives — *this* is what Paul will refer to as *kata sarka* ("according to the flesh") in 8:1-13.

Charlie Brown, that American icon of introspection, was admiring all the good his hands could do, when Lucy came by. Looking at his hands, Charlie announced, "These hands . . . these hands could have painted the Mona Lisa." Lucy stops to listen. Charlie, never one to disappoint an audience, continues, "These hands . . . these hands could have sculpted Michelangelo's David." From a distance Lucy looks at his hands with awe. "These hands," Charlie is building to a climax, "these hands could have written *War and Peace*." Unable to restrain herself any longer, Lucy reaches for one of Charlie's hands, looks at it closely, and observes, "Your hands have jelly on them." With his typical insight into human nature, of course, Schultz's cartoon was his way of saying that even the greatest works of man by his own efforts are still tainted by sin. Such is our fallen condition in the flesh.

2. The *Support* 7:18b-19

For to will is present with me, but how to perform what is good I do not find. [19]*For the good that I will to do, I do not do; but the evil I will not to do, that I practice.*

The word "for" tells us that Paul is explaining his claim in v. 18a. As new Creations in Christ we want to do the right thing, but as limited humans we simply do not have the inner power to pull it off consistently — this will require the power of the Spirit who dwells in me (8:1-4). My New Nature is prone to worship, but my Sin Nature is prone to wander. This flies in the face of humanism, which claims that man has the power within himself to solve his own problems. We are not saying man cannot send someone to the moon without God's enablement. The "will" in question is the ability to perform — and thus reveal — the righteousness of God (1:17; 3:21; 5:17, 21; 6:18-20); and this is what leads to our Sanctification:

---

2   On distinguishing *flesh* from the *Sin Nature* inherited in Adam, see note 5, Chapter 4, "Houston, We Have a Problem."

set apart to God in Christ as "holy" before the world (6:22b; compare 1:1-6). But something in Paul's subjective inner life finds it impossible to achieve this holiness. Again, the paralysis derives from discerning good and evil as a normal function of conscience (1:19-20; 2:14-15; 3:20; 5:20a) but then setting out to *do* the good in one's own ability (7:5, 7-12).

Through sheer discipline we may stop our smoking or drinking or swearing. But then our pride in doing so strikes us down as we look down on and judge other believers who do not seem to have our strength. Or through force we make ourselves pray for an hour or perhaps just a half and hour a day. But as we bow before the Lord on bended knee, we are thinking to ourselves, "My, what a great prayer warrior I am." So we see how all these efforts on our part do nothing to "deliver" us in our spiritual condition. We may achieve moral victory through our own efforts in one area, but then comes spiritual defeat in another and we really don't surpass the mere *letter* of the law (7:6) to display the righteousness of God.[3]

Paul is now ready to make the concluding observation that a "rat" lives inside of him — Sin working through his flesh — which drives him to do the evil he does not want to do.

3. The *Summary* 7:20

Now if I do what I will not to do, it is no longer I who do it, but sin that dwells in me.

Paul returns to the Sin Nature (*hē hamartia*, "the" sin) as the Agent of Despair. Let us recall how Paul is using "I" and "me" in 7:13-25 (see again our discussion of 7:14, above). "I" is one in Christ who has free will yet opts to fulfill the righteous requirement of the Law in his own ability ("me" = "the flesh," 7:18a). He realizes that the Sin Nature (the "Rat") takes over as soon as the flesh is engaged to fulfill the law's righteous requirement. In his book *Born Again* the late Chuck Colson echoes this principle for any human being:

> [I]t became clear to me that Watergate could work a healthy cleansing in the nation if it is understood for what it truly is. Were Mr. Nixon and his men more evil than any of their predecessors? That they brought the nation Watergate is a truth. But is it not only a part of a larger truth — that all men have the capacity for . . . evil, and the darker side of man's nature can always prevail in any human being. . . . Watergate raised so many questions. Can humanism ever

---

3   On the parallel between 7:6 and Matt 5 in this regard, see note 2 of the previous chapter, "The Do-It-Yourself Kit."

be the answer for our society? There is an almost sanctified notion that man can do anything if he puts his will to it. This was once my credo. Having seen through Watergate how vulnerable man can be, I no longer believe I am master of my destiny. I need God. . . . I am learning how God can break us in order to remake us.[4]

This surfaced in a discussion I had with a Christian brother on a separate issue when he said, "Well, don't you trust me?" I replied, "Trusting *you* is not the issue. I don't trust your Sin Nature . . . and I don't trust mine either. It's not that we can't work together but we need to admit that evil dwells in each of us — that is, in our flesh" (7:18a). It's the same old Rat.

Thus, it is not that we are too weak in our self-reliance to overcome temptation. We are *not weak enough,* and this awareness drives Paul to his own Admission of Despair, so that he will finally capitulate to *grace* by the Spirit rather than *law* by the flesh (6:14; 7:6) as he will elaborate in Romans 8:1-14.

C. ADMISSION of Despair   7:21-25

1. The *Statement*   7:21

I find then a law, that evil is present within me, the one who wills to do good.

Paul uses the word "law" in Romans in a number of ways: The Law of Moses (2:11-13; 3:19); the Law of conscience (2:14-15); the Law Principle (dominion by law) (3:21; 6:15; 7:1-6); the Law of Faith (3:27); the Law of God (6:15; 7:1, 4-16, 22, 25); the Law of Sin (7:23, 25; 8:2); the Law of my Mind (7:23); and the Law of the Spirit of life (8:2). Now, Paul has found a new law; in fact the Greek word for "find" at the beginning of the verse is the word from which we get the exclamation, "Eureka!" So, what is this new law that Paul has discovered concerning the operation of evil within us? It is "another law" (7:23) that he will finally identify in 7:25b — a law that is closely linked to the Law of Sin but *governed by the flesh* (7:5, 18).

Here Paul is taking the approach of a moral scientist in order to identify this "new" law. As a moral scientist, Paul has just made a new discovery, meaning he has observed something new regarding his failure to do righteousness according to God's standard (7:15-20). Do you remember the Scientific Method from ninth grade?

Observation > Hypothesis > Testing > Theory > Law

One reason why the Theory of Evolution is such a misnomer is that it should never have gotten to the level of a "theory." A theory cannot be formulated until there is an observation. The entire concept is built on the idea that there must

---

4   Charles W. Colson, *Born Again* (Old Tappan, NJ: Revell, 1976), 11-12.

be positive mutations from lower species to higher species, but scientists have never made one observation of a positive mutation from a lower species to a higher one. It makes one wonder if Darwin was visiting Fantasy Island instead of the Galapagos Islands, when he came up with his "theory." But Paul had no lack of observations on which to formulate *his* hypothesis, and he had ample occasion to *test* that hypothesis as a Law-abiding Jew (7:15-20).

Paul had a moral Observation (7:15-17): the things I do not want to do I am doing, and the things I do want to do I am not doing. That observation led to a Hypothesis (7:18-20): there must be something evil (Sin Nature) within me leading me to do these things I do not want to do. From the Hypothesis the scientist tests his observation and guess in a controlled environment to see if it can be repeated. If the Observation can be repeated over and over without exception, the scientist postulates a Theory. If the Theory can be verified without exception, the scientist is justified in concluding that we have a Law. And that is what Paul does in 7:21. Something within him is allowing the Sin Nature to have its way with him against his will. No exceptions. It is there in every single one of us.

Paul now explains the underlying process that drives the Law of Sin in the well-intentioned believer: when we engage the *flesh* to fulfill good intentions, it invariably enslaves us to Sin, *just as in the unbeliever* (7:5).

2. The *Support* 7:22-25a

22For I delight in the law of God according to the inward man. 23But I see another law in my members, warring against the law of my mind, and bringing me into captivity to the law of sin which is in my members. 24O wretched man that I am! Who will deliver me from this body of death? 25I thank God — through Jesus Christ our Lord!

Again, the word "for" tells us that Paul is *substantiating* his statement that evil is present within him (7:21). And "I" is still the Christian who has determined to fulfill the righteous requirement of the Law in his own inability (the *flesh*). Note Paul's prolific wordplay on the notion of "law":

- **Law of God** — this is God's standard of righteousness
- **Law of my Mind** — conscience-mediated awareness of, and agreement with, the standard of righteousness defined by "the Law of God" (see 2:15)
- **Law of Sin** — the Sin Nature (*hē hamartia*) leads to "death" when "activated" in my body ("members" refers to the *body*, 6:12-14) by awareness of the Law of God (7:7-12)
- **"Another" Law in my Members** — a "flaw" inherited from Adam that opposes the Law of my Mind and enslaves me to the Law of Sin; it is the **Law of the Flesh** (7:24, 25b), and only the **Law of the Spirit of Life** can release us from this slavery (8:2).

The present participles "warring" and "bringing" describe the ongoing pull of the Law of the Flesh in his members that enslaves him to his Sin Nature when incited by the Law of God, the perfect standard of righteousness. It is like the force of gravity acting on a book sitting on a desk. I might not be *aware* of this force until I pick up the book. When I attempt on my own to "hold up the book" — to live according to that perfect standard — the law of gravity wears me out with its continuous force until the book falls; that is, this "law in my members" (the Sin Nature working through the flesh) keeps on working until I exhaust my strength and stop trying. Some have more natural strength than others, but in time everyone will "put the book down."

The Law of the Mind seems to work from the inside out, while Sin gains its beachhead in the flesh ("in my members") from the "outside" through the law. This does not mean that the "body of death" is itself evil; God created it, and it was good. But the human body can be used as an accomplice to the Sin Nature to bring us defeat and despair.[5]

The body "houses" our flesh which is in turn exploited by Sin to defeat the "inward man" trying to meet God's righteous requirement. Paul describes this state as "wretched." Some believe that this could not possibly describe Paul as a believer, so it must depict his pre-conversion state. But without going into all the exegetical details, it describes the life of an "incarcerated" believer trying to live the Christian life through his own power — by the flesh.

To quote James D. G. Dunn:

> In a word, it is not the cry of the non-Christian for the freedom of the Christian; rather it is the cry of the Christian for the full freedom of Christ . . . If we have understood Paul aright, and if Rom. 7,14-25 is a transcript of Christian experience, then we must not hide or ignore this. Proclamation of a gospel which promises only pardon, peace and power will result in converts who sooner or later become disillusioned or deceitful about their Christian experience.[6]

In alluding to "this body of death," Paul intended to be very graphic: It was sometimes Roman practice to chain a murder victim's body to his murderer as punishment. Paul likens his wretchedness to just this kind of sentence: chained to a rotting body! Paul's best efforts to fulfill God's righteous standard were doomed instead to serve the Sin Nature with the "dead body" that houses his

---

5   Perhaps that is why God delayed puberty in the human being longer than any other mammal, most of which can reproduce within a couple of years after birth. Perhaps God wanted parents to use those years to help their children strengthen the inner man so that the onslaught from the outer man could be withstood.

6   "Rom. 7,14-25 in the Theology of Paul," *Theologische Zeitschrift* 5 (September/October, 1975): 268, 272.

flesh. Paul then realizes the only solution is to leave law's dominion and return to the realm of *grace* (6:14; 7:1), and this is what he finally realizes he has done in Christ: thank God, the Lord Jesus Christ has delivered him from this dreadful incarceration (7:25a)!

H. A. Ironside illustrates this realization in his story of a young Christian Navajo Indian who had never been off the reservation until Dr. Ironside brought him to Oakland. When the new believer arrived on Sunday night he was taken to a group of Christian young people who were discussing law and grace. He listened as they argued various aspects of the topic, and then the leader called on him to say a few words. He said something like this:

> Me been listening to you talk about law and grace, and the longer me listen, the more me think you don't know what law or grace is. Let me tell you what I think. When Mr. Ironside ask me to go to Oakland with him, we get on big train down in reservation. I never been on train before, and we ride, and ride, and ride all day long. Finally we come to Barstow out in desert. Me very tired, so me get out of train to walk platform and stretch legs. While me walk around platform, me see sign that say, "Do Not Spit Here." Me look at sign and me say, "What strange sign white man put up — Do Not Spit Here." While me look at sign, before I know what happen, me spit. I look all around platform and I see many people spit here. I think to myself, *How strange. Sign say*, "Do Not Spit Here," *but many people spit and I spit.*[7]

When the Indian saw the sign, he replicated Paul's experience in 7:18-21: "I desire to do what is right, but I find myself doing what is wrong." Here, then, is the basic Christian struggle that saps one of all spiritual energy and enthusiasm. The Indian then noted the remedy for this slavery.

> Then we got on train again and come . . . to Oakland, and some friends meet us at the train and take us to beautiful home. I never been in such home. Mr. Ironside take me in and shows me soft chair and excuses himself for a while, and I left alone in room. I look around and everything is so nice — soft, thick rug on floor, beautiful walls painted lovely color, pictures hanging on the wall — everything so nice. I walk around room and I think to myself about something, and I try to find sign that say, "Do Not Spit Here," but I cannot find sign. I think to myself, "Too bad all this lovely room going to be ruined when I spit on floor!" Then I look around floor

---

7   Adapted from H. A. Ironside, *Illustrations of Bible Truth* (Chicago: Moody Press, 1945), 40-42.

and see nobody been spitting there, and then it come to me — when law say, "Do Not Spit Here," it make me want to spit, and I spit, and many people spit. But when I come into grace and everything lovely and nice, I don't want to spit and I do not need law to say, Do Not Spit Here.[8]

When the Indian "entered the room of grace"[9] he displayed the intent of Romans 5:17, that "those who receive abundance of grace and of the gift of righteousness will reign in life." This "reign in life" is in turn fleshed out in Romans 8 in the full deliverance and freedom of the "sons of God."

3. The *Summary* 7:25b

So then, with the mind I myself serve the law of God, but with the flesh the law of sin.

Here Paul recapitulates the entire argument of 7:13-25. Recall that the "Law of the Mind" is our conscience-mediated agreement with the Law of God — His *righteous requirement* (*dikaiōma*, 1:32; 2:14-15, 26). Paul now confirms in the example of his own life that the "law in my members" opposing the Law of my Mind (7:23) is in fact the **Law of the Flesh.** In my Adamic self-reliance, I am caught in a tug of war between the Law of the Mind and the Law of the Flesh by which Sin enters. Once hosted by the flesh, Sin — like a parasite — *enslaves* me, and that is the Law of Sin.

This leads to a sense of resignation that Robert McGee calls the Shame Game, namely "the wrong belief that there is something wrong with us that can never be repaired."[10] Behind this lie there is another: "I must always be what I have been and live with whatever self-worth I have. I am what I am. I cannot change. I am hopeless." It is actually "the Rat" — the Sin Nature — that can't be repaired. We can't escape it. The shame in this case is a "deep feeling of guilt, sadness, and hopelessness that we experience when we become convinced that past failures, bad habits or poor appearance have made a permanent scar on our self-worth." Here is some of the self-talk that gets us caught up in the Shame Game:[11]

- Since I lost my virginity, I will never be worthy of someone who will really love me.
- Ever since I was held back a year in school, I haven't been able to do well.
- My dad said I was a failure and he is right. I will never succeed at anything.

---

8 Ibid.

9 This contrast between the "Room of Grace" and the flesh-based "Room of Good Intentions" is well depicted in Bill Thrall, Bruce McNicol, and John Lynch, *TrueFaced* (Colorado Springs, CO: NavPress, 2003).

10 McGee, *Search for Significance*, 101.

11 Ibid.

- When my parents got a divorce, I realized what a loser I really am.
- My parents forced Ritalin® down my throat. It kept me from reaching my potential, and now it's too late.
- I am so ugly. No one worthwhile will ever be attracted to me.
- I can never escape the shame and guilt of the abortion I got years ago. My Christian friends would instantly reject me if they knew.
- Drugs are ruining my life, but I can't change.

According to McGee, there are three primary reasons for this kind of shame:

1. **Too many failures in the past**

   All of us experience failure in our endeavors to one degree or another. But repeated failure can cause one to believe that he is a failure with no hope of success at anything.

2. **Bad habits in the present**

   Most of us have some bad habits we would like to break. Some are pretty harmless. But other habits can be destructive or shame-inducing, such that each time we give in to the habit, we only feel that much worse about ourselves. After repeated attempts to break the habit, we simply give up, thinking it is hopeless. That is when we are caught in the trap of shame. We would be ashamed to let others know how hopelessly enslaved we are to this habit. And, of course, God does know. We walk in darkness.

   For example, John is a sex addict. Unable to have a close relationship with his father and missing the love of his mother, he repeatedly pursues relationships with older women, even after he is married. He joins Sexual Addicts Anonymous (SAA) but tells me, "In SAA we speak of a higher power, but it is all so secular. How I wish it were safe enough in the church for a support group to wrestle with addictions like mine. I believe in Christ, but I'm too ashamed to admit my problem to other Christians. I haven't gone to church for years."

3. **Our appearance**

   McGee writes:

   In our society, our appearance is considered very important. Magazine ads, billboards, television commercials and programs are filled with people who we would call very attractive. Our problems begin when we compare ourselves to these unrealistic "beautiful people" standards. We wrongly believe that to be successful and accepted, we must be as attractive as these men and women. Unfortunately, very few of us are. Most of us tend to feel ashamed of some aspect of our appearance.[12]

Shirley is twenty-nine and overweight. Her appearance says, "I don't care about me." She admits with tears that she is afraid she is losing her husband. He has been accusing her of being a slob and nagging her to lose weight. She thinks he is seeing another woman. "I'm fat and I know it," she cries. "He doesn't have to remind me . . . I can't lose weight. He likes me to cook him fattening, rich foods. He is thin and can eat all those foods that I'm not supposed to eat. How am I supposed to lose weight when he's eating all the things I love? It's impossible."

The devil will use these pitfalls of relying on our flesh to trap us in the Shame Game. Even Paul had reason to be caught up in the Shame Game in these same three ways:

- Horrible mistakes in the past — he killed Christians;
- Present habits — his default system was to rely on his human strength which was considerable but it drove him to struggle with pride; and
- Personal appearance — his very name meant "small."

But Paul knew the way out of the Shame Game. It is not through some inner power, but a power that penetrates from without. Only the supernatural power of the risen Lord Jesus Christ can deliver us (Rom 5:10). God took Paul's past and buried it; he took his present and ignored it; he took his appearance and utilized it. Christ gave him a *new man* to put on, a *new goal* to live for, and a *new hope* to die for, and it drove him to share the means of achieving this deliverance in Romans 8. The contrast with Romans 7 couldn't be more striking.

William Backus describes the attitudes of Paul and Silas that enabled them to live a new dream.[13] They were brought before the Roman authorities at Philippi, beaten, and thrown into prison. Bleeding and wracked with pain, they lay on the cold prison floors with their feet in the stocks. The mission was not looking too successful, and their approval rating was not very high. They could easily have blamed God for the whole situation. After all, why did He have to call them to be evangelists? But it was because of their faith in a transcendent supernatural Being — a power *outside* of themselves that took residence *within* them — that they did not despair. Their strong belief system, grounded in the truth of their position in Christ, made them realize they had nothing to lose. That belief was in the person, the power, and the presence of Jesus Christ. For them to live was Christ, and to die was gain (Phil 1:21). If they were released from prison they would go on with

---

12   Ibid., 110.

13   William Backus and Marie Chapian, *Telling Yourself the Truth* (Minneapolis: Bethany, 2000), 118-19.

their work; if not, other evangelists would rise up to replace them (1:12-18). They did not complain, blame others for their physical agony, or agonize in silence. Instead, they prayed and sang praises to God so that their voices were heard throughout the prison. God heard them and opened the prison doors.

We may be in a prison of darkness and despair caused by past failures, persistent habits, or rejection by others. And the Rat will use these negative experiences in our lives to spin his lies. Don't let the Rat get to you. Romans 7 helps us to acknowledge Satan's strategy and focus on God's truth. When you know the truth, it will set you free. The keys of God's truth can open the prison doors of darkness and despair. Yet freedom for freedom's sake is not our ultimate goal; we are freed from the power of sin to "reign in righteousness to eternal life" (5:21) and thereby reveal the righteousness of God to all Creation (1:17). We are set free when we forsake our self-reliant flesh and follow the Spirit (7:5-6). And that is just where Paul is headed.

CHAPTER 12

"WAR AND PEACE"
Romans 8:1-4

War . . . I hate it. It is surely one of Satan's greatest weapons. With the slick technology of smart bombs and unmanned drones, modern warfare can depersonalize the carnage of war. But when I watch documentaries or movies about Gettysburg or the American Revolution I cringe again at the horrible waste of human life — real people, real sons of real parents, face each other off at ten or twenty yards. Men created in the image of God are mowed down like so many weeds in an overgrown field. Loss of life, especially in young people, depresses us. Who can forget the scene in *Saving Private Ryan* when the government car pulls up to the Ryan farmhouse with the news that three of Mother Ryan's four boys have been killed in World War II — she faints dead away. None of us can truly feel her pain; we can only imagine.

The waste of physical life in war is a huge tragedy. But as I ponder these wars, my mind drifts to another hidden war, one potentially more devastating than all the wars in history. It is the war being waged in the spiritual realm for control of our lives. Ephesians 6 draws back the veil covering the spiritual world to reveal demonic forces — fallen angels that war against us. While we may preserve our *physical* lives we may lose the battle for our *souls*. And this battle is waged not only to keep our souls out of *heaven*, but also to keep the lives of those in Christ from making a difference *on earth*, from having an impact for the kingdom of God that will count for eternity (Matt 16:24-27). Our enemies are also "youthful lusts" (1 Pet 2:11-12) that are inflamed by the world to create conflict among God's people (Jas 4:1-4) — conflict is rooted in an internal battle between the flesh and the Spirit (Gal 5). In Romans 8 the outcome of this battle determines whether we realize God's kingdom purposes in and through us as the people of God.

Paul introduced us to spiritual warfare in Romans 6 by depicting our Sin Nature and God as opposing generals. Paul's appeal to those in Christ was to use their "members" as weapons of warfare in the King's army and thereby be delivered from the tyrannical rule of the Sin Nature to an ironic *freedom* as "slaves of righteousness" (6:16-20). Such freedom was contingent on living not under the dominion of *law* but under *grace* (6:14-15), so we were warned about how readily the Sin Nature uses the law to gain a beachhead in the flesh and drag us back into the Arena of Despair: a slavery to Sin that brings defeat, disillusionment, and despair (Romans 7). Paul now aims to show *how* we are to live under grace and enjoy full deliverance from slavery to Sin to bear the fruit of righteousness, the incentive for which is a quality of life unknown by the world, something the Bible calls *eternal life* (6:21-23).

Thus, we leave the agony of defeat (Romans 7) and come with joyful anticipation to the thrill of victory in Romans 8, what some have called the "Red Rose of Romans," the Fulfillment of the Vision. Godet called it "that incomparable chapter."[1] Newell wrote: "The believer is like the storm-tossed mariner who has come to his home harbor and casts anchor when he comes into the light of Romans 8."[2] Here Paul virtually trumpets full deliverance to life and peace, and the key to this deliverance is the power of the Holy Spirit. Conspicuous by His scarcity in Romans 7 (a single introductory allusion in 7:6), the Spirit virtually *pervades* Romans 8 (19 times).

The Spirit can deliver us from Sin and "Death" (defeat, disillusionment, despair) to an abundant life (8:1-17), and He desires to deliver us through Suffering to a glorious inheritance (8:18-39). The entire chapter is therefore integrated by the **life** and **hope** that the Spirit supplies us as children of God, so that we might live a righteous life *now* and rule with Christ as "sons indeed" over *the world to come*. In the first major section Paul explains how the Spirit "displaces" the Law of Sin and Death (8:1-11), so that we may be fully released from the tyranny of Sin and Death to live out our calling as mature "sons of God" (8:12-17). So central is Paul's explanation that we will take three chapters of this book to unpack this liberating truth (8:1-11).

I.	**SIN**		(1:1–3:20)
II.	**SALVATION**		(3:21–4:25)
III.	**SANCTIFICATION**		(5–8)
	A.	**Freedom from Wrath**	(5)
	B.	**Freedom from Sin**	(6)
	C.	**Freedom from Law**	(7)

---

1   Frederick Godet, *Epistle to the Romans*, (New York: Funk & Wagnalls, 1883), 287.

2   William R. Newell, *Romans: Verse by Verse* (Grand Rapids, MI: Kregel, 1994), 287.

I. PRINCIPLE of Deliverance 8:1-4

Here we look at the first four verses which introduce us to the Principle of Deliverance from the Law of Sin and Death (7:23a, 25b; 8:2). Following the "carnage" of Romans 7, Paul wants to shift his readers' thinking from **death** through the flesh (introduced in 7:5) to **life** through the Spirit (introduced in 7:6), beginning with his victorious proclamation.

A. PROCLAMATION of Deliverance 8:1

1. The *Text*

Most translations rely on a Greek text that reads something like: *There is therefore now no condemnation to those who are in Christ Jesus.* Preachers typically use this verse as a guilt reducer, reminding us of our position "in Christ": we have been completely forgiven of all our sins, past, present, and future (= justification). So when we still drag around a wheelbarrow full of guilt, we need to recall that there is no longer any condemnation; we should stop beating ourselves up. It preaches well. However, 98% of existing Greek manuscripts conclude the verse with a qualifying clause:

There is therefore now no condemnation to those who are in Christ Jesus, **who do not walk according to the flesh, but according to the Spirit.**

This reading suggests that absence of condemnation depends on walking according to the Spirit rather than the flesh. Which text is right? Some would settle this discrepancy based on *external evidence* — that is, the *most numerous* manuscripts (98%) or the *oldest* (2%). That debate is beyond the scope of this book, but even if we accept the oldest manuscripts as more reliable, and the qualifying clause above is not present in 8:1, the truth of 8:1 is tightly argued all the way through v. 4 and therefore depends on the same condition as in 8:4, that we walk according to the Spirit, and not the flesh.

Looking at the author's logic in this way contributes to what is called *internal evidence,* another factor that helps us decide which manuscript tradition is preferable. Here, the internal evidence includes the intended meaning of the word translated "condemnation," a word which we have already encountered in Romans 5:16 and 18. Does it mean condemnation to hell or something different from that?

2. The *Technicality*

The most reputable dictionary available on the Greek NT (BDAG) points out a critical difference between two words[3] that play a key role in our understanding of 8:1 in light of 5:16 and 18:

Krima = the **courtroom verdict** (5:16a) — a statement of one's legal standing or Position *as a result of judgment* (= "guilty")

Katakrima = the **sentence** handed down (5:16a, 18a) — the Condition that *results from the verdict* (= incarceration leading to death)

The relationship between *krima* and *katakrima* in 5:16 establishes the meaning of *katakrima* in 8:1, where its use parallels 5:16, 18. The word *krima* denotes Adam's "guilty" verdict (5:16a). To be consistent, if Paul had wanted to denote a sense of *judicial* condemnation in 8:1, he would have used the word *krima*. So Paul is not alluding to the judicial condemnation we escaped when Christ took on our sins, was found guilty, and died on our behalf. In what sense, then, *do* we escape condemnation if not by Christ's judicial condemnation on our behalf?

It is not a statement of Position, but of Condition. We left our Position back in Romans 6. Truly, our Position in Christ is the basis for an abundant life (Rom 6:23). But the *basis* is not the *building*; the foundation is not the superstructure. So in Romans 7, Paul was addressing our miserable Condition as we serve the Sin Nature through a misdirected focus on law-keeping. If a Christian pursues life by reverting to the "flesh" in his present experience (6:19; 7:5, 14, 18, 25), the tyranny of his Sin Nature working through the flesh will incur *katakrima* ("penal servitude," MM, 327-28), for the wrath of God is poured out impartially against *all* sin (1:18). Our freedom in Position has already been won by Christ's death (4:25a), but the man of 7:24 is still in a wretched, enslaved Condition because of the Law of the Flesh (7:25b).

So as we enter Romans 8, Paul anticipates his release from this slavery and praises Jesus Christ (7:25a), the One who delivers us from this Condition by his *life* (4:25b; 5:9-10). Clearly, Paul is still dealing with our Condition, and the Spirit provides the key to releasing the Christian from his ongoing "penal servitude" according to the flesh. So just as Paul uses "walk" to advance from Position to

---

3   Walter Bauer, *A Greek-English Lexicon of the New Testament and Other Early Christian Literature*, rev. and ed. by Frederick William Danker (Chicago: University of Chicago Press, 2000), 518, 567 [hereafter BDAG].

Condition in Ephesians 4:1, he also uses "walk" in Romans 8:1-4. And — just as in 6:19; 7:5, 14, 18, 25 — "the flesh" should be seen to refer to our continuing human inadequacy or "inability" inherited from Adam and carried forward in this present life (5:12, 19).[4]

Consider Bob, a seminary graduate and evangelist, in fact, a very successful evangelist. But his giftedness and success seduced him away from his family like a wanton mistress. In time his wife left him; he lost his ministry and found himself bankrupt. In his wretchedness he said, "Where is this God I have been preaching? I trust the cross for my salvation, but I don't see that I am any different than before I became a Christian. I sense no power from the Holy Spirit. I've been a jerk all my life. It would be better for everyone if I just died." That despair is voiced by a man who read Romans 8:1 too narrowly as an affirmation of justification. He believed and preached the message of justification (the substitutionary *death* of Christ) but he desperately needs to hear and believe the message of *sanctification* (the substitutionary *life* of Christ).

This substitutionary life of Christ offers real hope that the wretchedness of Romans 7:24, the self-condemnation, can end. But how? This leads us to the Precept of Deliverance.

B. PRECEPT of Deliverance   8:2

For the law of the Spirit of life in Christ Jesus has made me free from the law of sin and death.

The verse begins with "for" to explain why "there is now no condemnation to those who do not walk according to the flesh but according to the Spirit" (8:1). We have already seen the Law of Sin and Death at work in Romans 7, but there is a higher law, the Law of the Spirit of Life, which "trumps" the Law of Sin and Death to free the wretched man of 7:24 from his enslaved Condition. The verb "has made . . . free" (*ēleutherōsen*) is in the aorist tense which may refer to the past, but not necessarily. One can argue that a newborn child has not *sinned*, even though he has inherited a sin *nature*. Hence, some grammarians think the aorist in Romans 3:23 should not be translated, "For all *have sinned* . . . ," but rather in a *gnomic* sense, expressing a general rule or principle or law of life, "For all *sin*."[5] Similarly, then, use of the gnomic aorist here would affirm a general principle: "makes me free."

---

4   Regarding Paul's use of "flesh" in Romans, see note 1, Chapter 1; note 5, Chapter 4; and notes 9 and 10 (with associated text) in Chapter 8.

5   On the parallel use of the gnomic aorist in 5:12c and 20b, see notes 4 and 15 and associated text in Chapter 4.

In commenting on this verse, Cranfield believes this is an *ingressive* aorist (an action which begins at a point in time and continues as an ongoing process):

> First of all it must be said that this "has set free" refers to the *beginning* of an action, not to its completion . . . The completion of our liberation from the power of sin and of death is not until our death and resurrection . . . Paul is affirming that the Roman Christians are people, the bonds of whose enslavement to sin, to the tyranny of self, God's Spirit has *begun* to loosen . . . The liberation of which Paul speaks *is setting free* to resist sin's reign over one's life.[6]

An ingressive aorist in this context, then, would signify that once I opt to walk according to the Spirit, the law of the Spirit of life *is setting me free* from the law of sin and death. If *ēleutherōsen* is translated as a *gnomic* aorist, the verse would read, "For the law of the Spirit of life . . . *sets me free* from the law of sin and death" as a general principle. In any case, this is not much different from Cranfield's ingressive sense.

Borrowing from our previous analogy of the law of gravity for the Law of Sin and Death (see our discussion of 7:22-25a), suppose I lift a rather heavy book lying on a table to see how long I can hold it up. Since the moment I pick it up the law of gravity begins working to oppose my efforts to hold it up, I will sooner or later have to put the book down, no matter how strong I am, There is no hope of continuing to hold up the book in my own strength. However, in the world of physics, there is a "higher" law to help me. It is the law of *displacement*. This is what causes a helium balloon to rise. Depending on the weight of the book and the size of the balloon, if I tie a helium balloon to the book, it might help me hold up the book. The heavier the book, the more helium balloons are needed, but we can safely conclude that enough balloons tied to the book will enable me to hold up the book as long as I wish, or even carry the book away.

In our Christian lives the "heavy book" is God's perfect standard of righteousness. I may see the book and decide it would be a wonderful way to live but when I pick it up, the Law of Sin and Death begins to oppose my efforts and works to make me put it down (Romans 7). Not until I depend on a higher power (Jesus Christ, 7:25a) can the higher Law of the Spirit of Life in Christ Jesus displace the Law of Sin and Death.

Someone might well object, "I have asked my Savior to deliver me from my sinful life-style, but it has not worked." But consider this: tying only one balloon to the book may not hold or lift the book up, but it is a *law*; if I keep tying balloons to

---

6 C. E. B. Cranfield, "Paul's Teaching on Sanctification," *Reformed Review* 48 (Spring, 1995): 220-21, emphasis added.

the book, sooner or later the book will go up. The law of displacement begins to work with the very first balloon. When I come to Jesus the first time and pray, "Lord, I simply cannot love brother Bob in my own strength the way you want me to. Please live in me. Love him through me." Balloon number one. The more consistently we pray a prayer like that, the more we focus on Jesus and the more "balloons" we tie to the book. It is only a matter of time until the book goes up, and I find myself loving brother Bob through Christ who strengthens me.

Some of our sins are sins of *commission*, meaning: things we know we are doing wrong and wish to stop. Others are sins of *omission*, meaning: things we know we are to do and should start doing. Either way, when we go forward in our own strength (the "energy" of our flesh), the law of sin and death begins to pull us down. So exactly how do we engage this "displacement" of one law by the other? Whenever we look to the substitutionary life of Christ, the law of the Spirit of life enables us to quit our old, bad habits and begin new, good ones.

C. PLAN of Deliverance 8:3

For what the law could not do in that it was weak through the flesh, God did by sending His own Son in the likeness of sinful flesh, on account of sin: He condemned sin in the flesh, . . .

1. The Flesh = Our Frail Humanity Inherited from Adam

Charles Darwin's theory of evolution had an impact on far more than biology. Social Darwinism bought into the idea that man is getting better and better in a *moral* and *social* sense. Hence, the notion of postmillennialism became popular: man is getting so good he can bring in a kingdom of righteousness for a thousand years, after which Christ will come. Science can solve the ills of society. Eugenics (eliminating weak genes) was an easy sell. But one notorious proponent of eugenics and Social Darwinism proved that mankind is far from getting better. Hitler used the best science of his day to play God with the human race and commit the greatest atrocities imaginable against mankind. The "weakness" remained because it resides in our flesh inherited from Adam (Rom 6:19a). Every aspect of our being has been affected by the Fall: our minds, darkened; our emotions, degraded; our wills, degenerate; our bodies, decaying. While humanism puts its faith in the powers of man, its end result will always be disillusionment. No, those who look to men to solve mankind's problems will be sorely disappointed.

When one of my daughters was about four years old, she was so in love with Christopher Reeves that she would climb up on my lap and try to give me a spit curl so I could look more like Superman. One day as she was curling away, I said, "You know, Laura, I really am Superman." Her eyes got wide. *Really?*

"Sure. You want to fly?" Of course she did. So I put her on my back and walked out into the street. "OK. Are you ready?" *Ready.* So I started to run down the street, slowly picking up speed (very slowly). She began kicking me like a horse. *Come on, Superman,* she cried, *let's fly.* I finally ran out of steam and stopped. *What's wrong?* "I forgot my cape." *Let's go get it.* "Can't. I think mom has it in the laundry. We'll have to try again when it's washed and pressed." I never got off the ground, of course, that day or any day.

Have we come to the place where we realize we are not Superman? The vision of Christ-likeness is asking us to fly; unfortunately, we cannot fly on our own. We cannot fulfill the law, God's perfect standard of righteousness, in our own strength, the flesh. But there is a Super Man living within us who has supernatural power; *He can* fly. So how does He do this within us? It is the effect of "displacement."

2. God's Plan = The Substitutionary Life of Christ

God sent His Son to do what we cannot. Christ took on human flesh to become our substitute in death — God "condemned sin" in Christ's flesh — and released us to life (5:18, compare Heb 2:14-18). But once we identify with him in death, he also wants to be our substitute in life (Rom 6:4-5). Our deliverance in Christ is not so much a *changed* life as an *exchanged* life; it is *trusting,* not *trying.* We trusted his substitutionary *atonement*; why not trust his substitutionary *enthronement*? He lives in us; why not let Him *replace* us at the controls so *we* become the righteousness of God in him (Gal 2:20; 2 Cor 5:21)? Paul's meticulous choice of words now makes this explicit.

D. PURPOSE of Deliverance   8:4

. . . that the righteous requirement of the law might be fulfilled in us who do not walk according to the flesh but according to the Spirit.

1. "Righteous Requirement" = Standard of Righteous Behavior

As we have seen, the word for righteousness in Romans (*dikaiosunē*) represents an umbrella concept or "genus" which is further specified by a variety of "species" — it encompasses both righteousness *credited* to us in the courtroom of heaven (our New Position, as in 4:3) and Christ-like righteous *behavior* on earth (our Intended Condition, as in 6:13, 16). Paul uses *dikaiōma* ("righteous requirement of the law") as the "species" of *dikaiosunē* that strictly denotes *righteous behavior,* not "justification."[7] After Paul uses *dikaiōma* to denote God's

---

7 As developed in our exposition of Romans 5:16, translating *dikaiōma* as "justification" does not adequately convey Paul's intent to designate righteous *behavior*—not just judicial *status*—as the ultimate goal of Christ's work on our behalf (5:18). Paul's choice of *dikaiōma* in 8:4 to describe this righteous behavior in light of our inability in Adam reflects our need to receive the abundance of the free gift of grace in Christ (5:17b) in order to fulfill the intended goal of our "absolution-and-release" (*dikaiōsin*)

righteous requirement for our behavior (1:32, "the law of God"), the same word explicitly links this righteous behavior *in us* (5:16b) to Christ's righteous work *for us* (5:18b). That is to say, God's free gift of grace in Christ's death and life *freely received by us* (4:25; 5:16b, 17b) ironically *fulfills in us* the very righteous requirement by which we are no longer bound (8:3-4).[8]

However, this "righteous requirement" is fulfilled in us *only* when we walk "according to the Spirit" and not by the self-reliant "flesh." So what does it mean for us to "walk according to the Spirit"?

2. "Walk" = Conduct of Life (see Eph 4:1, 17; 5:2, 8, 15; Col 3:7; 4:5)

Those in Christ who are free from condemnation (8:1) are better described by "walking" than by "working." But in *walking* by the Spirit, they will also be *working* for God's kingdom. We need to distinguish "walking by the Spirit" from other ministries of the Spirit that are often claimed as the means to full deliverance and freedom in Christ.[9] Some say we must be *baptized* by the Holy Spirit for power.[10] They usually believe in two baptisms of the Holy Spirit: one which puts us into the Body of Christ, and another by which we are baptized for power. Yet, there is only "one baptism" (Eph 4:5) and given the context of the Body of Christ (Eph 4:11-16), this "baptism" cannot be referring to water. It is the *singular* baptism of/by the Holy Spirit.

Others affirm that the *filling* of the Holy Spirit is what gives us power to bear fruit. If so, it is not even mentioned in the two greatest fruit-bearing chapters in the NT: Galatians 5 and Romans 8. In the two instances where the Greek verb *plēroō* is used (Eph 5:18ff and Acts 13:52), it refers to group worship. And in all the instances where the verb *pimplēmi* is used (John the Baptist, Zacharias, Elizabeth, the Upper Room, Peter, and Paul), the filling did not depend on first dealing with sin. The filling came on the person only for a short period, was for a special witness, and came with unequivocal physical effects.

---

to life (*zōēs*) (5:18b; see note 12, Chapter 4, "Humanity, We Have a Problem"). This goal is *God's righteousness revealed through us to the world by faith* (1:17; 5:17b, 21b; 6:19-22).

8   The mention here of fulfillment of the Law marks a crucial turn in Paul's argument that the purpose of the "gospel of God," to reveal the righteousness of God (1:1, 16-17): this righteousness is revealed when that Law is fulfilled in us (8:4) *not by the letter of the law* but *by the grace of Christ's ongoing work in us* (6:14; 7:4-6). The same truth can be inferred from two other high-profile NT passages. In the Sermon on the Mount, Christ affirms that all the Law is to be fulfilled *in him*, so that to be "great" in the Kingdom of God one must embody *his* righteousness and exceed even the greatest *self-sufficient* righteousness—it is the *perfect* righteousness of God (Matt 5:17-20; 48). This is modeled for us by Abraham, our father in faith, whose imputed righteousness did not fulfill the Law until he obeyed God and his faith was *perfected* (Jas 2:21-23); thus, like Abraham we enact God's imputed righteousness not by *law* but by *grace*—Christ's resurrection life in us received through faith (Rom 4:13-25; 5:17b).

9   See "Digging Deeper: The Basis for the Abundant Life in Romans 6:23," Chapter 7, "Freedom through Slavery."

10   Stanley M. Horton, "The Pentecostal Perspective," in *Five Views on Sanctification* (Grand Rapids, MI: Zondervan, 1987), 129-30.

By contrast, in Galatians 5 and Romans 8 we find the verbs "walk" and "lead"; from our perspective we *walk* with or by the Spirit; from His perspective He *leads* us. The following chart contrasts the differences among these three ministries of the Holy Spirit.

BAPTISM	LEADING	FILLING
1 COR 12; ROM 6	ROM 8; GAL 5	LK 1; ACTS 2, 4, 9
Indwelling	Enabling	Intoxicating
Permanent	Progressive	Periodic
"Fact"	"Faith"	"Feeling"

We can see that *baptism* by the Holy Spirit is a permanent indwelling — He seals us until the day of redemption (Eph 4:30). But the Holy Spirit's *leading* (Rom 8:14) is a progressive enabling that prevails over the lusts of the flesh to bear righteous fruit to holiness (6:19). In other words, as we grow in Christ, we log more and more time walking by the Spirit. This requires that we exercise faith, for there are times the Holy Spirit will lead us into a desert with adversity, just as He did with Jesus (Lk 4:1). As covered in the section on Romans 6:23 under "Filling of the Spirit," *filling* seems to come at the Holy Spirit's sovereign discretion for special ministry and is not expected to last hours or days on end until we knowingly sin. The person filled knew something special was happening; he could feel it, but it was never described as the key to full deliverance and freedom in the Christian life. Conjuring up formulas by which we can co-opt the Spirit into filling us smacks of manipulating God, or what might be called "magic."

So what is the Purpose of our Deliverance? It is that Christ's righteous work (*dikaiōma*) might be fulfilled (*plerōthē*) in us (8:4); in short, it is *Christ-likeness* (8:29). And how will we know we are fulfilling that purpose by walking by the Spirit? While the Scriptures give accounts of those who spoke in tongues and those who went around witnessing, the only reliable evidence of one who is walking by the Spirit is that they demonstrate the fruit of the Spirit as opposed to the works of the flesh (Galatians 5). One who is full of anger, envy, and lust is walking by the flesh; one characterized by love, joy, and peace is walking by the Spirit (see also Eph 4:22–5:11). We need to recognize that we are in a *war*.

Watchman Nee says we need to learn to *Sit* (our Position in Christ, Eph 1–3), *Walk* (our Condition on earth, Eph 4–5), and *Stand* (against the wiles of the devil, Eph 6). But we cannot Stand until we learn to Walk; and we cannot learn to Walk until we learn to Sit — to reckon on our foundational Position in Christ. Nee offers the illustration of a tank driver during the Sino-Japanese War and a sniper who kept shooting at the tank to no avail, as long as the driver remained in his amply protected position. But the tank driver could not tell where the enemy fire was coming from; so in frustration he stopped the tank, opened the hatch, and began looking around with his binoculars. Bang. The sniper shot him dead. He never should have left the tank, his protected *position*.[11] We need to learn about all the blessings we have in our new Position in Christ — to Sit (rest on the Rock, abide in the Vine) — before we can learn to walk by the Spirit. Paul has taught us to Sit (Romans 6); now he is trying to teach us to Walk (Romans 8).

Those who are trying hard yet suffering defeat in this battle against Sin need desperately to *rest* in their foundational Position and learn the Law of the Spirit of life (Rom 8:2): to let the Holy Spirit lead them through the darkness and deserts by faith. Through Him they can bear His fruit in the midst of any storm. There will still be pain in this life, sometimes very excruciating pain. But Jesus knew something about pain. Though he was acquainted with grief, he knew how to walk by the Spirit and he endured the cross on our behalf for the joy set before him. Likewise, the Spirit will be there to sustain us and imbue our lives with "eternal life quality" (6:22-23), even when we are led down paths of great pain (8:23-27).

So, for those of us who are on the front lines and know it, be of good cheer. By one free gift that *leads to righteous behavior* (*eis dikaiōma*, Rom 5:16), the "appointed" Son has already won the victory through "the Spirit of holiness" (1:3-4). Now this "firstborn of many brethren" (8:29) wants to lead many sons to glory (8:18-19; compare Heb 2:10), as God's *righteous requirement is fulfilled* (*dikaiōma plērōthē*, Rom 8:4) in those who walk by that same Spirit. Tragically, some of God's soldiers do not even know they are in a war, and they are in the greatest peril. They could go through their entire Christian lives, not realizing that their enemies (the world, the flesh, the devil) are blocking God's intent to reveal His righteousness in them (1:17). What a waste.

---

11   Watchman Nee, *Sit, Walk, Stand* (Fort Washington, PA: Christian Literature Crusade, 1976).

CHAPTER 13

"LADY AND THE TRAMP"

Romans 8:5-8

One of Walt Disney's most beloved animated movies is "Lady and the Tramp," a love story about dogs. But with this simple dog story I find more than just a lady's efforts to win her man; I also see a picture of the Christian life. We easily identify with the main characters in this love story as we root for Lady in her efforts to tame the Tramp. The movie illustrates that there are three kinds of dogs, just as there are three kinds of Christians. The first kind of dog is governed by Law. He is caged and has never known true freedom. Or the minute he is out of the house he has a chain around his neck. He walks down the sidewalk straining against the chain until his throat is rasping for air. He wants to chase after this dog or that butterfly, but cannot because of the chain. This dog knows law but not freedom.

This is the kind of dog Tramp vowed he would never be. He hated doghouses, chains, fences, leashes — anything that would restrict his freedom. He is the stray. At one point he and Lady sit on a hilltop while he boasts of his freedom. "Come away with me, Pidge," he pleads. "Look at the horizon. We can go anywhere, sleep any place we please. No leashes, no fenced in yards for us. We'll be free." Of course, this kind of dog has freedom. But absolute freedom carries its own dangers. While running hither and yon, the stray dog always risks being run over by a car. The threat of the dogcatcher lurks behind every corner. So the possibility of an untimely death or a miserable existence in the dog pound awaits the stray dog at the end of every alley and at every crossroad. He knows license, but he courts death daily. He knows a *form* of freedom, but he does not know *liberty*.

By the end of the movie Lady finally succeeds in making a family man out of the Tramp; no one stands prouder than Tramp when Lady has her first litter. Tramp has been transformed. He is a new dog. You might say he has found a new *leash* on life; he has been "born again." Oh, he still has lots of spunk. But now he lives with Lady in her master's house. Yes, he is still free to go and come as he chooses but he now has a master he loves. And although in his freedom he may run wherever he wishes, his love for his master and the security of a warm home and plenty of food always bring him back to his master. The Tramp has discovered *liberty*. You might say he has discovered the *Law* of Liberty. He has all the benefits of being free but he also enjoys the peaceful security of living the kind of life his loving master has designed for him that he might flourish and reproduce. For tramp to have sought security from a form of legalism (e.g., the dog pound) would not have brought peace but rather defeat leading to despair (Rom 7).

The Law of Liberty is precisely what Romans 8 teaches. Some Christians live under the law, "caged" or always stretching the leash and choking under the restrictions of the law. They know law, but not freedom. That is Romans 7. Other Christians boast of freedom but revel in license, just like the Tramp. They know license, but not true liberty — they live at increased risk of death or the "dog pound." That is Romans 6. But in Romans 8 God has provided the Law of Liberty to lift us above the doghouse of law or the gutter of license. Through his Holy Spirit we experience the Law of Liberty, and Paul now explains how it works. We learn to enjoy all the benefits of being free as well as the security of the restrictions set up by our wonderful Master for our own good and protection. Let us see how in Rom 8:5-8. As we move into these verses, we leave the Principle of Deliverance and enter the Process of Deliverance.

1. **Victory over Sin**   (8:1-17)
   a. **Delivered from the Law of Sin and Death**   (8:1-11)
       1) *Principle* **of Deliverance**   (8:1-4)
       2) *Process* **of Deliverance**   (8:5–8)
           a) **Walking According to the Flesh**   5a, 6a, 7-8
           b) **Walking According to the Spirit**   5b, 6b
       3) *Prospect* **of Deliverance**   (8:9-11)
   b. **Delivered from a Life of Sin and Death**   (8:12-17)

II. PROCESS of Deliverance   8:5-8

In Romans 8:5-8 we learn how to enjoy all the benefits of being free as well as the life and peace that comes from following the lead of our wonderful Master and thereby fulfilling His righteous requirement for those made in His image. By the end of the chapter this fulfillment will be realized in conformity to the image of His Son (8:29).

A. Walking According to THE FLESH

5a, 6a, 7-8

1. The *Root*

5a

For those who live according to the flesh set their minds on the things of the flesh.

The word here for *set their minds* on appears several times in Scripture, either as a verb (*phroneō*) or as the noun "mind" (*phronēma*). For example, in Matthew 16:23 after Peter has tried to dissuade him from dying on the cross, Jesus rebukes Peter, saying, "Get behind me, Satan; for you are an offense to me; for you are not *mindful* of the things of God, but the things of men." This context suggests that the verb means "to think about or to care about." In another instance Paul excoriates certain Christians "whose God is their belly, and whose glory is in their shame — who *set their mind* on earthly things" (Phil 3:19). Again he writes, "*Set your mind* on things above, not on things on the earth" (Col 3:2). In clay tablets discovered on excavations of ancient Greek sites, *phroneō* always means "to have a set direction in mind."

Putting all this together, we suggest that *phroneō* plays a foundational role in the Process of Deliverance. It means: "to focus one's mind in a given realm with a view to finding life and fulfillment in that realm." As previously discussed in our exposition of Rom 6:8-11, we become what we think about. Thus, one who "minds" the things of the flesh "sets his mind on the things of the flesh with a view to finding life and fulfillment in that realm." However, this lust of the flesh is part of the world system that directly opposes God and His will (1 Jn 2:16), and He specifically instructs us to abstain from fleshly lusts which war against our "lives" (1 Pet 2:11). There is no way we can fulfill God's righteous requirement (Rom 8:4) or conform to that pattern when we are governed by the dictates and desires of our flesh — we will not reign in the righteousness that brings life (5:17, 21; 6:19, 22).

How does the mind play such a key role? Three things make up man's inner personality: his mind, his will, and his emotions. With the will we make daily or life decisions, our choices. But what governs these choices? We may think that we choose to do whatever we set our minds to do. But that overlooks the vital role of emotions in our choices. In fact, most of us do what we *feel* like doing. There are exceptions, of course, but it is very hard to go against our emotions — they govern most of our choices *and* they are very hard to control.

With the mind we can at least have input into our choices. In fact, if we *think* about one thing enough, it can turn into a desire. And if we think about it to the point that it "consumes" us, that thing will become a *burning* desire. It certainly works that way in relationships. To love people biblically, we must think about them positively. If we think about them in a consistently negative way, we can end up hating them. But if we consistently reflect on them in a positive light, we will build a strong emotional attachment.

By the same token, if we *stop* thinking about someone, it is only a matter of time before we stop loving that person. When I headed off to college, I met nineteen classmates who thought they would marry their high school sweethearts. But only two of the nineteen couples married. Why? Among others, one reason is the old adage, "Out of sight, out of mind." If they stopped seeing the old girlfriend, it was just a matter of time before she was "out of mind." We might coin another adage, "Out of mind, out of heart."

This principle applies across the board. People in love with money think a lot about money. People in love with sports think a lot about sports. People in love with learning spend a lot of time learning. We build an emotional attachment to whatever we think about on a regular basis. Sometimes emotions cause us to make choices we know (in our minds) are not healthy for us, like the Christian girl who marries an unbeliever. In her mind she knows she shouldn't, but all that time spent dating she thinks a lot about her boyfriend. And then she falls in love with him. By then it is very hard for her to resist his offer of marriage — *or* premarital sex. It seems clear, then, that whatever we set our minds on will eventually grab our emotions. Perhaps that is why the old KJV translated Col 3:2 as, "Set your *affection* on things above." Our mind has a tangible influence over our emotions.

Recalling that the flesh includes all we carry forward from Adam — our unredeemed *body*, *soul* (inner personality: mind, will, emotions), and *spirit* — and that it houses our Sin Nature (Rom 7:18, 20), what then does it mean to "live [or walk] according to the flesh"?

- Pursuing the lusts of the body until we are consumed by them
- Falling in love with love so that we hop from one relationship to another, even if we leave a trail of multiple spouses and children blowing like leaves in the wind
- Seeking our significance in something that will pass away, whether stockpiling money or building our own kingdom in business, athletic prowess, winning, etc.
- Seeking *any* spiritual fulfillment apart from Jesus Christ

The list will contain whatever we hope will give us "life," and it could just as well consist of a set of prescribed behaviors designed to please God and earn His favor. This, we may recall, is mere legalism, which is equally rooted in flesh. Many pursuits are morally neutral in and of themselves — they may be oriented to the flesh or to the Spirit. The difference is *orientation*. Paul will now explain why "those who walk according to the flesh" and set their minds on the things of the flesh in hopes of finding life or fulfillment in them are in fact deceived.

2. The *Results* 6a

For to be carnally minded is death.

The phrase "to be carnally minded" (literally "the mind of the flesh") recalls 7:14, ". . . for I am carnal, sold under sin." So who are the carnally minded? It is simply those whose minds are set on things of the flesh to try to find "life" and fulfillment. By now it should be clear that walking according to the flesh only brings death, but it is not the *spiritual* fate of the unbeliever; the mind follows our Condition — in this case unrighteous behavior — which is subject to God's wrath *in this life*, whether in unbelievers *or* believers (1:18). Paul goes on to clarify that the "mind of the Spirit" is only available to believers (8:8), so it is death for believers he has in view. As we have seen, this death entails defeat, depression, and despair, and can even end in *physical* death. For example, tragedies like *Romeo and Juliet, Hamlet,* and *Oedipus Rex* all follow this path. Or how about Willie Lohman in *Death of a Salesman* or the wasted lives in *West Side Story* or the last scene in Steinbeck's *Grapes of Wrath?* All these dramas offer essentially the same message: "the best laid plans of mice and men oft go awry."[1]

Years ago I met a pastor who had allowed a moral compromise in his ministry. In order to offset the guilt, he began drinking. Drinking led to drugs. The FBI got involved. The pastor was convicted and sent to prison. After his release from prison he left his wife and four children so he could continue living "according to the flesh." He finally died of an overdose in his early fifties. Living according to the flesh as a believer will inevitably lead to defeat, disillusionment, and despair, and sometimes even premature physical death (see 1 Cor 11:30; 1 Jn 5:16). And why?

3. The *Rebellion* 7-8

[7]*Because the carnal mind is enmity against God; for it is not subject to the law of God, nor indeed can be.* [8]*So then, they that are in the flesh cannot please God.*

The connective "because" here is giving us one more reason why someone walking according to the flesh cannot be free from despair which is caused by the Law of Sin and Death. The carnal mind-set of someone walking according to the flesh is at odds with God. He is, after all, an eternal, spiritual being. Someone living for the physical world, which is passing away, is His enemy. As James puts

---

1 An English paraphrase of the concluding object lesson from Robert Burns' Scots poem, "To a Mouse" (1785).

it, "Don't you know that friendship with the world is enmity with God?" (Jas 4:4).

The last half of v. 7 tells us *why* someone with a carnal mindset is at odds with God. It is because their mind is not in submission to the law of God. Obviously, if a person after the flesh is not in submission to God's law, he cannot fulfill the righteousness of God's law. The carnal mindset is not only in rebellion against the law of God, it is not capable of being subject to it. Why? Because the two are *mutually exclusive*.

Now it is clear why v. 8 concludes, "indeed, those who are in the flesh cannot please God." Following Paul's use of *sarx* in 7:5, only an unbeliever can be "*in the flesh*" (Position). If it is impossible to please God when one has *no choice* as an unbeliever but to rebel against God, how absurd then for a believer — one who is free to walk according to the Spirit — to *choose voluntarily* to walk according to the flesh (Condition) and thus *revert to moral paralysis:* not only does he **conceal** God's righteousness (1:17; 6:15-22; 7:7-25), but he also **forfeits** the prospect of a greater legacy with Christ as a mature "son of God" (8:14-19).

Looking ahead to Romans 8:12-25, it is clear that when we pursue fulfillment after the flesh we chase that which is merely fleeting, for "all flesh is like grass and the beauty of it like the flower of the field; the grass withers and its beauty fades" (Isa 40:6-8) and "he who sows to his flesh will of the flesh reap corruption" (Gal 6:8). A believer who is oriented to things that are passing away (dying, wearing out) has thus opted out of his "obligation" (Rom 8:12a): to build on the eternal and not the temporal (8:12b-25). Only that which is aligned with God's law will stand the test of time and eternity, for "the heavens will pass away with a great noise, and the elements will melt with fervent heat; both the earth and the works that are in it will be burned up" (2 Pet 3:10). Poof — there goes the Taj Mahal. Poof — there goes the NFL Hall of Fame.

All that is of the flesh goes against the grain of God's Word, for the flesh is passing away but the Word of the Lord stands forever — its entire thrust moves us to live for the world to come. God has another Hall of Fame that will last forever, with this inscription on the plaque over the entrance: "Now faith is the substance of things hoped for, the evidence of things not seen" (Heb 11:1). We cannot see, hear, feel, smell, or taste that world, so it requires *faith*, the evidence of things not seen. All in the eternal Hall of Fame hang their hope on heaven instead of earth. Abel, Enoch, Noah, Abraham, Sarah and countless others. These names shine like stars amid the darkness of those who choose to live for this world instead of the next (Phil 2:15-16).

In sum, "according to the flesh" is a statement of one's Condition. One who is *in* the flesh (Position) cannot please God — flesh can only lead to flesh; so an unbeliever's Condition always aligns with his Position. But tragically, a believer can opt to pursue a Condition ("according to the flesh") so absurdly ill-suited to his Position "in Christ," in whom he has received the Spirit (Eph 1:13-14), the guarantee of his inheritance in the "Hall of Fame" (Heb 11). When we line up this insight with the truth of another plaque in that Hall — "Without faith it is impossible to please God" (11:6) — it is clear that pursuing the flesh entails a lack of faith. Anyone who has been freed from sin yet pursues the flesh — in either ignorance or willful rebellion — cannot fulfill his or her calling to display the righteousness of God by faith (Rom 1:17) or presently enjoy the "eternal life" *quality* Christ's righteous work secured for us (6:22-23).

Paul has conclusively demonstrated why those who walk according to the flesh cannot escape the Law of Sin and of Death (8:5a, 6a); but he responds in parallel (8:5b, 6b) to show how we *can* escape this Law when we walk according to the *Spirit*.

B. Walking According to THE SPIRIT 5b, 6b

While some expositors try to assign these early verses of Romans 8 to our Position in Christ, this view is precluded by the word "walk." It refers to *lifestyle* — Condition, not Position. To "walk" means to "live or conduct one's life" in a certain way. So, to walk according to *the flesh* would mean "to live according to the desires and dictates of fallen man" (by Adamic self-sufficiency), and to walk according to *the Spirit* would mean "to live according to the desires and dictates of the Spirit." As we do this, the Law of the Spirit of Life is activated to deliver us from the Law of Sin and Death (8:2). So, how do we "tune in" to the Spirit?

1. The *Root* 5b

But those who live according to the Spirit [set their minds on] the things of the Spirit.

Here Paul compares the choice to live according to the flesh with the choice to live according to the Spirit. Since the second half of v. 5 parallels the first, we should insert the same verb *phroneō* ("to set one's mind on") as in v. 5a. We have described the vital link between the mind and the emotions; again we see that the mind *orients* the emotions by the object of its focus, whether the things of the flesh or the things of the Spirit. Rarely does the will escape the influence of the emotions. People choose to live according to the Spirit because they *set their minds* on things of the Spirit to find life and fulfillment.

So what are the "things of the Spirit"? Newell's list includes "salvation, the person of Christ, the fellowship of the saints, the Word of God, prayer, praise, prophecy, the blessed hope of Christ's coming, and walking as He walked before me."[2] But if something is not on Newell's list, is it fleshly? If we introduce a false dichotomy between the sacred and the secular, as though anything secular is something of the flesh, then our work, marriage, recreation, money, food and clothes, house and car would all be of the flesh. The *real* distinction between what is spiritual and what is fleshly is our orientation to the sacred or the secular. With the right orientation of our minds we can walk according to the Spirit in our jobs, our marriages, our social lives — indeed, in all of life.

Remember the Tramp? One of my sisters loves border collies. In order to train them, she needed sheep so she bought a farm in Kentucky, went to Scotland to learn shepherding, bought a hundred sheep, and began training dogs as a hobby. It is an impressive sight to watch her put a dog through its paces. They absolutely *love* to herd sheep. The dog quivers as it sits by her feet awaiting her signal to round up the sheep. Pure freedom. No leashes, no kennels, no fences. But they are under complete control of their master. Debbie controls them with a whistle. With one sound she sends the collie to the left or right. With others she can bring the dog around behind the sheep or have it sneak up on them like a soldier crawling along the ground, all from as far as a half mile away. And you would think the collie was in dog heaven. Perfect obedience, and believe me, a well-trained collie listens only to the sound of its master. When I tried, the dog just looked at me and cocked its head inquisitively: "And *you* are . . .?" He was properly *oriented*.

Like the Tramp, this border collie has learned to love the Law of Liberty. The dog is not running pell-mell through walls like a rat in a maze. There are no walls at all. It gets the job done by being oriented to its master's signals. Our Master also signals us through the Holy Spirit to go this way and that. It's called walking according to the Spirit and it is a matter of orientation: In every area of life we can be oriented to the Spirit.

So if the *Root* or basis of a walk according to the Spirit is to *set our mind* on the things of the Spirit, what *Results* can we then expect from walking according to the Spirit?

2. The *Results*   6b

But to be spiritually minded is life and peace.

---

2   William R. Newell, *Romans: Verse by Verse* (Grand Rapids, MI: Kregel, 1994), 297.

The phrase "spiritually minded" — literally, "mind of the Spirit" — involves the noun *phronēma*, just as in v. 6a. The word "but" again sets up a contrast with the first half of v. 6; in contrast to the death that results from the carnal mind, we can expect the opposite from the spiritual mind: *life* and *peace*. Setting one's mind on the things of the flesh is ill-fated, because all that is of flesh and blood will ultimately decay. If we consider all the anxiety, fear, and despair in the world, it is clear that much of this anguish stems from attachment to things of the flesh. A woman worries as soon as wrinkles appear . . . or varicose veins . . . or cellulite on the hips and thighs. A man frets when his hair begins to recede and fall out . . . or his retirement investments tank . . . or his GM products wear out in three years. To set our minds on these things spells defeat, disillusionment, and despair; they are all doomed . . . the body to the grave, the car to the junk yard.

"All flesh is like grass, and its beauty is as the flower of the field. The grass withers, the flower fades, but the Word of our God shall stand forever" (Isa 40:6-8). And the things of the Spirit are recorded for us in the Word — the Spirit wrote them. So, as we read His Word we focus our minds on the things of the Spirit that stand forever, and whatever we do in alignment with God's Word will also stand forever. These acts or attitudes will not see corruption, pass away, or burn with the wood, hay, and straw (1 Cor 3:12-13). What is done in obedience and submission to God's Word will be like footprints in the bedrock of eternity. But acts and attitudes of the flesh will be like footprints along the seashore and vanish with the tides of time.

This is what Jesus meant when He said, "whoever desires to save his life will lose it, but whoever loses his life for My sake will find it" (Matt 16:25). This is not about going to heaven; He is talking to believers: "Now that the question of heaven is forever settled, what will you do with your life? If you live it only for yourself, for the temporal things of the flesh, then it leaves only a temporary imprint in the sand; its worth, significance, and purpose lost forever. But if you lose your life in the world's eyes for Christ's sake — living in accordance with the desires of the Spirit — then your life will be preserved with eternal worth, significance, and purpose."

So, let us imagine a typical day. It begins with our default setting on the flesh. Some people tell me their default setting, when they wake up, is on the Spirit. If so, good to go. But if you are like me, I must begin each day with a decision to take up my cross and follow Him. Something happens during the night, do not ask me to explain it, but even if I go to sleep praying, worshipping, or meditating on God's Word, by the time I wake up, my default setting is on the flesh. I must consciously hit CONTROL + S (controlled by the Holy Spirit). I do this by purposing to bank on my Position in Christ that day and follow Him wherever He may lead.

Off we go. As I am walking along according to the Spirit, I am controlled by Him and enjoy His fruit (Gal 5:22). I am also being cleansed by the blood of Christ from any unknown sin in my life because I am walking in the light (1 Jn 1:7). Suddenly, I notice a temptation, and a tug of war begins (temptation = tug of war). This temptation is either from the world, the devil, or my Sin Nature. Most of them come from the Sin Nature (Jas 1:16-18). I am confronted with a choice. I can present my members as instruments of warfare to the SN or to Christ. Another way to put it: I can yield to the temptation or yield to the Holy Spirit. If I yield to the Holy Spirit, the Law of Liberty (the Law of the Spirit of Life in Christ Jesus) unleashes the power of the Holy Spirit in my life. Victory comes either instantaneously or after many "balloons" are tied, depending on the strength of the temptation or the force of the "stronghold" in my life. But victory will come. "If we walk by the Spirit, we will not fulfill the lusts of the flesh" (Gal 5:16).

How will we know if the Holy Spirit or the Sin Nature is winning? By the amount of time we spend characterized by the fruit of the Spirit as opposed to the works of the flesh. But make no mistake about it. The victorious Christian life is more trusting than trying; it is more of a walk than a work; it more of a Done than a Do. The focus is on our Position instead of our Condition. We must rest in His power. But a life of rest is not a life without responsibility. Our responsibility is threefold in this passage:

1. **We learn what spiritual things are.** My thought here is that we can orient everything in our lives to a spiritual, eternal purpose: our money, our marriages, our jobs, our recreation — all of it. When we are oriented to eternity (His Kingdom) instead of time (my kingdom), then there is no dichotomy between the secular and the spiritual. Everything can be spiritual. We are locked and loaded for the world to come. That is the essence of a spiritual mind-set.

2. **We set our minds on spiritual things.** I do not see a formula here. It will be different for different people. But remember, it is an orientation. On Tuesdays I fly to Midland, Texas, to teach a seminary course. I often stay with my brother-in-law, Charlie Younger, who is an orthopedic surgeon. I have to get up at 4:45AM to make the plane back to Houston so I can get to staff meeting on time at 9:00AM. One evening I was talking to Charlie and said, "I hope I am not disturbing you in the morning." He said, "Oh, no, I am up." "You are? I have never seen your light on." "Oh, well, I'm in the bath tub." "In the bath tub?" "Yes, that's my Bible and prayer time. I spend a half hour every morning reading my Bible and praying in the bath tub." Hmmmm. I don't know many men who start their day in the bath tub, especially before they go in for surgery. But that is how he *orients* his day to spiritual things.

Again, no formula here. But there are some principles. Somehow we have to get spiritual thoughts into our minds. Again, the mind is like a field. It does not care what we plant. It will grow whatever we plant. If we plant fleshly thoughts, they will grow. If we plant spiritual thoughts, they will grow. We are the sowers. We get to pick the seeds we plant in the field of our minds. Prayer, Scripture, music, radio, TV, fellowship, worship — all these things we have heard for years help us plant spiritual seeds into our minds. We cannot orient to spiritual things until we think about spiritual things.

3. **We help our children set their minds on spiritual things.** What we feed our children's minds does so much to shape their futures and mold their lives. When we import the world system into our homes via the media and allow our kids to absorb the thoughts of the world without any oversight, soon their souls begin to circulate the temporal values of the world in their blood stream just like a crack addict. By the time they are teenagers, they are "world"-aholics, and their times in church, Sunday School, and even small discipleship groups are often not enough to offset the worldly germs in their system.

Elizabeth Elliot, widow of Jim Elliot, who was killed by the Auca Indians in S. America, preserved his memoirs in *Shadow of the Almighty*. It reads almost like Scripture. Here is a quote that reveals some of his own godly heritage: "How I praise God for you all. What a heritage falls to them whose surroundings from childhood have been illumined by the Book of God, whose winds have been freighted with the prayer and concern of others for their souls."[3]

Jim's dad was a minister who not only loved the Word of God, he lived the Word of God. I turned to the beginning of the book and was not the least surprised to read, "Fred Eliot read the Scriptures daily to his children, seeking to show them the glory of Christ above all else, striving always to avoid legalisms or a list of 'don'ts.'"[4] He prayed with his children as well as for them. And their front door stood open to welcome missionaries from many lands. Do we wonder, then, why Jim Elliot grew up with a burning zeal to serve the Lord and specifically as a missionary? No, for our thoughts are like the coal we feed into the furnace of our emotions to get our train rolling. And whether that train reaches the depot of God's service or Mammon's depends only on which track it is on.

And remember: *You will become what you think about.* It is the strangest secret in the world. Paul now explains the prospect of more life when we think about

---

3   Elisabeth Elliot, *Shadow of the Almighty, the Life and Testament of Jim Elliot* (San Francisco: HarperCollins, 1979), 131.

4   Ibid., 25-26.

and become what God has in mind for us rather than our Sin Nature acting through flesh.

CHAPTER 14

"HOLY SMOKE"
Romans 8:9-11

In 1938 Captain Lou Zamperini held the American record for the mile run and went to Berlin to compete in the Olympics.[1] There he provoked Adolf Hitler by tearing the swastika from the victor's stand, and the world began to take notice. In WWII with the Army Air Corps he fought over the islands of the Pacific. After he was shot down by the Japanese he set another record by floating on a small raft in the middle of the Pacific for forty-seven days. The Japanese eventually captured him and held him POW for two and a half years. Subjected to torture and ridicule, Lou Zamperini weighed only seventy pounds by the end of the war — he was a broken man. His psychiatrists said he was at the edge of physical and mental collapse which they ascribed to a deep-seated hatred for the Japanese. They concluded there was no help for him unless he could overcome his hatred. Zamperini recognized his need to forgive, but it was a futile struggle.

One night in October 1949 Zamperini's wife invited him to a Billy Graham Crusade in Los Angeles where they lived. As the story of Jesus Christ penetrated his heart for the first time, he heard a just and holy God offer His own Son Jesus Christ to die for the crimes he had committed against God and man. All that the Judge asked in order for him to get off scot-free was to accept this pardon by faith. That evening Lou Zamperini stepped forward at the invitation to receive Christ as Savior. As he tasted the sweet forgiveness of God, he found it within himself to forgive his enemies. He got permission from General McArthur to return to Sugamo Prison, where he sat with twenty-five of the men he had known all too well. He explained God's love and forgiveness through Christ, and some of them also received Jesus. When he came back to the United States Lou began a very successful program to introduce young boys to Jesus Christ.

---

1   Lou Zamperini and David Rensin, *Devil at my Heels* (New York: HarperCollins, 2003).

While Zamperini's story is extraordinary, in other respects it is all too ordinary. *All too many of us receive the great forgiveness of God only to disregard the third person of the Trinity as a real person who came to take up residence within us* (Jn 14:17). It was not until two years after his return that Lou read R. A. Torrey's book, *The Person and Work of God the Holy Spirit*. "For the first time in my life," he said, "I realized the Holy Spirit was a real person. He had come to live within me. I had been a believer for over two years without knowing that." As it sank into his heart, "Tears came to my eyes. I knelt by the bed where I was reading and asked the Holy Spirit to forgive me for my rudeness and neglect over the past couple of years."

> Go not my soul in search of Him;
> You will not find Him there.
> Or in the depths of shadows dim
> Or in the heights of upper air
> For not in far off realm of space
> The Spirit has His throne;
> In every heart he finds a place
> And waits there to be known.
> Oh gift of gifts, Oh grace of grace,
> That God should condescend
> To make your heart His dwelling place
> And be your daily friend.[2]

As a believer tunes his mind to the Spirit in order to follow His lead (8:4-5), the Spirit's control sets him free from Sin and death to bring life and peace (8:1-2, 6) in that it *displaces* control by the "weak" flesh through which Sin gains its power (6:19; 7:23-25; 8:3). Habits which chained him are broken and miracles begin to happen: his fear of speaking with others is gone; or his tongue which had run like a wild stallion is harnessed and tame; his marriage, broken by a selfish, stubborn will, is mended and healed — all these and more become the experience of one who finally yields to the control of the Holy Spirit. It is because his need for One who can truly love and value him is finally met.

This truth about the indwelling Spirit of God is the theological crux of Romans 8:9-11. By the end of Romans 7 we saw how the Law of Sin and Death works like gravity to prevent a believer from fulfilling the righteous requirement of the law. Romans 8:1-11 tells us how we can prevail over sin and death by the indwelling Spirit. We were first introduced to the *Principle* of Deliverance: the Law of the Spirit of Life can trump the Law of Sin and Death to fulfill God's righteousness in us (8:1-4). But for the Spirit to prevail, we must submit to the

---

2   W. Cowper, "The Indwelling God," *The Silver Cross*, Vol. 30, Issue 12 (September, 1918), 9.

Process of Deliverance by following the Spirit's lead (8:5–8). Now Paul describes the vitalizing *Prospect* of Deliverance by the Holy Spirit from sin and death to righteousness and life (8:9-11).

1. Victory over Sin	**(8:1-17)**
a. Delivered from the Law of Sin and Death	**(8:1-11)**
1) *Principle* **of Deliverance**	**(8:1-4)**
2) *Process* **of Deliverance**	**(8:5–8)**
3) *Prospect* **of Deliverance**	**(8:9-11)**
a. **Who Can Walk According to the Spirit**	**9a**
b. **Why We Should Walk According to the Spirit**	**9b-11**
b. Delivered from a Life of Sin and Death	**(8:12-17)**

III. PROSPECT of Deliverance   8:9-11

Since it is those who walk according to the Spirit that are set free to fulfill the righteous requirement of the Law (8:1, 4) and please God (8:7-8), it is important to identify *who* qualifies to walk by the Spirit (8:9a) and *why* they should forsake their inclination inherited from Adam to seek fulfillment and life through the flesh (8:9b-11).

A. WHO Can Walk According to the Spirit   9a

But you are not in the flesh but in the Spirit, if indeed the Spirit of God dwells in you . . .

In vv. 5–8 *according to* the flesh was contrasted with *according to* the Spirit, where "according to" denotes a manner of living, or Condition. But v. 9a contrasts *in* the flesh with *in* the Spirit, where "in" signifies Position and distinguishes *believers* from *unbelievers*. Those *in* the flesh can only *walk by* the flesh — they "*cannot* please God" (8:8). But those *in* the Spirit have the choice of walking by the flesh *or* by the Spirit, because they have the indwelling Holy Spirit (Jn 14:17). A remote-control airplane cannot respond to the operator's signals unless the device is installed that can "receive" the signals. When the device is installed and switched on, the airplane comes under the operator's control and can do all kinds of stunts it could not do on its own. Anyone who has received Jesus has the "divine remote-control system" installed and can choose *by* the indwelling Spirit to receive life (8:11) and put to death the deeds of the body (8:13)!

So why doesn't *every* believer walk according to the Spirit? Satan and the world conspire to convince us that we can get more "life" by choosing self-indulgence or law-keeping through our "weak" flesh. Of course, this only re-enslaves us to Sin and death through the Law of the Flesh (7:23-25), and we do not "reign in Christ's righteousness to life" (5:17b, 21b). Paul thus offers his Spirit-indwelt readers this needed incentive to overcome Sin and death by the Law of the Spirit of life (8:2): following the Spirit *always* trumps living by the flesh, because only through Him can we serve the righteousness that brings life (6:13, 16-23; 8:10-11).

B. WHY We Should Walk According to the Spirit 9b-11

9 . . . ***Now if*** *anyone does not have the Spirit of Christ, he is not His.* 10***But if*** *Christ is in you, the body is dead because of sin, but the Spirit is life because of righteousness.* 11***So*** *if the Spirit of Him who raised Jesus from the dead dwells in you, He who raised Christ from the dead will also give life to your mortal bodies through His Spirit who dwells in you.* [modified NKJV][3]

Drawing on his conclusions in 8:6-9a, Paul is saying that in the face of prevailing death in the flesh, real life is totally dependent on the *indwelling Spirit of Christ*. To paraphrase: "**Now if** someone doesn't have the Spirit, they are not in Christ, **but if** someone *has* Christ, the Spirit can bring life through righteous behavior, even if the body is still dead [from Sin's dominion through the unredeemed flesh]; **so if** the Spirit *dwells* in you, the same power that raised Jesus will also vitalize your flesh-bound lives when you let His Spirit *invade* you." The mention of the Spirit in connection with Christ's resurrection is an obvious echo of Romans 1:4, where Jesus himself is our model of spiritual empowerment.

In these verses Paul finally explains how reigning in righteousness can bring life (see 5:17b, 21b; 6:18-23). Paul identifies the key difference between a believer (8:10) and an unbeliever (8:8, 9b) so that he can now highlight the reason why believers are promised life in the Spirit. The goal is to please God with *righteousness* (8:8, 10b), but because of our unredeemed flesh, this righteous behavior can only come through the Spirit within us (8:4, 10b); only then will the Spirit "also give life" (8:11).[4]

This requirement of walking according to the Spirit is implied in the present passage by two different verbs, both translated "dwells" (8:11 NKJV). The word at the end of v. 11 (*enoikeō*) is not the same as the word in vv. 9 and 11a (*oikeō*). The preposition *en* intensifies the action of the verb: while *oikeō* depicts the Spirit as a resident, *enoikeō* portrays Him as having the run of the entire house — *invading* our lives. I saw this illustrated when I was commuting to Dallas for graduate work and often stayed there with my friend. His wife took me to a very beautiful guest room where I would stay. It was wonderful to be their guest, but after a few visits, she just gave me a key to the whole house. By analogy, when we

---

3   The logic in 8:9b-11 is governed by the versatile connective *ei de* in 8:9b, 10, and 11 (**bold**). The thrust of each connective turns on Paul's logic in 8:10, as explained in the text below.

4   Just as Jesus was raised only *after* his "righteous act" (*dikaiōma*, 5:18b), we get that same "life" (6:4b, 5b) only by first walking according to His Spirit to fulfill God's "righteous requirement" (*dikaiōma*, 8:4). Here the word *life* (*zōē*) always refers to *spiritual* life and is linked to *righteous reign* through Christ (5:17, 18, 21); it is not *biological* life (*bios*). Accordingly, the "death" in view is primarily *spiritual* death.

became believers, Christ came into our lives (Col 1:29) to *dwell*, along with the Spirit (Eph 1:13). He could push His way around but He only goes where He is invited, as indicated by *oikeō* (Rom 8:9, 11a). But when I give Him the key to the whole house, it lights up like a Christmas tree — He is free to *invade* every aspect of my being, and I experience His controlling power (8:11b). It's not that we get more of the Spirit; it's that He gets more of us.

Digging Deeper: *When* and *Where* Does the Holy Spirit *Indwell* and *Invade* Us?

There is a lot of confusion over this question. The Holy Spirit did not typically indwell believers in the OT. Kings, high priests, judges, prophets, or groups charged with important tasks like crafting Temple artifacts were indwelt by the Holy Spirit, but it was not usually permanent. After sinning with Bathsheba, David prayed that God would not take his Holy Spirit from him (Ps 51:11) as He had done with Saul. However, following Ezekiel's prophecy (Ezek 36:25-27), John the Baptist told of One coming after him who would "baptize" with fire and with the Holy Spirit (Matt 3:11; Mk 1:8; Lk 3:16; Jn 1:33). Then Jesus told his disciples to wait in Jerusalem for the Holy Spirit to come upon them with power (Acts 1:8); they were utterly transformed at Pentecost from cowards to *commandos*, from weaklings to *witnesses*, from deserters to *disciples*.

1. So, precisely *when* do we receive the Holy Spirit? Here are some common theories:

a. During water baptism (Acts 2:38)? Robert Shank, a respected Church of Christ scholar, once told me that a believer receives the Holy Spirit *under the water* in water baptism. When I asked him about the thief on the cross, he said the thief was credited with "baptism by desire": he would have headed straight for the river to be baptized if he could. So then I asked about Cornelius in Acts 10 who clearly received the baptism of the Holy Spirit *before* water baptism. He said Cornelius was an exception to the rule. We suggest that where more than one exception to the rule exists (the thief and Cornelius and his family), it may not be the right answer.

b. Some time after receiving Christ as Savior (Acts 2, 8, 9, 19)? The people in each of these instances in Acts were believers for some time before receiving the Holy Spirit. But we should note that they were all Jews. As the chosen people of God, the Jews of the generation that put Jesus on the cross incurred special requirements to avoid the impending judgment on that generation (Matt 23:36; Acts 2:40), which was fulfilled when Titus razed Jerusalem in AD 70, one generation after Jesus' ministry began: a Jew would have to separate from that generation by water baptism in Jesus' name.[5] Then if they were believers (and why else would they separate?) they would receive the Holy Spirit, just as Ezekiel had predicted (36:25-27).

Cornelius was a prototype of *Gentile* reception of the Holy Spirit in that generation and every generation since then. Since Gentiles were not under the curse of Matt 23:36, they did not need water baptism in order to dissociate from the Jewish generation and receive the Holy Spirit. All that Gentiles had to do was profess belief in Jesus as Messiah, and they would immediately receive the Holy Spirit.

c. When we are born again (1 Cor 12:13)? This is the correct answer. If Romans 8:9b says anything to us, it is simply that anyone who does not have the Holy Spirit is not a Christian. First Corinthians 12:13 confirms that the Holy Spirit has baptized *every* believer into the body of Christ — both the person who has just believed and the person who has been a believer for ten years. Whether or not Cornelius was a believer before his encounter with Peter (Acts 10:43-44), there is no such thing today as a Christian who has not yet been baptized by the Holy Spirit.

Since every Christian has the Spirit he must receive the Spirit the very moment he believes. He is no longer "in the flesh"; he is "in the Spirit" and the Spirit is "in him" (Eph 1:13). Also, 1 Corinthians 12:13 uses the word "all," even though *not* all speak in tongues (12:30). This contradicts the teaching that requires speaking in tongues as evidence of baptism by the Spirit. Speaking in tongues is not listed among the fruit of the Spirit (Gal 5:22). Those who seek more evidence of indwelling should look for the *fruit* of the Spirit, not the gifts of the Spirit.

2. So, *where* does the Holy Spirit take up residence within our beings?

First Thessalonians 5:23 distinguishes **body** from **soul** (made up of *mind* [Prov 2:10; Ps 139:14], *emotion* [1 Sam 18:1; 30:6], and *will* [Job 6:7; 7:15]) and **spirit**. Thus, we are tripartite beings — even unbelievers share these three components. Some teach that unbelievers are made up of only *body* and *soul*, but this would seem to contradict the experience of Pharaoh and Nebuchadnezzar, whose *spirits* were troubled within them (Gen 41:6; Dan 2:1).

5　In every case in the Book of Acts, baptism by the Holy Spirit did not occur until a professing believer in Messiah (often identified by John's baptism) *publicly acknowledged the Lord Jesus by name* as the promised Messiah. A major problem among Jewish believers was fear of ostracism by their *rulers* (Jn 7:47-52; 9:22; 12:42). This would lead to reticence to be water baptized because that entailed *confessing Jesus by name*. Thus, although water baptism saved them from the coming destruction (compare Rom 10:9-10) the warnings by Jesus and John the Baptist were primarily an incentive for them to overcome their fear of censure and *publicly identify with the Body of Christ*—a major theme in the Book of Acts.

The contrast in Romans 8:10 is between the human *body* and *spirit* — one decays while the other does not; one brings physical death while the other is the gateway to spiritual life. So here we see exactly where the Holy Spirit lives. It is not in our bodies; it is not in our souls; it is with/in our human *spirits* (Rom 8:16; 1 Cor 2:11-13). Since sin entered the world through Adam, we no longer have immortal bodies. After the fall, the human body decays and dies; man's spirit is also "dead" (Eph 2:1), *separated from God*. But when one believes, the Holy Spirit resides in (or with) our human spirit. This is what we mean by being born "again" or "from above" (Jn 3:3-8). The human spirit joined with the Holy Spirit is "made alive" (Eph 2:1 NIV), i.e., *regenerated*.

Reformed teachers use Ephesians 2:1 as a proof-text that the spiritually "dead" unbeliever must be regenerated *before* he can believe — like a corpse, his spirit can do nothing. But the spirit of the unbeliever is far from dead in the sense of a corpse. Most would agree that the conscience or "heart" is part of man's spiritual nature; the conscience of the unbeliever can certainly come under conviction by the Spirit (Eccl 3:11; Jn 16:8-11; Rom 1:19-20; 2:14-15). It is as dead as can be when "dead" is understood to mean separated from God. The believer is no longer separated from God since the Holy Spirit has come to live with/in his human spirit.

The tabernacle offers a good illustration with its three parts. The NT attests that the Holy Spirit lives in our *naos*, the "holy of holies" or innermost part of man's being. The "holy place" is analogous to the human *soul* (mind, emotion, will). This is why God is seeking those who will worship in Spirit and in truth (Jn 4:23-24). We can teach *truth* yet miss the *spirit*; we can come to Him with our minds and emotions yet fail to engage our spirit. He wants us to communicate with Him *in spirit*, because that is where He lives (compare 1 Cor 2:9-13).

3. *How* then does the Holy Spirit *invade* our lives? Several metaphors in Scripture symbolize our "invasion" — *full control* — by the Holy Spirit:

a. Wind (Jn 3:8; Acts 2:2). The Greek word for spirit is *pneuma* — the very word that also means "wind." Air. Most of us have had the unpleasant experience of a flat tire. As long as the tire is flat, the car won't go anywhere. The tire needs to be filled in order for the car to roll. "Deflation" is another picture of "death" (defeat, disillusionment, despair) in the Christian life, and our Sin Nature is the nail that deflates us. But the Spirit can "inflate" us again when he has "the run of the whole house"; the tire is full. The seven men chosen as "table waiters" in Acts 6 were "inflated" — "full of the Holy Spirit." Their lives epitomized His control.

b. Water (Jn 7:37-39). Jesus spoke of the Spirit as a spring of water bubbling up to quench our thirst and bring life. We are spiritual beings who develop spiritual thirst for the things of God (Jn 4:10-26). The unbroken believer always has an unsatisfied thirst. One way we can know that the Spirit has access to the entire house is that, like the woman at the well, we can't wait to share the living water — to testify of life in the Messiah (Jn 4:14, 28-30).

c. **Wine (Eph 5:18-22).** This passage refers primarily to group worship (for example, "submitting" requires at least two people), but it still applies to the individual. Wine can intoxicate to the point of controlling our thoughts and actions. When we are intoxicated by the Spirit rather than by wine we allow Him to control our thoughts and actions, encouraging psalms in our heart, songs on our lips, and thanksgiving for God's will in our lives. Of special note is that a parallel exhortation to thank God for His will is immediately followed by the warning not to quench the Spirit (1 Thess 5:18-19).

d. **Dove (Matt 3:16).** Metaphors of wind, water, and wine all point to internal things. The Holy Spirit is also likened to a dove, something *external*. The Holy Spirit is likened to a dove, not an eagle. He is not a proud bird with a golden tail, but a bird of peace and humility. When He opens His mouth, we do not hear a squawk or a screech, but rather a soft song in the morning. One controlled by the Spirit is never a Big Bird in his own eyes. Watchman Nee elaborates:

> The Holy Spirit is said to be like a dove, meek and gentle. The Spirit of God will incorporate His nature in us little by little until we, too, are characterized by the dove. Meekness, born out of the fear of God, is the Holy Spirit's sign for brokenness. One broken by the Spirit naturally possesses meekness. His contacts with people are no longer marked by that obstinacy, hardness, and sharpness which are the hallmarks of an unbroken man. He has been brought to the place where his attitude is meek and his voice is gentle.[6]

e. **Fire (Acts 2:3, 19).** We often speak of a Christian who is "on fire for Christ," living with energy for God; in fact the very word "enthusiasm" is a compound word that literally means "in-filling with God." Fire is a powerful energy source and can move a train down the track, a plane across the sky, or a rocket to the moon. And just like fire, the Spirit of God can spread to all areas of our lives and imbue our bodies with energy to come alive for Him — unless we quench Him (1 Thess 5:19). The Greek word for "quench" means "extinguish or put out" a fire, and no metaphor in Scripture fits the Spirit better than *fire*. Since the Holy Spirit is God, we often overlook the fact that we can restrict His access within our beings and thus "quench" Him. Even though He is omnipotent He does not intrude where He is not welcome.

---

6 Watchman Nee, *The Release of the Spirit* (n.a.: Sure Foundation Publishers, 1965), 85.

One way to put out a fire is to throw dirt on it. Similarly, if we pour enough dirt in the mind, emotions, will, and the body, and we will soon quench the Spirit. A little lust here, a little lie there; a little gossip here, a little greed there; here some bitterness, there some discord. Such dirt puts out the fire of the Holy Spirit — He is jealous and does not "share rooms" with our dirt (Jas 4:4-5). A second way to put out a fire is to remove its fuel. Remove logs from a campfire and it soon goes out. Neglecting God's Word withholds a primary fuel for the fire of the Spirit; Jeremiah's heart was burning like a fire when he had been feeding on God's Word (Jer 20:8-9).

A believer may well say, "What's wrong? I'm not *consciously* throwing dirt on the fire or holding back on fuel but I know the Holy Spirit is not in control." This believer may be trying to please God out of self-reliance (Romans 7). It can take years to reach the end, the point of utter brokenness. Not until our self-sufficient human resources — our cleverness, compassion, and determination — are depleted will we be broken and ready to give the Holy Spirit the key to our whole house. How can we tell? The body comes alive (8:11) with the fruit of the Spirit — I call it "Holy Smoke," because where there is smoke there is fire.

These various Scriptural analogies for control by the Holy Spirit can help us recognize when *Holy Smoke* is present. Yet C. S. Lewis reminds us that even if we *don't see* any smoke, it doesn't mean there is no fire:

> The presence of God is not the same as the sense of the presence of God. The latter may be due to imagination; the former may be attended with no "sensible consolation." The act which engenders a child ought to be, and usually is, attended by pleasure. But it is not the pleasure that produces the child. Where there is pleasure there may be sterility: where there is no pleasure the act may be fertile. And in the spiritual marriage of God and the soul it is the same. It is the actual presence, not the sensation of the presence, of the Holy Ghost which begets Christ in us. The sense of the presence is a super-added gift for which we give thanks when it comes.[7]

[END OF EXCURSUS]

In our discussion of Romans 8:9a, we introduced the analogy of a remote-control airplane When I was a boy, my father bought me one of those manually controlled airplane kits, long before all the fancy, radio-controlled toys we have now. So we assembled the plane, fueled it up, and fired the engine — it started right up. We

---

7   C. S. Lewis, *Letters to an American Lady* (Grand Rapids, MI: Eerdmans, 1967), 36-37.

couldn't wait to fly it, so we drove a couple of miles to the park. There was only one catch. Before we could turn the plane loose, it had to be tethered to a long string with a handle on one end. I would hold the handle, and the plane would fly around and around in a circle. If the plane could talk, I am sure it would have had mixed emotions about its new lease on life. It certainly could fly, but it was severely limited. It could only fly in circles, never getting anywhere. It was pretty boring after awhile.

Years later I came home from college for a visit and jogged down to the park for some exercise. As I neared the field where I used to fly my little plane, I could hear the loud whine of model airplane engines. When I passed by, I was amazed to see these great big model airplanes flying all over the place with no strings attached, doing loops and rolls with wonderful freedom. How did they fly so freely? By remote-control, of course. If *those* planes could talk, they would express the exhilaration of flight with no strings attached. But there was one condition. They did pretty much whatever the operator asked them to do. If any plane decided to go off on its own and got too far away to receive the signals from its owner/operator, a crash was inevitable. Oh, it might fly on its own for a while, but it was only a matter of time before it came down.

The Christian in Romans 7 is still flying on a string, but only going in circles. But those in Christ who operate by the Law of Liberty (or the Spirit of Life, 8:2) will enjoy the exhilaration of flying with no strings attached — by Spirit-control. This Christian knows that if he goes off on his own, it is just a matter of time before he crashes and burns. If he is smart he will keep flying according to the Spirit so he can do the marvelous loops and rolls that display the righteousness of God and joyfully testify of abundant life in Christ.

CHAPTER 15

"HOW TO GROW UP"
Romans 8:12-13

According to the late Art Linkletter, kids say the darndest things. Any of you who are parents can vouch for the fact that kids also do the darndest things, as I recently confirmed in an article in *Readers Digest* on "How to Eat like a Child." Here, for example, is how a child eats spaghetti: "Wind too many strands on fork and make sure at least two strands dangle down. Open mouth wide and stuff in spaghetti. Ask for seconds, and eat only half. When carrying plate to kitchen, hold tilted so remaining spaghetti slides onto floor." How to eat an ice-cream cone? "Ask for double scoop. Knock top scoop off while walking out of ice-cream parlor. Cry. Lick remaining scoop so slowly, it melts down outside of cone and over your hand. Stop licking when ice cream is even with top of cone then eat hole in bottom of cone and suck the rest out the bottom. When only cone remains with ice cream coating inside, leave on car dashboard." How about French fries? "Wave one fry in air while you talk. Pretend to conduct orchestra. Place four fries in mouth at once and chew. Turn to your sister, and stick out tongue coated with potatoes. Close mouth and swallow. Smile." But my favorite is spinach: "Divide into little piles. Rearrange into new piles. After five or six maneuvers, sit back and say you are full."

Yes, kids say and do the darndest things, but they also often bring frustration, grief, and even anger. We long to see them mature and contribute productively to their homes, churches, and country as respected adults who reflect the years of commitment their parents poured into them. Our Father in heaven desires the same for His children. But what if a Christian fails to make the kind of progress the Father hopes to see in his children as they grow? I am sure that as immature or carnal Christians we also bring Him our share of grief and frustration. As everything tends to revolve around a child's needs and wants, so also with immature Christians — we live selfishly. Church is mainly to satisfy our needs and wants; prayer is self-centered. We are often like a stubborn, petulant child who thinks he knows better or even defies his parents. Surely our heavenly Father longs for the day when we grow up to become the "sons" he chose us to be, fully equipped by our "portion" from Him to serve Christ and the kingdom of God, reigning and bearing the fruit of His righteousness and His life in us (5:17b, 21b; 6:15-23).

Given the fleshly temptation towards self-indulgence (Romans 6) and self-righteousness (Romans 7), Christian "adolescents" may be reticent to give up their freedom or the "security" of prescriptive living ("law"). Other believers shrink from the risk and responsibility of growing in Christ. These Christians are afflicted with the "Peter Pan Principle": they conceive of heaven as a Never-Never Land where there is no risk, responsibility, or work. Jesus is seen as Peter Pan and the devil as Captain Hook. We are just cheerleaders, watching them fight it out. Having offered his readers the *teaching* of "life in the Spirit" (8:1-11), Paul now invites us to *follow* the Spirit and thereby "graduate" from **law** to **grace** as mature believers in Christ (8:12-13; compare 6:14; 7:1, 4-6).

1. Victory over Sin		**(8:1-17)**
a. Delivered from the Law of Sin and Death		**(8:1-11)**
b. Delivered from a Life of Sin and Death		**(8:12-17)**
1.	**Mandate to Deliverance**	**12-13**
	a. *Rationale* **for Deliverance**	**12-13a**
	b. *Result* **of Deliverance**	**13b**
2.	**Motive for Deliverance**	**14-17**

I. MANDATE for Deliverance   8:12-13

If we have trusted in the cross of Christ as our only hope for eternal life, then we qualify as prospects for deliverance from the power of sin to become "portraits of righteousness." As prospects for full deliverance to maturity in Christ, to become "sons of God," we are called to *appropriate* the Spirit's lead by Paul's Mandate to Deliverance ("Grow up!"). Within this mandate is the Rationale for Deliverance (8:12-13a) and the Result of Deliverance (8:13b).

A. RATIONALE for Deliverance   12-13a

[12]*Therefore, brethren, we are debtors — not to the flesh, to live according to the flesh.* [13]*For if you live according to the flesh you will die.*

"Therefore" (*ara oun*) introduces a conclusion in 8:12-17 based on the preceding text (8:1-11). The moment we became believers our identity was transferred from the realm where the flesh reigned to the realm where the Holy Spirit reigns; by virtue of this New Position in Christ, "we are [therefore] under obligation" (NASB): called to emancipate from the flesh (7:25) and serve by the Spirit as mature "sons of God." Indeed, all creation awaits the climactic unveiling of these "adopted" sons (8:14, 19) who have fulfilled their spiritual "obligation," by analogy with the stipulations of Roman adoption (*huiothesian*, "the placing of a son," 8:15, 23), which carried certain responsibilities.

Digging Deeper: The Background of Roman Adoption and Sonship in Romans 8:12-23

In Rome a child under age seven was called an *infant* (Latin) or *nēpios* (Greek), a **babe**. From then until age fourteen a male was an *impubes* (Latin) or *teknon* (Greek), a **child**. At puberty he became a *filius* (Latin) or *huios* (Greek), a **son**. Although he could sit at the family council he could not conduct the affairs of his estate, including the exercise of property rights, until age twenty-five. But even at twenty-five he was still under what the Romans called the *patria potestas* (paternal power, power of the father).[1] This meant that his natural father had authority over the son until the father died[2] — *except* in the case of adoption.

To finalize adoption, the natural father took his son to the marketplace and sold him three times to the prospective father. A father could sell his children to pay off his debts, but he could also buy them back twice after paying off his debt. But with the third sale his *patria potestas* was broken, and the child was no longer obligated to his natural father in any way;[3] he was adopted "for good."[4] Such adoptions could take place at any age. In fact, Nero became emperor of Rome through adoption by Claudius. Since Claudius had no heir to his throne he simply chose to adopt one of his favorite generals. When an adoption took place, there were four consequences:

1. The adopted son lost all rights in his previous family, and his natural father lost all rights over him.
2. In the new family the adopted son gained rights equivalent to blood relatives (this is only true of Roman adoption, among the various cultures in the Bible).
3. His previous life record was wiped out, including any debts.
4. He began a new life with a new name, new rights and new status.

So, how does Paul apply this to the Christian life? Every unbeliever has a father just as every believer does. Paul says that all non-Christians are by nature children of wrath (Eph 2:3). Their spiritual father is the devil. But when a non-

---

1   Max Kaser, *Römisches Privatrecht*, trans. Rolf Dannenbring (Durban, South Africa: Butterworth & Co., 1968), 61.
2   Ibid., 256-57.
3   Ibid., 258.
4   Ibid., 264.

Christian receives Christ, he is born into a new family with a new Father, God, and all four consequences of Roman adoption also apply:

1. Our former father has lost all his rights over us, and we have no obligation to obey him.
2. We have rights in the new family on an equal basis with the only begotten Son Himself.
3. The record of our old life with its debt of sin has been completely wiped out.
4. We have begun a brand new life in a new family with a new status as new creatures.

One more key feature of Roman sonship completes Paul's analogy to the "obligation" of Christian maturity. A Roman son was under the care of a **tutor** (compare Gal 4:1-8) who trained him in morals and education and served as guardian and executor of his estate until age fourteen. At fourteen the child underwent a ceremony in which he was given the *toga virilis* — the apparel of manhood. A **curator** now took the place of the tutor, but his role was similar. The son could exercise a few legal rights and was allowed much more freedom but was still under the authority of the curator, who provided counsel and protection and administered the boy's property. Finally, at age twenty-five, the boy was considered a full-fledged son who could exercise full rights and privileges. No more tutors or curators, although he was still under the power of his father.

Paul draws on all this imagery in the passage before us. The believer's "biological father" (in Adam) was the devil, who had absolute *patria potestas* over him. His tutor and curator were the flesh, which trained him in self-sufficiency and self-gratification. As an unbeliever he was obliged to obey the flesh but through adoption he was transferred into a new family. Our Father in heaven paid the price to buy us out of the market place, which ended the *patria potestas* of the devil, the old father. Now we are under a new Father, the Father of our Lord Jesus Christ. While Jesus is our Father's only *begotten* son, we are His *adopted* sons. As such we no longer have any obligation to our former tutor, the flesh. Now we have a new tutor or curator — the Holy Spirit — whom God the Father has appointed as our protector, teacher, guide, and counselor; in sum:

IDENTITY	FATHER	TUTOR/CURATOR
Old: In Adam	*The Devil*	*The Flesh*
New: In Christ	*God*	*The Spirit*

[END OF EXCURSUS]

Such is the inherent nobility and grandeur of "adoption" for a child of God. Of course, the *legal* act of adoption does not automatically transfer one's *allegiance* and *emotions*. Although the child is adopted into a new family and "no longer obligated to the flesh — to live according to its leading and desires" (8:12) — he might still be partial to his old father and his old tutor, the flesh. His attitude toward the flesh would be like that of Russian astronaut Gherman Titov when he was asked what he believed about God and said, "I don't believe in God. I believe in man — in his strength, his possibilities, and his reason."[5] This is exemplary "flesh" — man with all his strength, possibilities, and reason, calling us to self-sufficiency. Now here is the problem: we believe in God; yet just like Titov we can go right on living as if it all depends on *us*, and it is just as useless to God as Titov's philosophy of secular humanism.

To warn us of the consequences of continuing to live the way our old tutor taught and trained us, Paul goes on to say, "Now, if in fact you live according to the flesh you shall *die*" (8:13). The Greek conveys this as a strong warning with an emphatic *gar* and an intensive verb form: *you are about to die!* Again, the Roman law of *patria potestas* included the *power of life and death* (*ius vitae necisque*) over children.[6] In the case of adoption, a child who ran back to his former family could be put to death by his new father. The analogy for believers is 1 John 5:16: the sin unto death. Our heavenly Father holds the power of life and death and can put us to death as an extreme and final measure of discipline. He simply brings His errant child "home." But *death* and *life* throughout Romans 5–8 look beyond the mere physical aspects. The child of God who runs back into the world to serve his old tutor, the flesh, will find himself among the "living dead" — a moral state actually worse than before he was adopted into God's family. In fact, says Peter, "it would have been better for them not to have known the way of righteousness, than having known it, to turn from the holy commandment delivered to them" (2 Pet 2:21).

We see this illustrated so often with children who have been raised in Christian homes but leave their Christian faith to follow the flesh. Invariably, it leads them to a life of immorality. They *feel* liberated, but the allure of pleasure or relief from life's difficulties brings a "sting in its tail": defeat, disillusionment, despair, and even premature death. Angela is just such a child of despair. Raised in a Christian home, in name at least, Angela chose to pack her bags and pursue pleasure as far as it would take her. Little did she realize it would end in a living death. At 5'6" she has physically withered to a weight of only 87 pounds, she has a husband who

---

5   Gherman Titov, cited by Ray Stedman in a 1975 sermon ("In the Arena"), Peninsula Bible Church, Palo Alto, CA.

6   Kaser, *Römisches Privatrecht*, 257.

beats her, has been in a mental ward three times, and has had three illegitimate children, all by age twenty-four. All she has to live for are her children, but they all hate her, according to relatives. If we choose to serve our former tutor after we have been adopted into God's family, then we too will find ourselves, to one degree or another, slaves to sin and death.

While a child may resist being led by this new tutor as an unwanted imposition, he is actually being *set free* compared to the slavery he endured when he was led by the flesh. The baby or carnal Christian (1 Cor 3:1-4) still lives a life oriented to the lusts of his old tutor the flesh and finds himself enslaved again to the Law of Sin that indwells the flesh when he succumbs to those desires (Rom 7:17-18, 20-21, 23, 25b). Only a mature son puts himself at the disposal of his curator, the Holy Spirit, and fully submits to his mentor's quiet, internal prompting. Paul now affirms the result of this transformation.

B. RESULT of Deliverance 13b

But if by the Spirit you put to death the deeds of the body, you will live.

Paul uses a synonym here for flesh ("body") to make it clear that self-reliance is to play no role in our deliverance to maturity in Christ. This is graphically illustrated in Ezekiel 44:18, where the priests of God who will serve in the future temple of God are a type of the Christian, the believer-priest, as we serve God today: "They shall not gird themselves with anything that causes sweat." Now, why in the world is God so concerned about sweat? Because sweat comes from the flesh and symbolizes how odious self-reliance is in the sight of God, who has provided the strength of His indwelling Spirit to empower us. Trust in the flesh — self-effort — can never produce the fruit of the Spirit.

Suppose you went to the ghetto to adopt a child. During his early years this child learned foul, dirty habits. He has become an expert shoplifter. He learned to speak in the gutter. He eats with dirty hands. He doesn't bathe very often, so one set of clothes last a week and he constantly smells. When you adopt little Johnny and bring him into your home, he has to learn a totally new lifestyle to suit his new identity: John has to learn to bathe himself, wear clean clothes, brush his teeth, wash his hands before eating, comb his hair, and clean up his speech. How absurd to think that John could learn these things all by himself. In England he would be assigned a *governess*; in Greece, a *paidagogos*; in Rome, a *tutor*.

And so it is in the Christian life. Now that the believer has been adopted into a *new* family, the customs and practices are radically different from the old family. A new tutor, the Holy Spirit, is assigned to lead him to deliverance, with a harmony between divine sovereignty and human responsibility. The Holy Spirit — our tutor, our trainer — teaches us to replace the old habits with the new. This is his work. He's in charge. How ridiculous to suppose that young believer could learn these things all by himself. But he must *cooperate* with the tutor. How can the tutor do his work, how can the tutor teach him anything unless little he cooperates?

So what am *I* supposed to do? Surely God doesn't expect me to sit back on my duff while I wait for Him to wave some magic wand to make me spiritual? Indeed, we *do* have an "obligation" (8:12, NIV), and Romans 8:13 spells it out: we are to put to the death the foul deeds (practices) of the flesh ("body" = flesh) incited by our Sin Nature inherited from Adam. Here we see the Law of Displacement in action: when *we follow* the Holy Spirit, *He leads* us to righteous behavior (8:4, 14) which in turn "displaces" the deeds done through the flesh by the Sin Nature from Adam (7:24-25), and they "die of neglect." The sanctifying work belongs to the Spirit. That is His responsibility. Our responsibility is to cooperate. We must be available and teachable.

I used to live next door to a former touring professional golfer named Don Massengale. After making his living on the PGA tour for over a decade, he became a club pro and gave lots of lessons. One day I asked him if he enjoyed teaching. He responded, "Sometimes I do, sometimes I don't. I enjoy teaching when someone really wants to learn." Well, how do you know when they really want to learn? "They hang around me all the time. Hungry to learn. Whenever I give them a tip, they are out there beating balls until they are ready for the next tip. Golfers like that always improve, and it is fun to watch. But a lot of club members buy packages of lessons, you know, eight lessons for so many dollars. And after coming in for a lesson, I might not see them again for a month. And when I ask them if they have been practicing what I suggested at their first lesson, they can't even remember what I suggested. That kind of teaching isn't much fun."

I suppose it is the same with the Holy Spirit. He can only teach us when we are available to learn. The young believer must place himself completely at the disposal of the tutor if he is to develop into a mature son who can bring honor to his Father. And the Spirit's tool to teach us is His sword, the Word of God. He knows when we are hungry to learn by how much time we spend with the sword. The Word of God is not only full of "tips" from the Holy Spirit; it is also His cleansing agent to wash away our dirty habits, our deeds of the flesh (see John 17:17). *His mission* is to speak what the Father tells Him; but *our obligation* is to follow His lead (8:14a).

It is like flying from Houston to Hawaii. We can't *run, walk,* or *swim* that far — the only way is by air. When we fly, there is that exhilarating experience of counteracting gravity as the airplane takes off. Most of us don't remember Bernoulli's principle, but two opposing forces are at work: gravity and aerodynamics. Gravity drags us toward the center of the earth, we cannot escape it. But we can *counteract* it by relying on the "aerodynamics" and "navigational system" of the Spirit. How foolish would it be for us to flap our arms like a bird in the back of the plane just to get credit for counteracting gravity! Yet so often we locate the "beacon" of the Spirit and then flap our wings. Imagine if I rushed to the cockpit right after take-off (before 9/11) and said to the flight crew, "Hey, guys, how'd ya do that?" They would kick me right out: "Sit down and relax. We're flying the plane. Don't worry about how it works. Just count on us." That is all God asks. Just trust the pilot who knows the destination and how to get there.

Yes, kids say the darndest things, and they are funny. But every parent longs for his children to grow up. Recently I went hunting on a West Texas ranch and shot a large axis deer, a nuisance to the ranch owner but great meat to eat. The owner of the ranch was away on business, but his son was there to help me. I was impressed that this young man seemed so mature. I knew he was just about to enter college, but he acted like he was twenty-five. When I saw the owner again, I mentioned that his son was about the most mature young man for his age I had ever met. His father beamed with pride as he told me of many others who had told him the same thing. Surely our heavenly Father beams with just as much pleasure when one of the angels points out one of His grown-up, adopted sons.

This is very much the "feel" we anticipate when Jesus returns to proudly display his sanctified "brethren" before the Father (Heb 2:11-13). And it is precisely what Paul anticipates as he concludes the first half of Romans 8 (vv. 14-17) in light of the glory to be revealed, as described in the second half (vv. 18-23).

CHAPTER 16

"WHY SHOULD I GROW UP?"
Romans 8:14-17

One Mother's Day I was cruising over the comics with my eyes open for some Mother's Day wisdom. Of all places, I found it in a little comic strip called "Momma." In the strip, Momma is obviously lamenting the fact that she "ain't got no respect" from her children. She says, "My children neglect me. . . . They're also opinionated, stubborn, and hard to handle. . . . Why couldn't I have had children who adore and respect me and accept my better judgment . . . like the other one out of 150,000 mothers?" I think all mothers as well as fathers can identify with Momma and her situation. It would seem that every child goes through at least one phase in which he is opinionated, stubborn, hard to handle, and lacks respect for the better judgment of his mom and dad. Actually, this phase marks out the child as a child. It is usually not until he grows up that he realizes how wise his parents really are.

But if any parent can identify with the lament of Momma most, it has to be our Father in heaven. Surely He can say, "My children neglect me." How about, "They're also opinionated, stubborn, and hard to handle"? Yes. And, "Why couldn't I have had children who adore and respect me and accept my better judgment?" Indeed, all these descriptions fit God's children, for these are the very marks of childhood and immaturity. And our Father longs for the day when we grow up and — as mature sons and daughters — appreciate His wisdom, and respect His better judgment. He longs for that day not just to prove to us how smart He is, but that He might enjoy a close, intimate relationship with us, and that we, in turn, embrace His wisdom and gain the inheritance He has stored up for us. This intimacy and wealth that God wishes to share with His children is precisely what Paul outlines for us in Romans 8:14-17.

We have looked at the "Mandate for Deliverance" in vv. 12-13. God the Holy Spirit will displace the foul practices of our old life, as long as we do our part to cooperate with our Tutor. But this will require us to fully emancipate from the flesh as *children* to follow the Spirit as *mature sons*. What incentive do we have to grow up? Why not just live in a Christian Never, Never Land? Romans 8:14-17 is designed to entice us to maturity by describing in more detail the benefits or "perks" of being delivered from the tyranny of Sin to maturity as "sons indeed" who bring honor to their Father. It is a far Greater Life when we are led by the Holy Spirit, consisting of Greater Freedom (14-15a), Greater Fellowship (15b-16), and a Greater Future (17).

1. Victory over Sin		**(8:1-17)**
a. Delivered from the Law of Sin and Death		**(8:1-11)**
b. Delivered from a Life of Sin and Death		**(8:12-17)**
1. Mandate for Deliverance		**12-13**
2. Motive for Deliverance		**14-17**
a. Greater Freedom		**14-15a**
b. Greater Fellowship		**15b-16**
c. Greater Future		**17**

II. MOTIVE for Deliverance   8:14-17

A. Greater FREEDOM   14-15a

14*For as many as are led by the Spirit of God, these are sons of God.* 15*For you did not receive the spirit of bondage again to fear.*

With the opening "for" (*gar*) Paul explains what it is to "live" (8:13): it is letting the Spirit mold us into mature sons of God who fulfill God's "righteous requirement" (8:4). The moment we are adopted *out of* the family of unbelievers and *into* the family of God, the Spirit of adoption (8:15b) is assigned to "fit" us as the portraits of righteousness we were created to be in the image of the Father by conforming us to Christ's image (8:29). The "fitting" has a distinctly *prospective* focus, as these "portraits" are to be "released for display" to all Creation (8:18-21).

As we saw in the previous chapter (see "Digging Deeper"), the Greek word for adoption is a composite word: *huios* (son) + *tithēmi* (to place). This process of being "placed" as a son came to denote not only the initial adoption but also the eventual transfer of full legal rights and privileges at maturity, so it occurred in two steps. When a child became a man at age fourteen he was placed as a son into the family council and could exercise certain rights. However, he still could not exercise his full rights as a son — he had no rights over his property until age twenty-five. So it is noteworthy in this connection that Paul speaks of *two* "placings" as a son: one on earth (vv. 14-15) and the other in heaven (v. 23). Similarly, while many of the rights and privileges of a son are to be enjoyed while we are on earth, the full benefits are not attained until our body is redeemed.

And as long as we are on earth we still have the Holy Spirit, to *train* us to walk worthy of our royal family and thus *fit* us to receive our full property rights and royal inheritance (8:17).

If we simply equate "son" with being born again, then *every* Christian (including "baby" or "carnal" Christians) is led by the Spirit. However, this is simply not true. The carnal Christian, by definition, is "led" by the *flesh* (8:5a, 6a, 7a). If we follow the distinction here between a *child* of God (8:16) and a *son* of God, then it all makes sense.[1] The son is *mature in Christ,* being led by the Spirit — the present tense of "being led" signifies a daily, ongoing "following." Over the years the mature son has let the Spirit guide him, teach him, and train him, and the result is cumulative wisdom from God which informs his righteous behavior.[2] The Christian being led by the flesh is not mature — he is not following his new tutor and is *bound* by fear of the cost of a righteous life. In being led by the Spirit, the son thus has greater freedom. He is fully released from the "spirit of bondage" that keeps us from freely receiving the Father's love to display His righteousness boldly (1 Jn 4:17-18). He is free from domination by sin in the flesh in this life and has the truth abiding in him, which makes him free indeed (Rom 8:21; also Jn 8:32-36).

I remember being asked years ago by a family in our church if I would visit their son in a psychiatric ward at the medical center in Houston. When I walked into the room, he took one look at me and asked, "Are you a preacher? What are you going to do, lay hands on me and speak in tongues?" *Well, no, I hadn't planned on that, but do you want me to?* "No, and I don't even want to talk to you. I bet my

---

1   We should note at this point that Galatians 3–4 uses the term "son" in a different way. There Paul is writing to Greeks, with different contextual implications for *adoption, pedagogues, guardians,* and *tutors.*

2   This corresponds to Paul's teaching in 1 Cor 2:6–3:4 that only the spiritually mature can receive such wisdom (2:6-16); those who are "fleshly" are unable to do so (3:1-4). Within this passage we get a sense for how this wisdom is communicated by the Spirit:

> *"No eye has seen, no ear has heard, no mind has conceived what God has prepared for those who love him"* — but God has revealed it to us by his Spirit. The Spirit searches all things, even the deep things of God. For who among men knows the thoughts of a man except the man's spirit within him? In the same way no one knows the thoughts of God except the Spirit of God. We have not received the spirit of the world but the Spirit who is from God, that we may understand what God has freely given us. This is what we speak, not in words taught us by human wisdom but in words taught by the Spirit, interpreting spiritual truths to spiritual men. (1 Cor 2:9-13, NIV marginal reading)

Such wisdom enables us progressively to discern truly righteous behavior (compare Heb 5:13-14). John frames this process as a function of our "consciences" or "hearts" when we obey God's commands with a keen sensitivity to the *internal conviction* of the Spirit (1 Jn 3:18-24). As He more consistently *abides* in us (Rom 8:11), we "hear" Him more clearly and we let Him prevail over the deeds or practices of the flesh in our lives (8:13) with righteous living. This builds greater confidence that we are becoming more consistently oriented to "what God has prepared for those who love him" (1 Cor 2:9) in the hope of a greater inheritance together with the reigning Son (Rom 8:15b-17).

parents sent you!" *Why don't you want to talk?* "Because you don't have anything for me. I have freedom." *Why do you have freedom?* "Because I can do whatever I want. I can come and go as I please. I just came back from Austin. I went there for the weekend to party. And I took that TV with me [pointing to the hospital TV]. Walked down the hall with it and then brought it back. I'm free, and I don't need what you're selling."

I headed for the door, but just as I was about to walk out, I felt an urge to confront him and said, *You're not free. In fact, you are one of the bigger slaves I have ever met.* "What do you mean, I'm a slave? Come back here and explain yourself. No one talks to me like that." *You are a slave of this world. Look at your hair.* (He had a really weird hairdo.) *Who told you to cut it like that? Look at your clothes.* (He was wearing some really weird clothes.) *Who told you to dress like that? You are a slave to the world system that dictates how you cut your hair and what clothes to wear. And look at your freedom. You are so proud of it you are a slave to it — always having to prove it to everyone and then brag about it. You are a slave to the max.*

I had never spoken to anyone like that before in my life and have not since, but the Holy Spirit used it. Mark prayed to receive Christ that night. Later, after his release from the hospital, he led his younger brother to Christ. That younger brother went on to attend seminary and is now an adjunct professor for Grace School of Theology. Mark went on to learn the truth, and the truth set him free from his living death.

It will become increasingly clear in Romans 8:18-39 that full maturity develops *only as we accept the risk* of present trials and suffering in order to "look like the Father" in this world. Paul thus expands on the benefits of being led by the Spirit, starting with greater fellowship with God, both now and for eternity.

B. Greater FELLOWSHIP 15b-16

1. Superior *Intimacy* 15b

But you received a Spirit of adoption by whom we cry out, "Abba, Father."

According to the Roman adoption ceremony, a child never had the privilege of calling his father, "Father," until he was placed as a son. And that privilege is what we see in v. 15: Abba, Father. The word "Abba" originally meant "Daddy." It was a term of endearment and intimacy, one of the first sounds a baby would make in the Aramaic language. But in Romans 8 it is not the little child who says "abba." The Aramaic word "abba" would not mean much to the Romans, who spoke Latin. Why, then does Paul include this term Abba in the text? If we look at the use of this word in Scripture, we find that it is a term of *privilege*.

Rarely in the OT does anyone address God as Father (Isa 63:16 and perhaps 1 Chr 29:10). In fact, nowhere in the known literature of Judaism before the coming of Jesus Christ do we have any Jew calling God his own Father. Finally, in the NT we have Jesus addressing God as "My Father" some twenty times. Only once does Jesus call His Father "God," and that was on the cross when He said, "My God, my God, why have you forsaken me?" On the cross Jesus became the sin offering for us, separated from His Father, bearing our judgment. The close, intimate fellowship between the Father and His Son was broken for the first time since eternity past, so instead of addressing his Father with deep intimacy, Jesus calls Him "God." Every other time it is, "My Father." In fact, some 170 times in the NT he speaks of "the Father" or "My Father."

In the special case of John's Gospel, Jesus mentions the Father over a hundred times, but none in Matthew and only three times in Mark. This is because John always reserves the term *huios*, son, for Jesus in his Gospel. Nowhere in John's Gospel do we see other Christians being called the sons of God. They are only called children, little children, believers, or disciples. The term "son" was reserved for Jesus. And it is only Jesus who addresses his God as Father.

In the Garden of Gethsemane it was Jesus who cried out in prayer, not as a baby but as a dependent son, "Abba, Father." It is noteworthy that *abba* only occurs one time in the Gospels and that was from the lips of Jesus in the Garden. We suggest, then, that abba was a term of great intimacy on the part of a mature son with intimate fellowship and dependence on his father. This is the intimacy Paul has in mind in Romans 8:15, as opposed to John's gospel where "children" are in view. Here, then, we see the mature son calling his Father "Abba" after he is "placed as a son," adopted, being led by the Spirit of God (8:14) — just as Jesus Himself was "appointed" or "placed" as a Son by the Father when *He* was empowered by "the Spirit of holiness" (1:4).

This is the adoption in view in Hebrews 1, with its attendant royal inheritance — a reign over the world to come (Heb 2:5-9). The OT basis for this inheritance is a "reward" covenant, known as a "covenant of grant."[3] When a servant showed exemplary faithfulness, his lord might choose to reward him by adopting him and giving him a piece of land. In the adoption ceremony the lord would say, "Today I have begotten you; you will be a son to me, and I will be a father to you." It is this OT cultural practice that the NT authors have in view: Jesus came to earth as a Suffering Servant, but He ascended as a Son (Rom 1:3-4)[4] and received

---

3   Moshe Weinfeld, "The Covenant of Grant in the Old Testament and the Ancient Near East," *Journal of the American Oriental Society* 90 (April-June 1970): 184.

4   Martin Hengel (*The Son of God* [Philadelphia: Fortress, 1976]) has argued that there are actually *three* phases to the sonship of Christ: before the earth, on the earth, and after the ascension.

the inheritance of a faithful Son (Heb 1:4-14), along with His "companions" (*metochoi*, 1:9, 14). Thus Paul can also say that His companions share the Son's intimacy with the Father, as well as His inheritance, for they too fulfill their "obligation" as faithful, adopted "sons of God" who are led by the Spirit in the face of suffering (Rom 8:12-17).

One father was deeply impacted by this superior intimacy when his daughter got the news that her fiancé had suddenly been killed in a car accident. Deeply distressed, she went into her room and shut the door. Her mother heard her sobbing and finally said to her husband, "I think you better go up and see her; she needs a father right now." So he quietly went to the room where his daughter was sobbing. When he cracked open the door he saw her kneeling beside the bed with her head buried in her hands and crying out, "Oh, Father, Father, Father . . ." He quietly shut the door again, went back downstairs, and said to his wife, "She's in better hands than mine." This daughter had privileged intimacy with her Father in heaven. Is the Father the One to whom we pour out our hearts and with whom we share our troubles, burdens, joys, and triumphs as we face the trials of growing up to become "mature sons"? The greater intimacy we have with the Father amid suffering is rooted in the superior *assurance* of being in His family that we would expect from such a "Spirit of adoption."

2. Superior *Assurance*   16

The Spirit Himself bears witness with our spirit that we are children of God.

Assurance of salvation is one of the most important foundations of the spiritual life — it is the difference between a "have-to" and a "thank you" kind of life, the difference between *faith* and *works* as the way to please God. If I think I have to persevere in good works in order to make sure I will go to heaven, then I cannot logically have full assurance of salvation until I die. And that is just what some major branches of Christianity teach. Roman Catholics claim we *can't* be sure in this life where we will go when we die. Arminians say we must be faithful until death or *lose* our salvation, and most Five Point Calvinists claim we *never had* salvation if the "right" works are not evident. Obviously, none of these approaches offers reliable assurance of salvation, since their source of assurance depends on the ongoing production of good fruit.

So what happened to 1 John 5:13, which says that anyone who has believed on the name of the Son of God can *know right now* that he has eternal life? It is not a future hope or anybody's guess. It is certain knowledge — now. And what is the basis of this knowledge, this assurance? Simply God's promises — the Bible tells me so. That's why we don't have to wait until we die to have the "blessed assurance" that we will spend eternity with our Maker. Perhaps the best known and most loved verse in the Bible is John 3:16, which says, "For God so loved the world that He gave His only begotten Son that whosoever believes in Him shall not perish but have everlasting life." It is a promise.

The promises of God are essential for our assurance, and they are our primary source. However, they are not our only source. There is also what we call secondary or "corroborating" assurance: it is our Christian walk, our *experience*. Some will recoil from this statement, saying, "Then we are right back to what everyone else is saying about perseverance until the end of our lives." No, we are not. Our experience can never be our primary or essential source of assurance. But it *can* serve as a back-up — Romans 8:16 is a case in point. To deny this is just as unbiblical as claiming one cannot have *any* assurance in this life. Neither extreme is biblical.

Each of us goes through times of darkness and gloom, storms that often stem from our own failures and sin. During those times "in the pit" we are easy targets for a spirit of fear that can lead us to wonder whether God will cut us off or, worse yet, whether we are Christians at all. An adopted child especially needs reassurance. Since our family has adopted two children from Russia, we have firsthand knowledge of the bonding issues adopted children have. The older they are when adopted, the more difficult the bonding, because they aren't sure to whom they really belong. It can take months or even years for a sense of belonging and bonding to develop. And if the adopted child comes from the slums, he may feel especially unworthy of the grace and love of his adopting family.

These observations have relevance to Paul's argument, since adoption provides the backdrop for his portrayal of the Father/child relationship in Romans 8. When I need assurance as a newly adopted child, I am not concerned about my privileges as a mature son. I just want to know that I am in the family, that I am one of His children. This assurance comes primarily from the promises of God. But during later times of adversity and self-doubt, it comes secondarily from the Holy Spirit, and Paul will expand on this ministry of the Spirit in our suffering in the second half of Romans 8.

In Ephesians 1:13 the Holy Spirit is the seal from the Father that marks us as His permanent possession. In 2 Corinthians 1:22 the Father gives us the Holy Spirit as a down payment (*arrabōn*) to assure us that we belong to Him. We are presently "on lay away," but at the appointed time the redemption of our body will be complete. And here in Romans 8:16 the Holy Spirit has been appointed our legal guardian until that final day of redemption — our official tutor to teach us and train us for a life in the royal family. The very presence of our tutor from heaven assures us that the King of the universe truly has adopted us.

For the mature son, however, there is a *superior assurance* available — he has experienced the power of the Spirit; he has allowed the Spirit to lead him, guide him, teach him, and train him; and through the years the Spirit has put to death one foul deed or practice of the flesh after another (8:13). Each time the Spirit does another work in his life, the growing son has further assurance that he is a child of the King and growing into His likeness.

Unfortunately, the carnal believer knows little of this internal testimony or power of the Holy Spirit. He has rejected the leadership of his appointed tutor. Instead he has chosen to go back to this old tutor, the flesh. As he walks in darkness, he is like a near-sighted man that stumbles along, unable to see heaven before him or hell behind him. "He cannot even remember the day his sins were purged" (2 Pet 1:9).

The point is that a believer who logs more time walking with the Spirit, experiencing His power, watching the scales of his old life peel off like the skin of a snake — this maturing believer has greater and greater assurance of his salvation. That is one of the benefits of growing up. And greater assurance only enhances our intimacy with God, thus leading to even greater fellowship. But besides the promise of Greater Freedom (8:14-15a) and Greater Fellowship (8:15b-16), Paul offers one more powerful incentive to grow up — the promise of a Greater Future.

C. Greater FUTURE   17

And if children, then heirs — heirs of God and joint heirs with Christ, if indeed we suffer with Him, that we may also be glorified together.

By calling Jesus "the firstborn of many brethren" (8:29), Paul alludes to the rule of *primogeniture*: the birthright of the firstborn. In OT times this meant that the firstborn son inherited twice as much as the others. Here in 8:17, Paul is therefore claiming that while all of God's children are His *heirs*, those willing to suffer with Christ will be *joint-* or *co-heirs* with *Him*, the Firstborn. In other words, those who remain faithful in suffering with Him have a greater inheritance together with Him when He returns — a Greater Future.

This is not meant to promote envy or jealousy in heaven. We will have no flesh or Sin Nature in heaven, so there will be no works of the flesh, either. Rather, Jesus is motivating us with his promise of a Greater Future, but it will not be revealed until His second coming when He establishes His millennial kingdom (see Matt 19:28-30). Christ uses various concepts to explain this Greater Future to His disciples. Sometimes He pictures it in terms of rewards for faithful service (Matt 16:27). Other times He calls it an "inheritance" (Matt 19:29). Here Paul is doing the same thing: with the backdrop of adoption laws in mind when Paul writes Romans 8, he aims to motivate his readers with the promise of their future inheritance.

As children of the King, all believers are heirs. We all inherit a glorified body and live with the King for eternity. But, if we take up our cross (suffer) and follow Him, we will have a greater inheritance, a Greater Future, when the King comes. Although some make no distinction between a *child* and a *disciple*, this confuses the *free gift* of eternal life to anyone who believes in Jesus Christ with the *high cost* of following Him. We see this in Luke 14:15-35, where the free supper of salvation differs radically from the high price of being His disciple. How blessed to be like the 144,000 of Revelation 14 who were willing to follow Him wherever He went and will be richly rewarded. But the price is high, the cost is steep.

Scholars who make no distinction between *believers* and *followers* claim that those who are not willing to pay this price and follow Jesus wherever He goes are simply not born again at all. They resort to Greek grammar in Romans 8:17 to claim that the *if* of v. 17b speaks of reality, or something that will actually come to pass in every case, so it is often translated "since" instead of "if." This leads to the conclusion that only those who suffer for Christ are elect.[5] But this is a misuse of the Greek language to support a theological position; Free Grace Theology does not force us into this all or nothing position.[6]

The Greek "*men . . . de . . .*" construction in this verse ("on the one hand . . . on the other hand . . .") marks a disjunction between "heirs of God" and "co-heirs with Christ," and it parallels the distinction between "children" (8:15, 21) and "sons" (8:14, 19).[7] Every believer is a child of God and therefore an *heir*. But *joint heirship* with Christ is offered to those willing to identify with Him and His righteousness to the point of suffering with Him (see 1 Pet 2:19-24; 3:14); and this hope affords us added motivation in our dark hours.

This is perfectly consistent with what Jesus taught as well as John, the disciple who Jesus loved. Perhaps none was closer to Jesus than John, who was among his first disciples and entrusted with special tasks. He lived thirty years longer than the others, who were martyred during the sixties. Finally, at the end of his

---

5   See Thomas R. Schreiner, *Romans*, BECNT 6 (Grand Rapids, MI: Baker, 1998), 428; and Moo, *Romans*, 506.

6   There are four ways to express a conditional ("if . . , then . . .") clause in Greek. The construction in Romans 8:17 expresses a "first class condition." This typically signifies *reality* or something that will *actually* come to pass, so that "if" (*eiper*) would be translated "since." However, the same condition often *assumes* the reality of the condition for the sake of argument, even if it *may not* actually be true. This is the case in Romans 8:17. See William N. W. Pass, "A Reexamination of Calvin's Approach to Romans 8:17," *Bibliotheca Sacra* 170 (Jan–March 2013), 69-81.

7   Ibid. Hence, not all "children" become fully mature as "sons" but all have some share in *eternal glory*, as indicated by 8:21.

life, in exile on a lonely island, John writes Revelation.[8] Imagine the intimacy of this man who lived only for Jesus for over seventy years and knew what it meant to be an "overcomer" (Jn 16:33; 1 Jn 5:4-5), a co-heir with Christ. In a vision from Jesus, John sees the New Jerusalem coming down out of heaven from God to a new earth and atmosphere. The God of heaven has chosen to make His tabernacle among men, so John asks what inheritance is reserved for men in God's city on this new earth (Rev 21:6).

Jesus answers by describing three categories of men. First, whosoever wants can drink of the water of life *freely*. John would have no confusion over this imagery; water was his metaphor for eternal life. John could remember this object lesson all too clearly from the well of Sychar in Samaria. There He told a lonely, empty, thirsty Samaritan woman that He could give her water so she would never thirst again. It was hers for the asking. Anyone who thirsts may drink the water of eternal life. It is absolutely free (21:6).

But then a second category of men is mentioned: "The one who overcomes shall inherit these things." Whereas the water of life was free for the asking, the Master had taught John that inheritance only came to the *victorious*. Salvation cost us nothing, but full inheritance would cost us everything. To *possess* God's kingdom could only be gained by selfless sacrifice. And as if to underscore the close intimacy that would come with this inheritance, a heavenly voice says, "I shall be his God and he shall be my son" (21:7).

John can hardly believe what he is writing. As mentioned previously, in all his works (the Gospel, three letters, and the Revelation thus far) he had never used the word "son" for anyone other than Jesus our Lord. Believers were always "children," "little children," "believers," or "disciples." Now the Spirit has told him to call the "overcomer" (the mature, grown-up believer) a *son*, an actual *heir of the Father!* John had used the inheritance illustration slightly differently from Paul. In John all children were *potential* heirs, but only a child who grew up became an *actual* heir. For Paul *all* children were heirs, but God's sons were *co-heirs*. Despite this variation, both Paul and John recognized God's use of inheritance as an incentive for victorious living in this life with a view to a Greater Future. Now John would also call the coheirs *sons*.

---

8 Many NT scholars believe all the NT books were written before the destruction of the temple in AD 70. The reasoning is: how could a Jew writing post-destruction of the temple not mention the most significant event in the history of Judaism during the past several centuries? The grammar of John 5:2 is also marshaled as evidence, where the present tense of *eimi* ("is") points to the existence of the Pool of Bethesda at the time of John's writings. The "historical present" is not an option since it never employs the verb "to be" (*eimi*).

John's third category of men was unbelievers, who have their "portion" in the Lake of Fire (Rev 21:8). So, John has two basic categories for humanity: believers and unbelievers. But among the believers there are two subgroups: those who have received the free gift of eternal life and those who have both the *gift* and the *inheritance* because they have grown in their faith.[9]

So then, who are God's sons? Those who are led by the Spirit (Rom 8:14) are His sons, and those who suffer for His cause (8:17-19) are His sons. The two are very likely the same group; that is, all those who are led by the Spirit and grow up are also destined to suffer with Him, as Paul affirms in 2 Tim 3:12: "All that will live godly in Christ Jesus will suffer."

A final benefit of maturity I have not yet mentioned is the *joy* of growing up. One of the great thrills of my own firstborn was riding the horse in front of K-Mart. It was not alive and it did not go anywhere, but to Jimmy it was big stuff. As soon as I put a quarter in the slot, he was bucking and holding on for dear life with a big smile. But that is just as far as some get in the Christian life: lots of fun and lots of motion, but no real progress.

When Jimmy was five, a friend of ours who trained horses invited us out to ride one Sunday afternoon. Jimmy was in for a brand new thrill. Now he sat astride a real, live horse. Nancy led him around and around her training track. Now he was starting to get somewhere, but in reality he was just going in circles. This is the Christian who has been at it for awhile. Although God can use him, much of the time he may only experience the despair of Romans 7, seeing no real freedom or lasting joy. It may beat sitting on a horse in front of K-Mart but it's still just going in circles.

But when he was eight I took Jimmy along to meet with some other families at a farm near Tomball. They had several horses, so Jimmy and I picked out Scout and Silver. Off we went, Tonto and the Lone Ranger. I had never seen Jimmy smile so big. Now he was on the open range. He was not confined to the front of

---

9   Another approach to Rev 21:8 actually strengthens the argument for a distinction between subgroups of believers with respect to future inheritance. The Greek word for "portion" is *meros*, the same word used in John 13:8-10. There, Jesus told Peter—a *believer* ("you are clean")—that if he refused to let Jesus wash his feet, he would have no *meros* with him, implying *loss of fellowship* with Christ but also *loss of future co-inheritance*. So, while Revelation 21:8 is traditionally assumed to refer only to the destiny of *unbelievers*, John could also be including carnal *believers* whose future co-inheritance ("portion") with Christ is burned up in the Lake of Fire (compare 1 Cor 3:11-15). John's point would then be to contrast those who inherit a *full* portion ("all things," Rev 21:7) with all who *lose* their inheritance, whether *believers* or *unbelievers* (21:8), for their failure to display God's righteousness and uphold his reputation before the world. For Paul, mature sons of God inherit a *full portion* with Jesus (Rom 8:17b-19), just as John's "overcomers," for they are led by the Spirit (8:14) and thereby fulfill His *dikaiōma* ("righteous requirement," 8:4; see note 7, Chapter 12, "War and Peace").

a shopping center or the circle of a training track. Now that was true freedom — and *great joy*.

So why shouldn't we live forever in some sort of Never, Never Land where there are no responsibilities and we can leave all the work for someone else to do? Why should we grow up? Paul gives us three good reasons. As we grow up, we will enjoy a Greater Freedom from our Sin Nature, a Greater Fellowship with our Savior, and a Greater Future when He returns. It is to this future that Paul now turns in view of present suffering.

CHAPTER 17

"THE GLORY OF GOD"
Romans 8:18-25

"So you think you've had it rough?" That was the eye-catcher on the front page of the Houston Post. It seems no matter how many bad hands we've been dealt in life, there is always someone who has had worse hands than we. Take the case of Roy Reep, whose streak of bad luck began at age three when his brother accidentally fired a .38 bullet into his face. "The bullet went through the roof of my mouth and knocked off the whole side of my face," says Reep. Six years later a friend pushed him off a barrel. When Roy hit the ground, his head split open. At age eleven, Roy's dad accidentally hit him in the head while chopping wood. Two years later doctors operated to correct a sinus condition. They found two teeth lodged in his nose, apparently from the shooting ten years earlier.

Roy then spent sixteen years without major mishap until he decided to enter the ministry. While driving to seminary in Greensboro, he was in a car wreck and broke both hips and his pelvis, puncturing his kidney and rupturing his bladder. He lay in a hospital bed for forty-two days as his organs healed. Then doctors put him in a full-length body cast to give his bones a chance to mend.

Roy finally married, but his luck did not improve. His wife accidentally shot him in the right side of his chest and his right arm. You guessed it. When Roy fell, he hit his head and neck and had to spend the next year in bed. After that, during a cataract operation, a vein burst in his left eye, leaving him blind in that eye. And then one night he took out his dentures and noticed a piece of bone protruding from his mouth. It turned out to be another tooth and a chunk of jawbone that was still left from his shooting injury at age three. Since then Reep has developed diabetes and suffers from a nerve injury to his hand.

Looking back over this formidable list of misfortunes, one might easily conclude that the fickle hand of fate had stacked the deck against Roy Reep. But Roy doesn't see it that way. Despite all his hard times he thanks God for keeping him alive. In his words, "Sometimes I sit here and cry about the mistakes I've made and wonder why He's been so good. He could have taken me away from here any one of those times. I can't understand why he didn't."

Romans deals with two huge problems that plague the Christian in his walk with God on the way toward maturity. One of those problems is *sin*; the second is *suffering*. Of course, some of our suffering comes from our sin, maybe most of it. But that kind of suffering should not shake our faith. After all, we sinned, so we deserve the consequences, many of which are quite painful. No, the kind of suffering that shakes our faith is undeserved suffering, especially when it *comes from* walking with God. It is our suffering "with Christ" that Paul first mentioned in 8:17b and now elaborates in the last half of Romans 8.

One old proverb says, "Life is a grindstone, and whether it grinds you down or polishes you up depends on the stuff you're made of." That sounds good but is non-biblical. It brings out the urge in me to fight life's battles on my own. I would rewrite it to say, "Life is a grindstone, and whether it grinds you down or polishes you up depends on the stuff *your faith* is made of." *That* I like. For suffering in this life is inevitable for all of us. And that suffering can either purify our faith from dross or pollute our faith with doubts. It all depends on what our faith is made of.

Some people build their faith on what they can see. Their motto is, "I'll believe it when I see it." But the definition of biblical faith is *the substance of things hoped for, the evidence of things not seen.* That faith comes to life in the darkness of the cemetery; it flies best in the fog by clinging to the promises of God with eyes blind-folded. So how do we get that kind of faith?

When the sea of life lays before us calm and smooth, our faith remains untested. But when the storm swallows us and the waves beat on our ship like a battering ram, up from the depths come the dragons of doubt. Does God really care about us? Is He really good? Is He really great enough to solve our giant problems? The Bible can seem like so many fairy tales. If only we could bury all these doubts and learn to deal with our suffering. If only there were something to help us endure the pain as our faith is tested.

If I make my own bed, then I need to lie in it. But if God permits trials as I grow up in faith, He will also provide the consoling truth that can sustain my hope through undeserved suffering (Rom 5:3-4). And that is how Paul wraps up his argument in Romans 8, offering four consolations to sustain that hope: the Glory of God (18-25); the Groaning of God (26-27); the Goodness of God (28-30); and the Greatness of God (31-39). The Glory of God helps us look to the goal *through* our suffering and to *endure* it rather than to be distracted from our calling.

D.	**Freedom from Despair**		**(8)**
	1.	**Victory over Sin**	**(8:1-17)**
	2.	**Victory over Suffering**	**(8:18-39)**
		a. The Glory of God	**(8:18-25)**
		1) The Glory is *Incomparable*	18-19
		2) The Glory is *Inevitable*	20-23
		3) The Glory is *Invisible*	24-25
		b. The Groaning of God	**(8:26-27)**
		c. The Goodness of God	**(8:28-30)**
		d. The Greatness of God	**(8:31-39)**

I. The Glory is INCOMPARABLE

8:18-19

*18For I consider that the sufferings of this present time are not worthy to be compared with the glory **about to** be revealed **to** us. 19For the earnest expectation of the creation eagerly waits for the revealing of the sons of God.* [**bold** = modified NKJV]

In light of the prospect of suffering mentioned in Romans 8:17b, Paul is quick to assuage any doubt over whether it is worth all the trouble to reign with Christ. When Paul says, "I consider," he is using the same banking or accounting term (*logizomai*) we have previously seen in Romans (4:3; 6:11). It is as though Paul adds up the sufferings of this time in the debit column and the glory which grows out of this suffering in the credit column. Paul is no armchair theologian; he has accumulated quite a "debit column" of suffering himself (see 2 Cor 4:8-12; 11:23-29). But even so, after tallying both sides, Paul can still conclude that the credit of glory so far exceeds the debit of suffering, it is not even worth our time to compare. So is this glory worth it?

It is to be revealed before the entire world! Conspicuously, the verb "to be revealed" (*apokalupsthēnai*, 8:18b) and the noun "the revealing" (*apokalupsin*, 8:19b) echo the very goal of the gospel (1:1, 16): the righteousness of God "being revealed" (*apokaluptetai*) by faith (1:17). Thus, those who are **to be revealed** to all Creation at Christ's return *in glory* are the very ones who **are revealing** the righteousness of God *on earth* (1:17; 8:10b). This high privilege is exclusive to "sons of God" who are willing to accept the call to follow the Spirit by faith and thereby endure "the sufferings of this present time" (8:12, 14, 18). It is the incomparability of both "revealings" in the sons of God — *righteousness now* and *glory then* — that explains why (*gar*, "for," 8:18a, 19a) the prospect of co-glorification with Christ is such a potent incentive for us to follow the Spirit in spite of suffering (8:17b).

So what will it look like? This climactic revealing of the sons of God at Christ's return (8:19) denotes an *unveiling*, as of a great sculpture or mural. Imagine Michelangelo is about to unveil his greatest work of all, as sculpture lovers from the world over gather at the appointed time. As Michelangelo enters, a hush falls over the audience. With everyone on tiptoe, every neck craned in anticipation, he takes hold of the veil covering the statue. Similarly, the earth itself "stands on tiptoe" with neck craned (that's what *apekdechetai* means in 8:19) to witness the unveiling of the sons of God.[1] God the consummate Artist will unveil His greatest work: His Portraits of Righteousness — the "bride of Christ" (Rev 19:8), "filled with the fruits of righteousness . . . to the glory and praise of God" (Phil 1:11).[2] And their glory with Christ will shine forever for all Creation to see.[3]

This prospect of co-glorification (8:17b-19) thus serves as the literary transition to 8:20-25, where the "revealing of the sons of God" is seen to herald the final consummation of God's redemptive purposes *for all Creation,* which is presently "subjected to futility."

II. The Glory Is INEVITABLE   8:20-23

A. The Groaning of *Creation*   20-22

20*For the creation was subjected to futility, not willingly, but because of Him who subjected it in hope;* 21*because the creation itself also will be delivered from the bondage of corruption into the glorious liberty of the children of God.* 22*For we know that the whole creation groans and labors with birth pangs together until now.*

---

1   The same verb (*apekdechomai*) is key to our understanding of the parallel verse in Gal 5:5: "For we through the Spirit *eagerly await* the hope of righteousness." This "hope" *is* in fact the "incomparable glory" we anticipate as mature "sons of God" who reveal the righteousness of God in *this* life by conforming through the Spirit to Christ's righteous image. Another audience is also watching: the angels await the revealing of these sons of God at the Judgment Seat (1 Cor 11:10; Matt 16:27; Mk 8:38; Lk 9:26; 12:8-9). The angel in Dan 4:13 is even called a "watcher." The cosmic scope of this "unveiling" is suited to the royal appointment of the subjects to be unveiled, *just like Jesus,* "in power according to the Spirit" (Rom 1:4; 8:4)—these "sons" are appointed to reign over the entire world, thus fulfilling the intended goal of 5:21b, "that grace might *reign* through righteousness to eternal life through Jesus Christ our Lord." The "cosmic unveiling" of royal sons within the framework of Heb 2:5-13 offers a striking parallel.

2   Thus fulfilling Rom 6:20-22; see further the APPENDIX, "What Does the Righteousness of God 'Look' Like?"

3   There is a close connection in John's writing between "glory" and "light." The believer to whom Christ is finally willing to *entrust himself* (Jn 2:23-25) is the one who "comes to the light, that his deeds may be clearly seen, that they have been done in God" (3:21). John's "people of light" (Jn 12:36) are in fact Paul's "sons of God" (Rom 8:14, 19) who will comprise the New Jerusalem. In that final consummation (Rev 21), "the bride, the Lamb's wife" (21:9) adorned with "righteous acts" (19:8) will transmit His light more brilliantly (21:22-27). This "incandescent" glory will be preserved through fire as a reward for faithful ambassadors to the world of the righteousness of God (2 Cor 5:10-21). As Christ then establishes his reign on earth, that which was not built on the foundation of Christ will be burned away as believers are "integrated" into the "temple of God" (1 Cor 3:11-17). Those who did not live in light of the future—did not keep their eye on "treasure in heaven"—will be relegated to relative "darkness" in the Kingdom of God (Matt 6:19-23).

To feel the full impact of what Paul is doing here, we need to review the broad scope and destiny of God's original work of creation. God first created the universe, including earth, in order to demonstrate His great power to the angels (Job 38:7). So the earth was originally made beautiful and ready to be inhabited (Isa 45:18). This is what we might call Stage One of earth's existence.

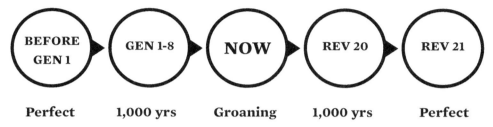

| BEFORE GEN 1 | GEN 1-8 | NOW | REV 20 | REV 21 |
| Perfect | 1,000 yrs | Groaning | 1,000 yrs | Perfect |

Fig. 1. Satan's Rebellion, God's Judgment, and the Refashioning of Creation

Sometime after the original creation,[4] Lucifer committed the original sin of challenging God's right to rule the universe. Such a challenge left God's character open to question, specifically His attributes of sovereignty and love. So Satan and the angels who followed him (one third) were cast out of heaven to earth (Isa 14:12; Rev 12:3). Apparently, they made such a mess of things that the earth was left in a state described in Hebrew as *tohu wabohu,* "without form and void." Whenever this phrase occurs elsewhere in the Hebrew OT, it refers to God's judgment (see Jer 4:23; Isa 34:11) and projects a sense of disorder. This state of judgment is described in Genesis 1:2 where we find three markers that would signify judgment, at least in the Jewish mind: darkness, salt water, and *tohu wabohu.*

Then God set into motion His plan for man. He *refashioned* the earth and the heavens (atmosphere) so that flesh and blood beings that need food and air might survive. When God finished "remodeling" (*bārā'* does not necessarily refer to *ex nihilo* creation; compare Ps 51:10), He looked it over and proclaimed it "very good" (as opposed to Platonism, which views material things as evil). A canopy of clouds protected the earth from the sun's ultraviolet rays, and a thick mist fed the plants and trees — a built-in sprinkler system. It was on *this* earth that Adam and Eve arrived. In this environment even fallen humans could live for long time

---

4   This may have taken place billions of years ago when time is viewed from the edge of the universe. Space/time is relative as opposed to the speed of light; we could have seven twenty-four hour periods from the vantage of planet earth but 14.3 billion years from the edge of the universe. On white holes and black holes and the event horizon, see Stephen Hawking with Leonard Mlodinow, *A Briefer History of Time* (New York, NY: Bantam Bell, 2005), 79-80; and D. Russell Humphreys, *Starlight & Time* (Green Forest, AR: Master Books, 1994), 31-40. On the literary design of Genesis 1 and its suitability to accommodate a variety of proposed cosmologies and time frames, see John H. Walton, *The Lost World of Genesis One* (Downers Grove, IL: InterVarsity, 2009).

periods. Adam lived to be over 900 and Methuselah lived to 969, close to 1,000 years. We might call this Stage Two of the earth's existence.

But like Lucifer, Adam went his own way and sinned under Lucifer's influence, so that even the ground was put under judgment. Man would have to toil, sweat, and struggle against the thorns and thistles to reap his crops. But from this small ripple in the Garden of Eden, sin soon spread to a full-blown tidal wave. Consequently, God told righteous Noah (Gen 6:8-9) He would send His own tidal wave and unleashed a universal flood.[5] The protective canopy of clouds collapsed and ultraviolet rays penetrated our atmosphere, forming a new "heaven" and earth. Human lifespan decreased sharply as disease and insects began their devastating march. This is earth's Stage Three, in which we now live.

What does the Bible predict for the future? Another refashioning of the earth (2 Pet 3:10) to bring it back to its original state of perfection, beginning with the unleashing of God's wrath during the Tribulation Period (Rom 2:5, 8-9; Rev 6:12-17; Amos 5:18-20). Following this Day of Wrath, Christ will rule from Jerusalem for 1,000 years in a new heavens (atmosphere) and a new earth like that before Noah's flood. Men will again live to be nearly 1000 years old. We might call this Stage Four. There will be peace on earth; the lion will lie down with the lamb (Isa 11).

At the end of the millennial reign of Christ, the earth and its atmosphere will once again be recycled by God (or created anew) to usher in Stage Five (the Day of God or Eternal State, 2 Pet 3:12). This will bring it back to its original beauty, glory and perfection before Satan & Co. trashed it up. In his spiritual, glorified body man will no longer depend on physical food and oxygen and will dwell in the New Jerusalem throughout eternity.

With this background to Romans 8:20-22, the earth is still presently groaning in Stage Three, her face riddled by disease and pockmarked by wars. The earth was subjected to futility when humanity fell (5:12) — she could not fulfill her purpose of reflecting God's glory. But she has a hope and expectantly awaits her restoration to her former state of perfection when she is "delivered from the bondage of corruption into the glorious liberty of the children of God."[6]

---

5   The flood was probably not caused by the forty days and nights of rain. More likely it was tidal action, caused either directly by God's word or by tsunamis from deep earthquakes and volcanoes from the deep, which would cause tidal action via tsunamis. Two thirds of the earth's crust is covered by water, and the Mariana Trench near Guam is deep enough (36,000 feet) to cover Mt. Everest.

6   Why does Paul say "the glorious liberty of the *children* of God" in 8:21 after referring to the glory of the *sons* of God in 8:19? Paul will soon make it clear that all who are *justified* are also *glorified* (8:30). Yet this *positional* truth of the future glory of *all* believers ("children . . . heirs of God," 8:16-17a, 21) will be *more conspicuous* in the *sons* ("co-heirs with Christ") whose Condition matches their Position by following the Spirit (8:4, 14, 17b-19). Thus, Paul very likely has *corporate* glorification in mind; the "co-heirs with Christ" ("sons," 8:19) are placed more conspicuously among *all* the "heirs of God" ("children," 8:21).

Just before the Millennium, the works of Christians will be tested by fire at the Judgment Seat of Christ, where the "sons of God" will be revealed and receive their inheritance. Many of these works will be burned up, for they were done out of self-reliant flesh, seeking the praise of men rather than God. But the works of mature sons will remain as gold, silver, and precious stones.

Earth's present groaning anticipates this future deliverance. The crunch of earthquakes in Haiti and Chili, the avalanche's rumble on Mt. Rainier, and the volcano's belch at Mt. Hood; the whine of tornados in Oklahoma, devastation of hurricanes in Texas and Louisiana, and littered bodies and debris of tsunamis in Indonesia and Sri Lanka — these are the groans of earth. She groans each fall as her leaves turn brown, her face turns white with snow and ice, and the fruit withers. She yearns to be restored to her original fruitful state. But we also groan, anticipating our own restoration as the *firstfruits* of the new creation (1 Cor 15:20-23; Jas 1:18-20).

B. The Groaning of *Believers* 23

Not only that, but we also who have the first fruits of the Spirit, even we ourselves groan within ourselves, eagerly waiting for the adoption, the redemption of our body.

This second mention of "adoption" again recalls the two stages of Roman adoption: 1) Placed as a son at age fourteen, with voting rights; 2) placed as a *mature* son at age twenty-five, with property rights. We have "voting" rights now (free to choose Sin or Righteousness, 6:16-19); but those who suffer with Christ will have "property rights" in the world to come (an inheritance in His Kingdom, 8:17b). They, like Paul, are waiting and groaning in present suffering. This "groaning" (*stenazō*) is the word used for a woman in labor, an analogy that carries over from the groaning of all creation in the preceding verse (8:22). This anticipation can encourage us in two ways:

1. Without the groan, there is no glory. This is something the angels cannot understand. In fact, in 1 Pet 1:13 it says the angels are down on their hands and knees, so to speak, to look carefully and search out the kind of salvation that would make groaning a prerequisite for glory. Of course, the salvation spoken of in 1 Peter 1:9 and 11 is not the "get into heaven" salvation (justification). If it were, then we could only get there through self-sacrifice and suffering (1 Pet 1:6). No, this salvation in 1 Peter is a salvation that points to the Judgment Seat of Christ where we see how much of our time on earth (our life) will be "saved" forever to

---

On this crucial distinction, see further note 3 above; see also Joseph Dillow, "Becoming an Heir of the World," Chapter 5, in *Final Destiny: The Future Reign of the Servant Kings* (Houston: Grace Theology Press, 2013), 76-88.

glorify God and how much will be lost, burnt up, or destroyed. (This is very likely what Peter has in view in 1 Pet 4:17a.)

But the good angels have never suffered, and they could not understand the Lord of Glory humbling Himself to suffer (the cross) before His glory (the ascension). Nor do they understand our suffering before glory. And this is one reason the mature sons of God will actually judge the angels in the world to come (1 Cor 6:3) — we will have endured something they never have nor ever will experience: suffering. So, just as in the case of a woman in labor, the groans are a necessary prerequisite for the glory to come.

On this side of glory we know this, but not experientially. For our first two children, my wife received an epidural. But ten years later our friends were using the Lamaze approach where the husband comes alongside as a coach to help his wife through natural childbirth, that is, without pain killers. So when Betty was pregnant with our third child, I went with her to Lamaze classes. When the great moment arrived, I was not much help — I just did not like watching her go through all that. But women understand the groaning experientially.

Years later I gained a better understanding. I woke up in the night with a pain so bad I knew it had to be a kidney stone. I did not tell Betty I was going to the hospital — I did not want to wake her up. So I drove the short distance to the emergency room, walked in, and before I got to the front desk with my insurance card, the receptionist said, "You've got a kidney stone, don't you?" *How did you know?* "Oh, all you men look the same when you have a kidney stone." So she took me back to a little cubicle, drew the curtain and called for a nurse to start an IV. The nurse poked me in the right arm. No blood. Two more tries. No blood. So she went to the left arm and poked me again. No blood. And again. No blood. Then she looked at me and said, "I'm having a bad night." *You're having a bad night?!!!* "I guess we'll have to wait for the doctor."

One hour, two hours, still no doctor. And that meant no morphine. Now when you have a kidney stone, you just can't sit still, you have to walk. So I began walking around the rectangle of cubicles right past the nurses' station, wearing that cute little gown that's so airy on the backside. Each time I passed the nurses station I groaned, just to make sure they didn't forget me. About the fourth time around, my nurse came out and said the only doctor on duty was still busy on the second floor. I would just have to wait. I finally got tired of walking and went back to my torture cell, *three* hours after arriving.

My nurse finally came in and started some small talk. "Are you Betty's husband?" Turns out she knew my wife who for years had been an advocate of conservative Christian values in our political system. Then this nurse who could not even start my IV said, "Well, I've had babies and I've had kidney stones. Kidney stones are worse. I think it is good for you men to have kidney stones so you can better appreciate what it's like for us to go through childbirth." Groan. At least I had a better understanding of Romans 8:23.

The doctor finally came down with "the glory" and put an end to my groaning. And when Jesus comes He will bring the final glory with Him. The groaning will be over.

2. We forget the groans and focus on the glory. No one wants to remember his wife in labor. No one takes pictures of his wife in labor. I have never seen a picture of a wife in labor. "Look, here's a picture of my wife in labor. Look how she is groaning." We take pictures of our babies. The baby is what we are waiting for. Little scrawny things. As Bill Cosby announced to his wife after their Lamaze experience, "Look, dear. You've given birth to a lizard." But what a beautiful lizard. We take so many pictures we make folders of them. We send them out through i-photo, email, and Facebook. We see bumper stickers that say, "Ask me about my grandbaby." If you do, out comes the folder. There has never been a bumper sticker which says, "Ask me about my daughter's labor." Why not? Who wants to remember the groan? We want to remember the glory. "Hey, here's the result of that painful experience." What was it like? "I don't even remember. But wow. Look at the result."

We Christians can learn a lesson from this. God says the glory is about to come. But *we walk around like we are going be in eternal labor*. That was the point of v. 22 where Paul has been taking about the groaning of creation, waiting . . . But now he gets personal and talks about groaning *as Christians*. We groan just like the woman in labor. But God wants us to stop focusing on our groans and start focusing on the glory:

> Oh that will be,
> Glory for me
> Glory for me
> Glory for me.
> When by His Grace,
> I shall look on His face,
> Oh, that will be,
> Glory for me.

Yes, the glory will be Incomparable. And though our groaning is inevitable, the point here is that since the Glory *trumps* the Groaning, it will also *replace* the Groaning for it too is Inevitable. For this reason, though the Glory is presently Invisible, we still have the full hope of seeing God's glory and should therefore persevere to the end.

III. The Glory Is INVISIBLE   8:24-25

24For we were saved in this hope, but hope that is seen is not hope; for why does one still hope for what he sees? 25But if we hope for what we do not see, we eagerly wait for it with perseverance.

Hope is among the three great themes of the NT; it almost always refers to that blessed hope when Jesus returns for His bride at the Rapture. At that time, the initial placing of sons (adoption) that took place in phase one while we were on earth will be consummated in phase two at the Judgment Seat of Christ. Some think that to focus on the Rapture and the rewards we receive is selfish. But remember, we shall cast our crowns before Him, for He alone is worthy to wear them (Rev 4:10). The more crowns, the more glory we bring Him. The real tragedy would be to stand before Him empty-handed, with nothing to show for our gifts and opportunities to serve Him on earth. Imagine the look in His eyes if I stood before Him with nothing to offer, no crowns, nothing to glorify my Lord — perhaps the same look He gave Peter after his third denial.

But surely someone will ask, "what tangible evidence is there of such pie-in-the-sky bye and bye? I have to see it to believe it." Thomas had to see to believe, yet Jesus did not say Thomas' faith was false. He *did* say that believing *without* seeing brings greater blessing (Jn 20:29). According to Heb 11:1, faith is the evidence of things *not* seen. In fact, Paul here implies that if we can see it, there may be faith, but there is no hope. We do not hope for something we can see; if we could already see it, there would be no groaning. Hope is challenged by what we *can't* see.

I will never forget the day I ran over my own daughter with the car! A parent's worse nightmare. We had an L-shaped driveway. I was heading out for some church work when my only daughter at the time, Christie, came out to wish me good-bye. I rolled down my window, gave her a little peck on the cheek, and began to back out. As I turned the wheel, the tire caught one of her feet and she instantly went down. I heard her scream and felt the car rise up on her body. Instinctively I drove forward and rolled over her again. Sheer panic set in as I jumped out of the car and scooped up her six year old body in my arms. I placed her in the passenger seat, and drove to the hospital like I have never driven before or since.

The whole time I was driving I was looking for blood to come out of her mouth as a sign of internal injuries. As she lay there groaning, I was hoping — hoping I had not ruptured something internal that could cause her to bleed to death. I could see the tire marks on her legs and the blood from scrapes on her legs. I could not even pray. Just groaned and hoped: "Oh, Father. Oh, God. Oh, Jesus." Groan and hope.

When we got there, my eyes were riveted on the x-ray machine, hoping the machine would reveal the true story. I *could not see* inside her — her own little groans that kept my hopes alive; all I could do was hope. Finally, the x-ray machine revealed no internal damage; the car had only rolled over her foot and lower legs.

At crucial times it seems that life rolls right over us. Right now all we can do is groan. Groan and hope. Wait for the x-ray machine to look into our hearts and tell us everything is all right. Not until then will the groaning stop. Jesus says, "I've given you a hope in that I've promised to return. When I do, if you have endured in suffering for my name's sake, the glory will far outweigh the groans. Though you cannot see the glory right now, it is *inevitable* and it is *incomparable*."

Our hope in suffering found in Rom 8:18-25 is the Glory of God. Paul urges us to shift our focus from our present groaning to our future glory. Someday we will forget the groans, but we will always remember the glory. C. S. Lewis put it this way in *Mere Christianity:*

> Hope means a continual looking forward to the eternal world. It does not mean that we are to leave the present world as it is. If you read history you will find that the Christians who did the most for the present world were just those who thought most of the next. It is since Christians have largely ceased to think of the other world that they have become so ineffective in this. Aim at Heaven and you will get earth "thrown in": aim at earth and you will get neither.[7]

---

7 C. S. Lewis, *Mere Christianity*, III, 10 (New York: HarperCollins, 2001), 118.

CHAPTER 18

"THE GROANING OF GOD"
Romans 8:26-27

C an God heal a broken heart? Of course. *Will* He heal a broken heart? That is another question. At Johns Hopkins University cardiologists did a study of a hundred people with what they called "Broken Heart Syndrome" and found that in this kind of stress the brain sends chemicals to the heart that weaken the heart by damaging its tissue.[1] Here's what Wikipedia says about "broken heart":[2]

> A broken heart (or heartbreak) is a common metaphor used to describe the intense emotional pain or suffering one feels after losing a loved one, through death, divorce, moving, being rejected, or other means. It is usually associated with losing a spouse or loved one, though losing a parent, child, pet, or close friend can also "break one's heart." The phrase refers to the physical pain one may feel in the chest as a result of the loss. Although "heartbreak" is usually a metaphor, there is a condition — appropriately known as Broken Heart Syndrome — in which a traumatizing incident triggers the brain to distribute chemicals that weaken heart tissue. The symptoms of a "broken heart" can be both psychological and physical:
>
> - A perceived tightness of the chest, similar to an anxiety attack
> - Stomach ache and/or loss of appetite
> - Partial or complete insomnia
> - Anger
> - Shock

---

1 Broken Heart' Syndrome: Real, Potentially Deadly but Recovery Quick," available at http://www.hopkinsmedicine.org/Press_releases/2005/02_10_05.html. Accessed October 26, 2010.

2 "Broken Heart Syndrome," available at http://en.wikipedia.org/wiki/Broken_heart. Accessed Oct 26, 2010.

- Nostalgia
- Apathy (loss of interest)
- Feelings of loneliness
- Feelings of hopelessness and despair
- Loss of self-respect and/or self-esteem
- Medical or psychological illness (depression, for example)
- Suicidal thoughts (in extreme cases)
- Nausea
- Fatigue
- The thousand-yard stare
- Constant or frequent crying
- A feeling of complete emptiness
- In extreme cases, death

The Bible addresses the broken heart due to undeserved suffering. Romans 8:18-39 deals not with the deserved suffering that comes from our own sin or foolishness, but the *undeserved* suffering that strikes the innocent man due to no sin of his own, or the righteous man precisely *because* he is living for Christ. One way a righteous man can suffer is from a broken heart.

In Psalm 69 David was full of heaviness after the death of Absalom. In v. 1 David says, "Save me, O God! For the waters have come up to my neck. I sink in deep mire, where there is no standing; I have come into deep waters, where the floods overflow me." David is hurting so badly he is falling apart. That's a broken heart. He feels as though he has been hit by a tsunami and is being sucked out into a sea of emptiness. In verse 20 we read: "Reproach has broken my heart, and I am full of heaviness; I looked for someone to take pity, but there was none; and for comforters, but I found none."

Notice that "Reproach has broken my heart." It wasn't his son's death; it was the insults, the verbal attacks. He looked for sympathy and comfort but found none. In fact, "They gave me gall for my food; for my thirst they gave me vinegar to drink" (v. 21). Does this remind you of anyone? Now make no mistake, David was far from perfect; the Psalm even refers to his sins. Yet his suffering was undeserved: "because for Your sake I have borne reproach" (v. 7); even the elders who sit at the gate speak against him "because zeal for your house has eaten me up" (vv. 9, 12).

I hope you never suffer from "Broken Heart Syndrome." But David did, and we can tell from the familiar words in the Psalm that Someone else did, too. How does God help in these times of undeserved suffering? We have suggested that at the end of Romans 8 God offers four sources of hope in suffering. The first was to shift our focus from present groaning to the glory that will be revealed when the mature sons of God are unveiled. The second is found in 8:26-27 — it is the groaning of the Spirit of God Himself.

2. Victory over Suffering		**(8:18-39)**
a. The Glory of God		**(8:18-25)**
b. The Groaning of God		**(8:26-27)**
1.	*Support* of the Spirit	26a
2.	*Supplication* of the Spirit	26b
3.	*Success* of the Spirit	27
c. The Goodness of God		**(8:28-30)**
d. The Greatness of God		**(8:31-39)**

I. SUPPORT of the Spirit   8:26a

Likewise the Spirit also helps in our weaknesses.

We first need to explain the word "likewise." What does the Holy Spirit do in vv. 26-27 that resembles what is going on in vv. 18-25? At first we look in vain for any similarity. There is *support* from the Spirit in v. 26a, but not in vv. 18-25. There is *prayer* in 26b, but not in vv. 18-25. There is *searching* in v. 27, but not in vv. 18-25. So what is similar? It is the "groaning." Creation groans in v. 22, Christians groan in v. 23. Likewise, the Holy Spirit groans in v. 26b. That is why we have called vv. 26-27, "The Groaning of God." We will find that the Spirit's groaning is a great source of comfort in the midst of suffering.

This suggestion is supported by 2 Timothy 1:7 where we are told that "we have not received a spirit of fear, but of power and of love and of a sound mind" to answer our weaknesses. So what are "our weaknesses"? Some Greek manuscripts read it as singular, "weakness." In this case interpreters assume that it most likely refers to our weakness in prayer. But most manuscripts read the plural, "weaknesses," with a broader range of possible references to include all of our weaknesses during times of suffering.

The same verse suggests that fear is a prominent weakness in suffering. Take for instance the patient just informed of terminal cancer. Fear cuts through that cancer victim like a surgeon's knife; fear of pain, agony, and death to come. But the Spirit can help that weakness with His calm assurance, peace and longsuffering. Another weakness we may encounter is our inability to control our circumstances. But the Spirit's answer to that weakness is His power to either change our circumstances or enable us to endure them. Another is loneliness. We feel all alone in our world of misery, often thinking that no one faces quite the same problems we have. But the Spirit comforts us with His love and reminds us that even our Savior endured suffering unto death.

Digging Deeper: The Semantic Range of "Weakness" in the NT

So, how else in Scripture does the Holy Spirit, the divine author, use this word "weakness" (*astheneia*)? If we look at the range of conditions covered by this word, there seem to be at least five different uses whenever we find the noun or verb in the NT:

1. **Sickness** (Jas 5:14). This is the most frequent use of the word. It tells us that the Spirit has a special ministry of supporting those sick in body when they lean on Him. Many testimonies and studies bear witness to the fact that those who are strong in faith recover more quickly.

2. **Uneducated Conscience** (1 Cor 8:9, 11, 12). We often do not know the Scripture well enough or have not grown enough in wisdom to know what is right and what is wrong before God. Here the convicting ministry of the Spirit helps us in that weakness in order to keep us from harm's way.

3. **Human Inability** (Rom 6:19). We cannot have victory in the Christian life through our own strength ("flesh").[3] "'Not by might, nor by power, but by my Spirit,' says the Lord of hosts" (Zech 4:6).

4. **During Persecution** (Heb 11:34). This is where that Spirit of power and of love and of a sound mind (2 Tim 1:7) can enable us to endure abuse, love those who persecute us, and keep our sanity in the process.

5. **Thorn in the Flesh** (2 Cor 12:7-10). Here Paul actually boasts about his weakness in the flesh, for he sees it as an opportunity for the Spirit to make him strong. This is the real beauty of our weaknesses. If we will just turn these areas over to the Spirit's support, He can turn our weakness into God's strength. Ultimately we can find glory in our own weaknesses.

[END OF EXCURSUS]

Romans 8:26a applies to all these circumstances. We will not find the Holy Spirit's help in any of them until we realize that He stands by us ready to help (*synantilambanomai*). This word "help" occurs only twice in the NT. It means "to come to the aid of, be of assistance to, help someone" (BDAG, 965). It is as if someone were about to fall, and the Holy Spirit extends a helping hand to hold him up, or a shoulder for him to lean on. The saying "God helps those who

---

3   In Rom 6:19, "the weakness of your flesh" may mean "the weakness *that is* our flesh." If *astheneia* is also singular in 8:26 (see discussion above), then Paul may well be echoing 6:19 in this context and thus underscoring *the Spirit's power to overcome the deeds of the flesh when we are afflicted by suffering* (8:13, 17b-18, 23).

help themselves" is not in the Bible. Actually, God helps those who *lean on Him*. That's why we are calling 8:26a "The Support of the Spirit."

We can view life in three stages. In the first stage, which only lasts about nine months, we find ourselves in total darkness. Yet in this darkness God is doing a work, some say His greatest work, His magnum opus. He is creating form, to be sure, but He is also creating senses — eyes to see, ears to hear, a nose to smell, a tongue to taste, and the capacity for touch — for us to utilize in the second stage of our existence.

The second stage of our lives can last up to seventy or eighty years. And during this stage God is also creating senses . . . *spiritual* senses in His spiritual children who have trusted in Jesus for life (1 Cor 2:6–3:4). He is building spiritual eyes to see His handiwork and purposes; spiritual ears to hear His still, small voice; spiritual olfactory nerves for the sweet aroma of sacrifices for His kingdom; tactile capacity to sense the leading of the Holy Spirit; and spiritual taste buds to hunger and thirst after righteousness. At times, however, we are so overwhelmed by this physical world that we use only a fraction of the full range of these spiritual senses; but they are being prepared for us to use in the third stage of our existence — ruling with Christ over the world to come, which lasts forever.

If time means anything, God is far more interested in developing our spiritual senses than our physical. But one particular feature distinguishes the first stage of our existence from the second: babies in the first stage don't self-abort. Some external force must be brought to bear in a physical abortion. But God's children can clearly self-abort in the second stage of our lives. By that we don't mean that one of God's children can cease to be His child. But he can certainly resist the work of the Holy Spirit in his life. He can quench and he can grieve the Holy Spirit by sin. He can lean on his own strength instead of the strength of God's Spirit, the very One He sent to support us amid suffering. James adds, "The Spirit who dwells in us yearns jealously" (Jas 4:5). What a tragedy, then, to abort the very work God is trying to accomplish in our lives by the Spirit Jesus sent to sustain us through the tough times.

Now we see that the Support of the Spirit as He consoles us during suffering is matched by the Supplication of the Spirit in our groaning before God (8:26b).

II. SUPPLICATION of the Spirit   8:26b

For we do not know what we should pray for as we ought, but the Spirit Himself makes intercession for us with groanings which cannot be uttered.

What a comfort to know that in the midst of suffering the Holy Spirit is praying on our behalf. In the first clause, *proseuchomai* ("pray") means praying in general.

However in the second clause, *enteuxis* ("intercession") means to draw close to a person so as to enter into familiar speech and communion with him.[4]

Suppose you have a business problem that can only be solved by Warren Buffet. So you write Warren a formal letter requesting a meeting. He grants your request, but when you fly up to Omaha you are so nervous you can hardly talk. But let's also suppose you were personal friends with Bill Gates. Gates sees your problem and says, "You know, Warren and I are really close. He donated thirty billion to our philanthropic foundation. Would you like me to put in a good word for you?" *Are you kidding??? Of course!!* So Gates walks right into Warren's office without knocking and says, "Hey, Warren . . . about this friend of mine down in Texas . . ." That is the freedom and boldness of access this word *enteuxis* conveys.

It is the same sense as in Hebrews 4:16, "Let us therefore come boldly to the throne of grace, that we may obtain mercy and find grace to help in time of need." The word "therefore" points back to God's open-door policy in 4:15: we have a King, a High Priest, who has felt our weaknesses and gains us access before God. There it is again — that word "weaknesses" (*astheneiais*) is the same word we encountered in Romans 8:26a. He knows how it hurts, He has been there; it would be hard to name a category of human suffering that He did not endure. Even His own spiritual children left and forsook Him. Israel, His chosen one, went off to play the harlot. Yes he surely does know how it feels. And now His Spirit lives inside of us and hurts right along with us as we go through undeserved suffering. He groans with us.

Some believe these groanings of the Spirit are the same as speaking in tongues. Suffice it to say, the word *alaletois* ("which cannot be uttered") means just that: the groanings cannot be uttered. They don't make a sound. The word for groaning in v. 26 (*stenagmois*) is an *internal* groaning that differs from *audible* birth pang groans (*synōdin*), as in v. 22, where the two corresponding verbs occur together yet are clearly distinguished. So a groan that cannot be uttered cannot be the equivalent of audible tongue-speaking.

Isn't it great to know that when we are hit with the sledgehammer suffering, the Spirit is there praying for us? When that blow comes, we are so numb with pain we don't know how to pray. We instinctively fall before the Lord in prayer and open our mouths but we can't produce adequate words to express our need. Well, there is good news. If we stay on our knees, even if we cannot articulate a coherent prayer, there is One praying on our behalf at that very moment. He knows how to pray, even when we don't. And if the fervent prayers of a righteous

---

4   Richard Chenevix Trench, *Synonyms of the New Testament* (Grand Rapids, MI: Eerdmans, 1969), 188-92.

man avail much (Jas 5:16b), imagine what the groans of the very Spirit of God can do. He hurts right along with us for He loves us and dwells within us.

3. SUCCESS of the Spirit 8:27

Now He who searches the hearts knows what the mind of the Spirit is, because He makes intercession for the saints according to the will of God.

How can we be sure the prayer of the Holy Spirit is of any avail? This is precisely the assurance we have in v. 27. The groanings of the Spirit may not be heard, but that does not mean they are unknown. God the Father searches our hearts — the very place where the Holy Spirit lives — He knows the mind of the Spirit. There is no need for audible groans.

Have you ever had a close friend or spouse who just seemed to know what you were thinking? You could sit together and communicate without words. Or you could begin a sentence, and they could finish it. This is because you all think so much alike; you are frequently on the same wavelength, and you are also so intimate that no words need be spoken in order to communicate. This is what this verse is saying. The Holy Spirit and the Father are always on the same wavelength. They are one, very intimate — each knows what the other is thinking (see 1 Cor 2:10-11). As a result, the Spirit's prayers are known perfectly by the Father. And they are also the most effective prayers ever offered since they are prayed according to the will of the Father.

If you want a passage to share next time you go to the hospital, try this one. When someone calls and tells me of a situation in the hospital or the home and asks me to pray, I gladly fall to my knees knowing all the while that I really don't know how to pray for the situation. Although I don't know God's will in the matter, that does not discourage me from praying, for I know the Spirit Himself is praying at that moment, and He knows the will of God and prays accordingly (compare 1 Cor 2:9-12). These prayers are always heard and return with the right answer, because the Spirit prays according to God's will.[5] Sometimes even prolonged suffering plays a central role in that purpose. Witness the cross!

---

5 The prepositional phrase "according to the will of God" literally reads *kata Theon*, "according to God," and is grammatically parallel to *kata pneuma*, "according to the Spirit," in 8:4-5 and also in 8:13, by implied contrast with *kata sarka* ("according to the flesh"). Thus, the intended sense in 8:27 is that those who walk "according to the Spirit" (*kata pneuma*) have a distinct advantage in their weakness because they allow the Spirit to intercede on their behalf and thereby "align" them with God's will (*kata Theon*). As we shall see, this intended "alignment" continues in 8:28 with another parallel phrase (*kata prothesin*), "according to plan." Hence, the "sons of God" who choose to "walk according to the Spirit" end up fulfilling God's purposes "according to plan." This in turn sets up the "golden chain" in 8:29-30, which affirms God's providence in fulfilling that plan.

Digging Deeper: Relying on the Spirit to Display Righteousness

As one who took on "the likeness of sinful flesh" (Rom 8:3; Phil 2:7; Heb 2:14), Jesus himself leaned on the Holy Spirit to set an example for us. In Matthew 12 the miracles done by Jesus are explicitly attributed to the power of the Holy Spirit. Why didn't Christ just use His own power? It was to set an example for us, as He too came "in the likeness of sinful flesh" (Rom 8:3). Christ voluntarily limited the use of His divine attributes when He came to earth. Though He was all-powerful, he chose to rely on the power of the Holy Spirit to perform His miracles. I would suggest, however, that Jesus used the power of the Holy Spirit primarily to display the righteousness of God — Paul's core purpose in Romans for the "gospel of God" (1:1, 16-17). Again, it was to set an example, that we might follow in His steps in spite of suffering (1 Pet 2:21). Isaiah 61:1-3 further explains (emphasis added):

> "The Spirit of the Lord GOD is upon Me,
> Because the LORD has anointed Me
> To preach good tidings to the poor;
> He has sent Me to heal the brokenhearted,
> To proclaim liberty to the captives,
> And the opening of the prison to those who are bound;
> To proclaim the acceptable year of the LORD,
> And the day of vengeance of our God;
> To comfort all who mourn,
> To console those who mourn in Zion,
> To give them beauty for ashes,
> The oil of joy for mourning,
> The garment of praise for the spirit of heaviness;
> *That they may be called trees of righteousness,*
> *The planting of the LORD, that He may be glorified."*

Clearly the Spirit enabled Him to persevere in the midst of suffering. Take for example the pain of rejection He felt on Palm Sunday. We only have a record of Jesus weeping twice. One of them is on Palm Sunday — He offers Himself as King, Messiah, only to be rejected (Luke 19:41). His heart is beginning to break, but He still has a long way to go. The crucifixion will not occur for five more days. How will He endure the Passion? We are told it is by the Spirit in Isaiah 11:1-2:

> There shall come forth a Rod from the stem of Jesse,
> And a Branch shall grow out of his roots.
> The Spirit of the LORD shall rest upon Him,
> The Spirit of wisdom and understanding,
> The Spirit of counsel and might,
> The Spirit of knowledge and of the fear of the LORD.

How would He endure? "The Spirit of the Lord shall rest upon Him . . . The Spirit of counsel and might." Jesus could endure because He leaned on the Holy Spirit. In the Garden when Jesus groaned, "Let this cup pass from Me," the Holy Spirit was groaning on His behalf, and through the scourging and trudging up the Via Dolorosa.

The Spirit's groaning empowers Him even as He dies. Upon the cross Jesus cried out, "My God, my God, why have you forsaken Me?" Some say He was so weakened from His scourging that He died within six hours. But I suggest that He died of a broken heart. Christ did not survive the usual three days on the cross before dying. In Gethsemane He sweats so profusely, it is as though He is sweating great drops of blood. "Please Father, take this cup from Me." It seems like more than He could bear and, in His humanity, it was. But the Spirit sustained Him right up to Golgotha. There on the cross the Son cried out to His Father once more, "My God, my God, why have you *rejected* Me?" The human rejection weakened Him, but the divine rejection broke His heart: "My heart is like wax; It has melted within Me" (Ps 22:14). Yes, the Holy Spirit was upon Him, but His heart was still breaking.

There may well be physiological evidence that this was the case. In describing the crucifixion, nationally respected ophthalmologist C. Truman David writes:

> Apparently to make doubly sure of death, the legionnaire drove his lance through the fifth interspace between the ribs, upward through the pericardium and into the heart. The 34th verse of the 19th chapter of the Gospel according to St. John reports: "And immediately there came out blood and water." That is, there was an escape of water fluid from the sac surrounding the heart, giving postmortem evidence that Our Lord died not the usual crucifixion death by suffocation, but of heart failure (a broken heart) due to shock and constriction of the heart by fluid in the pericardium.[6]

Where was the Holy Spirit? Wasn't He was resting upon Him? I thought He would sustain Him. Indeed, the Spirit got Him through the week. The Spirit helped Him carry the cross up the Via Dolorosa. And while Jesus hung on the cross with a broken heart, the Spirit was making groanings for the Son that could not be uttered. But the Spirit was praying according to the will of the Father. And he was heard (Heb 5:7). It was the Father's will that His Son should die in our place. And His Son loved us to the end (Jn 13:1).

---

6   C. Truman David, "A Physician Analyzes the Crucifixion," available at http://www.thecross-photo.com/Dr._C._Truman_Davis_Analyzes_the_Crucifixion.htm. Accessed October 26, 2010.

After Jesus rose from the grave he made His final *aliyah* — His ascent to sit beside His Father in the New Jerusalem. And as proof of His messiahship and His presence with His Father, He sent us the Holy Spirit. He sent us the Comforter to enable us, *pray* for us, and *groan* for us in the midst of our suffering. He will enable us to endure the Father's will as a *tree of righteousness, a planting of the Lord, that He may be glorified* when we, in His Son, reveal His righteousness on earth.

[END OF EXCURSUS]

What a comfort in suffering: the Support of the Spirit; the Supplication of the Spirit; and the Success of the Spirit! Aren't you glad the Spirit is a real person and not a machine? Ever heard of a golf cart giving a golfer advice on club selection? Ever heard a golf cart groan when its owner hit one out of bounds? A caddy can do those things, but even the best caddy in the world can't help unless the golfer trusts the caddy. The caddy's advice could be perfect but is useless until the golfer fully trusts in the caddy's complete knowledge of his strengths and weaknesses. The Holy Spirit is our "caddy." Until we learn to lean on Him and trust Him to turn our weaknesses into strengths, we will never see victory in the midst of our suffering.

Isn't this beautiful? I can certainly relate. I am a groaner. I moan and groan even when I have a cold. Yet there is a vast difference between my groans and the groans of the Holy Spirit. My groans don't do much good, but the inaudible groaning of the Holy Spirit is God-to-God communication. So when times are really tough, His groaning on my behalf meets my need and also accomplishes God's will. Don't ever forget it. When our pain and suffering — undeserved though it may be — crashes over us like an unexpected tsunami, our God groans.

> Our God groans when we're broken-hearted,
> Our God groans whenever we're blue;
> Our God groans when we feel rejected,
> Our God groans when friends are untrue.
> > The Spirit is there to help in our weakness;
> > He feels for us in our deepest pain.
> > The Spirit can utter what we cannot mutter;
> > He turns passing loss into permanent gain.
> Our God groans when we're broken-hearted,
> Our God groans whenever we're blue;
> Our God groans when we feel rejected,
> Our God groans when friends are untrue.

The trials of life come crashing like waves,
I feel like I'm drowning in sorrow's dark sea,
But there at the bottom of all of my suffering,
I know the Spirit is groaning for me.
Our God groans when we're broken-hearted,
Our God groans whenever we're blue;
Our God groans when we feel rejected,
Our God groans when friends are untrue.

CHAPTER 19

"THE GOODNESS OF GOD"
Romans 8:28-30

The story is told of an airliner that had an engine flame out mid-flight. But the captain came on the intercom to reassure the passengers. They still had three engines. Everyone was perfectly safe. Then a second engine went out. The captain still reassured everyone that a safe flight could be negotiated with two functional engines. A little while later the third engine stopped. This time the captain came on and said, "Well, it looks like we will have to land short of our destination, but not to worry, we can make it that far with one engine." Wouldn't you know it, the fourth engine went out, and the passengers looked out the window only to see the crew floating down in parachutes. Nevertheless, the captain's voice filled the intercom and said, "Not to worry, ladies and gentlemen. We are having a problem with the airplane, and we will have to make an emergency landing. The pilot and the crew have abandoned the plane and are parachuting to safety. There is no need to panic; the plane is on automatic pilot, and everything is under control . . . control . . . control."

As we look around at this world, it does appear that things have gotten out of control, does it not? The great genius Alan Greenspan, who directed our economy as chairman of the Federal Reserve during the greatest boom an economy has ever experienced, recently said "Oops" in reaction to the global economic meltdown experienced in 2008 and 2009. And that's only one thing. We could also name health care, the ongoing Middle East Crisis, swine flu, AIDS in the third world countries, not to mention earthquakes and tsunamis. It would appear that no one is in control. Of course, atheists and agnostics jump on the chaos of our current world events and shout, "See, we told you so. There is no God out there in control of these things, and if there is, then perhaps He just got the plane up into the air, and now that the engines are going out, He has parachuted to another universe to start a new experiment."

This cynicism flies right the face of the Bible, especially Romans 8:28-30, which says that not only is there a Creator God out there, but that He is very much in control. The Captain has not abandoned the ship or parachuted from the plane. So although things may seem out of control, whether on a global level or in your own life, God says, "No, I am still in control. What's more, I can work everything together for good to those who love Me and are called according to My purpose." It is in the midst of our suffering, especially undeserved suffering, that the accuser levels his forked tongue at God and accuses Him of being a divine sadist. That is precisely when we need to be reminded of the Goodness of God. This is the third of four consolations, or sources of hope, offered in Romans 8:18-39 to help us deal with the pain of undeserved suffering. We have already looked at His Glory and His Groaning on our behalf. Now we will see His goodness, first in His Providence (8:28), then in His Purpose (v. 29), and finally from His Perspective (v. 30).

2. Victory over Suffering		**(8:18-39)**
a. The Glory of God		**(8:18-25)**
b. The Groaning of God		**(8:26-27)**
c. The Goodness of God		**(8:28-30)**
1)	**Seen in His *Providence***	28
2)	**Seen in His *Purpose***	29
3)	**Seen from His *Perspective***	30
d. The Greatness of God		**(8:31-39)**

I. Seen in His PROVIDENCE 8:28

And we know that all things work together for good to those who love God, to those who are the called according to His purpose.

According to Webster, "Providence is the act of providing, exercising foresight, or preparing." And that is what Romans 8:28 is all about. It is God's way of providing for us and preparing us through the exercise of His foresight. And He uses all things to do this preparing work. And all these things work together for good. Let's take a look at the words involved in v. 28; their use by Paul will help us get a better grasp on the providence of God.

"We know" (*oidamen*) occurs five times in Romans, and it always refers to a definite knowledge that only Christians have. Only *we* know that all things work together for good. The world of unbelievers cannot fathom these things. When they see a mother's teenage son run away from home to live in a commune they cannot imagine any good coming out of that situation. When a seminary student comes home to find a note from his wife saying she has left him because she does not want to be married to a minister, the non-Christian wonders what possible good can come from that situation. But the believer intuitively knows that all these things can work for good because he knows the sovereign God of the universe is either directly or indirectly in control of these events. Either He caused it or He allowed it. One way or another He's behind it. If so, then there must be something good hidden within the apparent tragedy. If not, then our God is not good.

God's providence is all-inclusive: He works "all things" together,[1] whether good or bad. All things? Whenever we hear the words "all, every, never, or always," we start looking for exceptions. What about sin? How can sin work for good? Well, the greatness of our God is such that He can pick up the broken pieces of His highest will for our lives and remold them to make another plan which can still bring good into our lives and glory into His. A classic example would be David's life. After his terrible series of sins involving Bathsheba and her husband, Uriah, David cried out for God's mercy and vowed that if God would restore the joy of his salvation, then he would teach sinners the ways of God and many would be converted. Without his terrible failure, David could not be as effective in teaching others how to avoid the same trap, so God was able to redeem much good out of David's sin.

"All things." What about the stoning of Stephen? Saul of Tarsus was probably haunted for the rest of his life. Yet without Stephen, there might not have been a Paul. What about Jesus? It was sin that put Him on that cross, your sin and mine. Yet our God is so great that He can take the good choices and bad choices we make and use them for our good and His glory. That is a great God. In fact, such a God is far more sovereign than One who controls only animals or machines, which are not free to make choices. If I create ten computers and program them to sing, "Glory to Dave," when I snap my fingers, I am certainly sovereign over those machines. But they have no choice in the matter. Far greater is the sovereign Creator who in His providence can use both the evil and the good choices of the people He has created and use them for their good and His glory.

But what *kind* of good? The meaning of this text opens up a bit more when we see what kind of good Paul means here. There are two types of good in the Bible — external good and internal good. External good appears good on the outside. All men can see it. A guy in our church came by the other day to take me to play golf in his beautiful Corvette. And it was beautiful. I walked around it and whistled. My, my. He put it through its paces on the way to the course, and I was

---

1 The grammar in 8:28a is ambiguous. Both "all things" (*panta*) and the verb "work together" have the same form whether *panta* is the *subject* or the *object* of the sentence, so "all things" may be the *subject* of "work together" (as in NKJV) or the *object* of "he works together" (NASB). The immediately preceding allusion to God at the end of 8:27 (*kata Theon*, "according to God") makes the latter option seem more likely, "He works all things together."

impressed. So was everyone else on the road. Why, even I looked good in that Corvette, I mean really good. But it was all external. That is *kalos*, external good; good to the eye.

However, the word which occurs in v. 28 is *agathos*, a good that may not meet the eye. It may be internal and not seen by the eye at all — an inward benefit or improvement that may be evident only to the individual himself and God. Many times, perhaps most of the time, the good which comes from some tragic event can only be realized internally. On the surface, there would seem to be little benefit from having a leg amputated, a house that burns down, or a child that dies prematurely. But this verse never promises external good. It promises internal good, good which does not meet the eye. Just what that good is specifically, we shall discover in vv. 29-30.

But the verse does not claim that it works out for good for everyone. It is promised only to them who love God. Love Him how? The Greek word for "love" here (*agapaō*) does not refer to our emotions here as much as to our choices. For example, in Romans 9 Paul says God loved Jacob and hated Esau before either was born. This does not refer to emotions. It means God *chose* Jacob as head over Israel and rejected Esau. Jesus said unless you hate your father, mother, wife, children, brothers, sisters, and even your own life, you cannot be His disciple. This use of love and hate carries over from the OT. It has to do with our *choices*. To be His disciple, one must choose Him before all people or things, even one's own life. In another passage Paul says, "If any man loves not our Lord Jesus Christ, let him be anathema." Those that love God put His will first in their lives. These are the ones for whom God can work all things together for their good and God's glory.

Now Paul tells us something else about those for whom God works all things together for their good and His glory. He says they are "called," so we need to look more carefully at the idea of "calling." Some of us immediately think of the doctrine of "election" — that God sovereignly chooses some but not others to enjoy His favor — and God's choice of Jacob over Esau is often cited to support this view. But how does the word "called" fit the context? The adjective *kletos* is derived from the verb *kaleō*, used twice in 8:30 in exactly the same way as *kletos*. It is often translated "invited," as in Luke 14:7-24, arguably Jesus' best explanation of what it means to be "called." There it is obvious that the invited guests had the choice of *declining* his invitation, like Esau (Heb 12:16). The implication is that those who "love God" *freely accept* His invitation,[2] which is "according to purpose."

---

2 This understanding is at the core of Free Grace Theology and cuts against the grain of many strains of Reformed theology. At issue is the question of whether true believers, those who are "called," will

This does not mean that the calling *itself* was the "purpose," as the "election" view holds. If we read the phrase "according to purpose" (*kata prothesin*, literally, "according to plan") in parallel with "according to the Spirit" (*kata pneuma*, 8:1, 4, 13) and "according to God" (*kata Theon*, 8:27) we get a bigger picture: people are invited by God to follow His plan in alignment with the Spirit and God Himself.[3] As we have argued throughout, God's plan is worked out as "those who are called" display the righteousness of God by becoming mature "sons of God." Romans 8:28 thus assures us of God's providence as a primary incentive to fulfill our calling to righteousness.

If we then ask what God's plan *is* in that calling, Paul has already shown this plan from *our* perspective in our hope of future inheritance and glorification before all Creation as adopted sons in the Kingdom of God (8:18-23). Seeing that "the good" in our calling is often internal in this present life, Paul first situated that good within God's Providence in v. 28 and now integrates it into God's sovereign Purpose and Perspective in 8:29-30 — it will "align" with *His* plan.

II. Seen in His PURPOSE

8:29

That *whom He foreknew, He also predestined to be conformed to the image of His Son, that He might be* **[ ]** *firstborn among many brethren, . . .* [***bold*** = modified NKJV] [4]

---

necessarily show righteous behavior and/or avoid certain sinful behaviors. Calvinism has incorporated a system of "five points" epitomized by the acronym TULIP. Both sides of the debate hold that a change takes place when the believer is indwelt by the Spirit. The difference can be traced to the "I" in TULIP, which holds that God's grace is *irresistible* — in this case the "called" will *necessarily* show righteous behavior. However, as we have argued throughout, God's grace can indeed be resisted, to the point that the new identity in Christ (2 Cor 5:17) may not be externally evident; that is, a believer may *freely choose* to "walk according to the flesh," and thereby "grieve" or "quench" the Spirit (Eph 4:30; 1 Thess 5:19). A basic survey of the elements of Free Grace Soteriology is available in Dave Anderson's recent book by that title (Revised Edition, Grace Theology Press, 2012).

3 "God" is most naturally taken here to denote the *Father* as Author of the "plan." Regarding the use of parallel terms ("according to . . .") to show the "alignment" of *Father, Spirit,* and *plan,* see note 5 in the preceding chapter.

4 The NKJV reading of the connectives in 8:29-30 is somewhat misleading, so we show them here (**bold type**) in a way that better reflects the sequential logic all the way through v. 30:

[29]***that: whom*** *He foreknew, He **also** predestined [to be conformed to the image of His Son, that He might be firstborn among many brothers],* [30]***and whom*** *He predestined,* ***these also*** *He called;* ***and whom*** *He called,* ***these also*** *He justified; and* ***whom*** *He justified,* ***these also*** *He glorified.*

The first connective (*Gk hoti,* "that") introduces the entire sequence. Hence: (1) the opening connective in v. 30 (*de*) is best read as a linking "and" rather than the disjunctive "moreover" (NKJV); (2) the logic that continues in v. 30 is thus linked directly to the opening *hoti* in v. 29; and (3) the text shown in brackets has no connective—it is the direct complement (object) of the verb "predestined" and thus further delineates the nature of God's "plan" in predestination: His goal was *many brothers* who fit the image of His Son as "firstborn" (the Gk has no article) and can be "placed" *with* him as mature sons (1:4; 8:14-15, 17-19). This notion of conformity to the Son so as to be "placed" with Him as "adopted sons" is especially evident in Heb 2:10-13.

The word translated "for" (*hoti*) in the NKJV, NIV, and NASB is usually translated "that" but can also mean "for" or "because." Here we prefer "that," because it more likely introduces *what* Paul meant by "according to plan" in v. 28, rather than *why* "God works all things together for good." But before we get too far into the significance of this verse, let's take a look at the meaning of the words "foreknew" and "predestined" which have caused great controversy and not a little confusion in Christendom.

The first word is *proginōskō*, which is made up of the verb "to know" and the preposition "before." It just means "to know before"; hence, "foreknow" is accurate. However, one of Augustine's biggest mistakes was to confuse this foreknowledge with *predetermination*. As the author of double predestination — that God chose some to go to heaven and the rest to go to hell before He ever created them — Augustine held that whatever God *foreknew*, God *predetermined*. Theologians have been supporting this doctrine or reacting to it ever since Augustine died (AD 431). Those who oppose this teaching have trouble accepting a view of God that would create some people just to send them to hell. Those who support the doctrine counter that God did not create them just to send them to hell; He created them mainly to demonstrate His justice, and He could only do that by sending some people to hell. The sad result of this view is that God created the vast majority of people just to demonstrate His justice by sending them to hell.

Naturally, many theologians cannot stomach this view of God, which was supported by Gottschalk (AD 850), John Calvin, and his successor at the Geneva Academy, Theodore Beza. Thus, historian Will Durant, no friend to Christianity, concluded his discussion of Calvin and his effect on Geneva and Western Christianity by saying, "We shall always find it hard to love the man who darkened the human soul with the most absurd and blasphemous conception of God in all the long and honored history of nonsense."[5] So is there any way out of what Calvin called the "labyrinth" of equating foreknowledge with predetermination? Yes, there is.

The way out is to concede the obvious, that foreknowledge and predetermination cannot be equated. God does not predetermine what He foreknows. Rather, foreknowledge is only one "compartment," we might say, of omniscience. With foreknowledge God knows what *will* actually come to pass. But with omniscience

---

5 Will Durant, *The Reformation*, vol. VI in *The Story of Civilization* (New York: Simon & Schuster, 1957), 490.

He knows not only what will come to pass but also what might come to pass; omniscience includes the "woulda, coulda, shoulda."[6]

Consider the following example from 1 Samuel 23. Here we see how *both* God's foreknowledge *and* His omniscience affected David's decision making. David is running from Saul. First, David enquires of the Lord whether he should take his men to Keilah in the territory of the Philistines. In other words, would the Philistines wipe them out if they went there? The Lord says go. David's men aren't so sure, so David asks the Lord again, just to double check. Again the Lord says go, only this time He gives David a promise based on His foreknowledge: "Arise, go down to Keilah, for I will give the Philistines into your hand." God knew what would *actually come to pass* when David took his men to Keilah and went up against the Philistines, so David based his decision on *God's foreknowledge*. Of course, David went to Keilah and won the battle against the Philistines.

But when Saul heard that David was in Keilah, he was sure he had him trapped and could take him. Saul thus prepared his men to lay siege to Keilah. Since David knew Saul was plotting the siege, he called for the ephod that Abiathar the priest had brought to Keilah and asked the Lord two questions: 1) Will the men of Keilah surrender David and his men to Saul? 2) Will Saul come down to Keilah? Saul never came down, and the Philistines never handed David and his men over, because David high-tailed it out of town before Saul could get him. However, this time God answered the questions based on His *omniscience* (what *would* happen *if* David stayed):

God says Saul will come down, and the Philistines will surrender David and his men. Since neither of these things actually came to pass, we can safely conclude that these potentialities were not part of God's foreknowledge but rather His *omniscience*, which includes not only what *will* come to pass but also what *might* come to pass. Thus, David made his decision to flee from Keilah based on God's omniscience, not on His foreknowledge.

This reveals some important things about God's knowledge. When we come to a fork in the road with options A, B, and C, God already *foreknows* what choice we will make — option B, for example. But in His *omniscience*, He knows what would come to pass if we chose option A or option C. He does not predetermine our choices. He just knows what will happen if we choose any of the options before us. The choice is ours, even if He knows ahead of time what that choice will be. This distinction is essential for human freedom, the capacity to choose.

---

6   For grammarians, foreknowledge is in the *indicative*; omniscience includes both the *indicative* and the *subjunctive*.

This is not a trivial right. If we were created in the image of God, part of that image is the capacity to choose. He made us with mind, emotions, *and* will. This isn't to say that our capacity to choose has not been affected by the fall — it most certainly has. That is why we need God's *persuasion* (or "drawing," Jn 6:44) and the Spirit's conviction (Jn 16:8) to trust Christ as Savior.[7] However, if we equate foreknowledge with predetermination, then our capacity to choose has been nullified — we become little more than automatons or robots in God's hands. One of the many problems with this view is that it makes God the efficient moral cause of evil. This was the labyrinth from which Calvin could not escape; neither could his successor Theodore Beza, who turned Aristotle's four causes into *ten* causes in his attempt to exculpate God as the efficient moral cause of evil.

This brings us to the second controversial word in v. 29: "predestined." Does this word mean that God predetermined who would go to heaven and who would go to hell? Well, not in this passage, at least. Is there any mention of heaven, hell, lake of fire, the New Jerusalem? No. When we hear the word "destination" we think of a place. But the destination in view here has nothing to do with our ultimate *location*; it speaks of a *state of character*; that is, conformed to the image of Christ. In heaven we shall all be like Christ, for we shall see Him as he is (1 Jn 3:1-3). But while we are still on earth, God's great Purpose in His divine providence is to make us like His Son.[8] Jesus reveals the qualities of God to men. He tells us what God is like. And so, as we become like Christ on earth — we too reveal the qualities of God.

Recall the book's opening illustration about the artist and the beggar (see Preface). God sees His Son Jesus living within each believer and wants our lives to display a replica of His Son to the world. Therefore, it behooves us to respond like the beggar, "If that is the man you see, then that is the man I'll be." Like the image of a President embossed on the surface of an old coin, it is so tarnished and covered with grime it can hardly be seen; if we are to see the image clearly, the surface must be abraded. God sees the perfect, pristine image He wants and uses life's difficulties as abrasives to sharpen in us the image of His Son for all the world to see. As Jesus "has explained" God (Jn 1:18), so are we, his abiding presence on earth, to conform to his image and thus reveal God's *righteousness* (Rom 1:17). We are to be the salt of the earth and make men thirsty for Him (Matt 5:13). Since God's plan is not limited by time or space, He *will* accomplish His plan which culminates in the corporate glory of his people (Rom 8:14-25), even if *individual* believers reject His "invitations."

---

7 For a more complete exegetical argument on this point see the chapter entitled "Regeneration" in Anderson, *Free Grace Soteriology*.

8 See above, note 4, esp. the concluding sentence.

It is not always easy to see the Goodness of God. Why not? It is because we lack God's Perspective. We've seen the Goodness of God in His Providence (v. 28) and in His Purpose (v. 29). Now let's look at God's Goodness as seen from His Perspective.

III. Seen from His PERSPECTIVE   8:30

. . . and *whom He predestined, these He also called; whom He called, these He also justified; and whom He justified, these He also glorified.*

This verse concludes the famous "Golden Chain," so called by those of the Reformed persuasion because no one is "lost" along the chain. That is, everyone predestined was called; everyone called was justified; everyone justified was glorified. Therefore, it is argued, this verse must teach "perseverance of the saints," meaning that everyone who is justified will go on to be glorified.

Well, if by that we mean we are *eternally secure*, then yes, that is exactly what the verse supports. But Reformed people go beyond eternal security, at least those who support classical Dortian Calvinism, the origin of the Five Points of Calvin. By "perseverance of the saints" they mean that all who are justified will necessarily persevere in faith *and* good works, or they were never elect to begin with. In effect, they *infer* the promise of progressive sanctification until death. So certain are they that progressive sanctification is guaranteed to the elect, that William Perkins, one of the most influential preachers of Calvinism in the eighteenth century, actually plugged the word "sanctified" into the chain when he explicated this verse.[9]

In fact, however, sanctification is conspicuous by its *absence* in this verse, especially considering that Romans 5-8 is focused on freedom from the power of sin; indeed, that is what is at stake for believers: there *is no* guarantee of progressive sanctification in the Scriptures. For us to move on in maturity we must *choose* to cooperate with the Holy Spirit's working in our lives. We must choose to present our members to Christ (6:12-14) and we must choose to follow, or walk according to, the Spirit (8:1-14a).

It is noteworthy that the word "glorified" is in the Greek aorist tense, which usually conveys *action in the past* when used in the indicative mood, just like all the other finite verbs in the "chain" of 8:29-30. But surely we are not yet glorified. Foreknown, yes; predestined, yes; called, yes; justified, yes; but *glorified* — no. So, what is the point of putting this word "glorified" in the aorist tense just like the other indicative verbs here? There are at least two good alternatives:

---

9   W. Perkins, *The Works of that Famous and Worthy Minister of Christ in the University of Cambridge, M. William Perkins*, vol. 2 (London, 1631), 2:78; cited in Anderson, *Free Grace Soteriology*, Appendix B.

- **Our glorification as a "whole."** The "constative" use of the aorist tense denotes action over time *viewed in its entirety*. God is not bound by time and "sees" the entire time line of human history. Thus, by putting all the verbs in the aorist, Paul's point is that from God's perspective all these actions occur as an integrated whole. God sees right through the suffering of 8:18-39 to His goal, our conformity to Christ and the glory that will be revealed in the sons of God.

- **Our glorification as a "done deal."** The "proleptic" use of the aorist tense treats the future *as though it has already occurred*. It is used for emphasis. The future is so certain that it is as good as done. Again, this would help Paul's readers get their eyes off their current suffering by focusing on future glory.

Of course, it *is* true that no one is lost along this chain. Since all believers have been predestined to be conformed to the image of Christ they have all been called, as Paul has defined it in 8:28: "according to plan." If they were not called, they would not have responded (3:10-18). And all believers have been justified, or else they have not believed (3:21-26). And all believers will be glorified, but in what sense and to what degree? Certainly, every believer will receive a gloried body and spend eternity with God. But 8:17b-25 highlights the potential for those willing to suffer with Christ to bring Him even more glory, and this is limited only by our lack of response to His Spirit's leading in this life. The believer who walks according to the flesh will not bring as much glory to Christ as the believer who walks according to the Spirit. For this reason, the prospect of glorifying Him in the next life is one of our primary incentives to endure suffering in this life.

We will be like moons reflecting the light of the Son in eternity. Because we have no Sin Nature in heaven or the New Jerusalem, there will be no sense of lack, envy, or jealousy. And there will be no half moons in heaven. Every moon will be a full moon. The dark side of every moon is gone forever. But some moons will be larger than others, according to their faithfulness on earth. Some moons will have a greater capacity to reflect the light (character qualities) of the Son forever. After all, no moon has any light of its own. And there is only one Superstar in heaven. It will be our great privilege to reflect His light for His glory forever and ever.[10]

From God's perspective He sees the entire plan and purpose. It is as though life is a big jigsaw puzzle we are trying to figure out. To us it looks like a mess, but God sees the completed picture, and it is beautiful. One weekend while on an Indian Guides campout with one of my boys, I saw a trail of ants in the woods. I dropped

---

10 Regarding the connection between glory and "light" in the destiny of believers, see note 3, Chapter 17, "The Glory of God."

a piece of bread just off the trail and tried to direct the ants to the bread. Most of them could not be deterred, but one little ant broke off the main trail. Every time it went off in a direction that would take it far from my crumb of bread, I redirected the ant by putting my finger in its path. It must have taken twenty turns, but it finally made it to the bread, and oh, was it happy! But until it reached the bread, my finger made it very frustrated. My purpose was good. And the goal was good. But the ant panicked every time it ran into my finger. Little could it see or know I had something good in store for it.

God goes one better. Truly, the hand of God appears to be a barrier to our happiness from time to time, whereas all the while He is trying to direct us to a breadcrumb. But He also, through the revelation of His Word, swoops us up in His hand to let us see things from His perspective. That is when we learn of the breadcrumb at the end of the line. And that is when we can see the Goodness of God. Yes, His goodness can help us overcome the discouragement and depression of undeserved suffering. His Providence says all things work together for the internal good of those who put His interests before their own. His Purpose says that internal good is Christ-like character. And His Perspective says that Christ-like character yields glory for us in Him at the end of the road.

When I was growing up, our family said the same prayer at the evening meal. None of us had a personal relationship with Christ, but we prayed, nonetheless. And it went like this: "God is great, God is good, let us thank Him for our food." Now that I am a believer, I prefer the advice of Mother Theresa. She got tired of her sisters complaining all the time about the work. Problems, problems, problems. She said, "Let's not complain about our problems. In fact, let's not call them problems anymore. Let's call them gifts . . . gifts from God. And every day, let's thank God for our gifts." It changed the entire atmosphere. The nuns began coming to Mother Theresa and saying things like, "Mother Theresa, we have a small gift from God today." Or, "Mother Theresa, we have a really big gift from the Lord today." They began to see their problems from a new perspective.

Did you know that the Chinese had a corner on the silk market for three thousand years? It was an emperor's wife who discovered silk in 2700BC. Some of the mulberry trees were dying, so the emperor asked his wife to find out why. As she began inspecting the trees, she discovered some moths and cocoons. She watched as a small worm wove a cocoon for a home and came out a moth. Then she took one of these cocoons and put it in warm water. It unraveled. The silk thread of one cocoon was a half-mile long. They could make the most beautiful clothes with their silk. In fact, the Romans would exchange the weight of the silk for an equal weight of gold. Finally, the Roman Emperor Justinian (AD 522) sent two monks to China to come back with the silk secret. They smuggled some eggs from the silk worm in bamboo shoots, and that is how the Chinese lost their lock on the silk trade.

What solace and hope do we have when our lives are infested with worms, cocoons, and moths? Well, God can tease out the silk threads from even our worst mistakes and weave them into something beautiful. In fact, the righteous acts of the saints (Rom 8:4) will be woven by the Master Weaver into the white robes to be worn by the saints when they return with Christ at the Battle of Armageddon to the wedding feast of the Lamb (Rev 19:8-9, 14).

> Are the threads of your life all tangled?
> Have the plans that you dreamed gone astray?
> Do the bright tones clash with each other,
> And the dark ones cloud most of the way?
> Remember the Master Weaver
> Can straighten the tangled strands,
> And weave anew the pattern
> If you place the silk in His hands.
> The dark days and the bright ones
> Will be woven with infinite skill,
> For both joy and sorrow are needed
> His perfect plan to fulfill.
> Some day you will see the upper side,
> In its matchless symmetry,
> His plan with the threads all blended
> In an exquisite harmony.[11]

---

11   Lilliam M. Weeks, *Sunday School Times*, quoted by Walter B. Knight, *Three Thousand Illustrations* (Grand Rapids, MI: Eerdmans, 1947), 577.

CHAPTER 20

"THE GREATNESS OF GOD"
Romans 8:31-39

Where do you go when life turns upside down? John Crews, a missionary who organized short-term trips, told me a remarkable story about one of his trips to Puerto Rico. On an excursion and some down time with his wife, Diane, he went to a fun park where they had ten different zip lines of variable length and slope. What fun! But on about the fifth line John's harness slid to a halt right in the middle of the line, about 150 ft. over a gorge. He yelled for help. Operators came and began yelling instructions. They wanted him to pull this way and sway that way. He followed the instructions but ran out of strength after about twenty minutes. Slowly, beyond his control, the harness tilted upside down. There was John, out serving the Lord, hanging upside down, 150 ft over a gorge.

Life is supposed to be an exciting adventure, just one zip line after another. And it can be, until things grind to a halt somewhere along the journey and you find yourself hanging upside down, completely out of control. Jane Fowler found herself in exactly that kind of spot after her firstborn son died. She had longed and prayed for this baby. But only a few months after his birth, her little boy mysteriously died. To make matters worse, the police showed up and arrested her for killing her own child. The autopsy revealed *ethylene glycol* in the little boy's blood — *antifreeze*. Jane was arrested and convicted. She was given life in prison without parole. Only she knew she didn't do it. How could a mother poison a child she had longed for and prayed for? Her husband and her parents knew she didn't do it, couldn't do it. But there she was, in prison. Where does she go?

Sidney Lanier was stricken with tuberculosis. He felt lost in a sea of suffering and defeat. But one day he sat looking at the marsh on the coast of Georgia and was moved to write:

> As the march-hen secretly builds on
> > the watery sod,
> Behold, I will build me a nest in
> > the greatness of God.

And that is precisely what we would like to do in Rom 8:31-39 — build a nest in the greatness of God. At some point in life most of us run into a situation or set of circumstances that appears insurmountable — higher than Mt. Everest, wider than the Pacific, darker than the back side of the moon. What is worse, it is precisely at these times that the devil whispers in our ears that we have been abandoned by God. Something in our past, something we have done and are ashamed of has finally come back to haunt us. God is just not going to bail us out of this one. And why should He? We don't deserve to be.

We tend to stare at our problem sometimes to the point of immobility. My problem looks like Mt. Everest — insurmountable. But if only I could look down from God's throne room, high, high above the earth where I am seated with Christ at the right hand of God the Father. Then that mountain would look like a molehill.

The question is, How big is our God? Before we can see things from God's point of view, we have to have the correct view of God. Some people worship a little God. He can create the sun, moon, and stars, but He cannot solve our financial problems. He can chain the fallen angels in Tartarus until the Day of Judgment but He cannot restrain our tongues and our problem with criticizing and complaining. He can take away all the sins of the world, but He can't take away our bitterness toward those who have mistreated us. Just how big is our God?

That is when we need our fourth consolation or source of hope for suffering. We have seen the Glory of God (18-25), the Groaning of God (26-27), and the Goodness of God (28-30). Finally, we are ready for the Greatness of God (31-39). This will conclude our journey through chapter 8, the Red Rose of Romans. We need to see how the Greatness of God is able to still the sea of suffering that threatens to drown us from time to time.

This chapter attacks the two-headed Medusa of Sin and Suffering that wreaks such ruin and misery in our lives. The sword of the Spirit has already cut off the head of Sin (8:1-17). Now we are going to take a final whack at the problem of undeserved suffering with the Consolation of the Greatness of God as seen in the Provisions of God (31-34), the Presence of God (35-37), and the Power of God (38-39).

I. God's PROVISIONS
8:31-34

31*What then shall we say to these things? If God is for us, who can be against us?* 32*He who did not spare His own Son, but delivered Him up for us all, how shall He not with Him also freely give us all things?* 33*Who shall bring a charge against God's* **chosen***? It is God who* **acquits***.*34 *Who is he who* **pronounces sentence***? It is Christ who died, and furthermore is also risen, who is even at the right hand of God, who also makes intercession for us.* [**bold** = modified NKJV]¹

If God is for us, who can be against us? Imagine being at a sandlot football game. You and a buddy are choosing sides. Your buddy chooses Bob, and you choose Sam; he chooses Joe, and you choose John; he chooses Robert, and you choose . . . God. All of a sudden the choosing stops. Obviously, if God is your quarterback, your team will win. After all, He's the Supreme Being. He's the greatest; He's invincible. You're not gong to lose with Him on our side.

More literally, Paul has a *courtroom* scene in mind. On the Judge's seat sits God the Father—the same God who *justified* us while we were yet sinners will also *acquit* us of any charge the world may bring. Our personal defense lawyer, God the Son, intercedes on our behalf. Paul thus throws an open challenge to any prosecution the world might bring: "Who can be against God's chosen? Who can charge them with any crime? What sentence can be handed down on God's chosen when Jesus Christ speaks on their behalf?" *Jesus* will judge how well they hold up under persecution, but He is *for* them when they face the world's condemnation.

God first provides for our eternal destiny by offering up His own Son on our behalf, but then He provides for our preservation in the pressure cooker by freely

---

1 The participle *ho dikaiōn* ("the one who justifies," 8:33) in this context is *versatile*: while "acquit" fits better than "justifies" as God's response to "bring a charge" (*egkaleō*), this is to be seen in light of God's prior, greater work to "justify" us through Christ's death (5:8-10; 8:30). Similarly, the participle *ho katakrinōn* ("the one who condemns," 8:34) is a form of *katakrinō* ("to pronounce sentence in judgment") and thus related to the noun *katakrima* ("condemnation") in 5:16, 18; 8:1 (BDAG, 518-19). Paul's point in 8:33-34 is therefore this: since God is the one who *acquits* those "chosen" (*eklektōn*) to represent Him in the world (1:17) but only *Christ* has the authority to *judge* how well they do that in suffering (8:17b), they need not fear condemnation from the world—Christ is *for* us.

giving us all things. By offering up His own Son we have been justified; now with our personal lawyer interceding for us at the right hand of the Judge, we can be assured of having all our needs met in spite of present opposition. These are God's provisions for a victorious Christian life. It sounds like a reprise of Romans 5:8-10: salvation first; then comes sanctification. If God could accomplish the greater feat of atonement for sin by giving up His firstborn Son, surely He will freely give us all we need in Christ's life to deliver us from wrath ("condemnation," slavery to sin) to reveal God's righteousness amid suffering.

Some years ago I needed a pick-up truck and trailer to haul motorcycles because one of my sons had gotten into racing. I had never owned a truck and didn't know squat about them. But my son-in-law knew trucks. So, one weekend when his wife (my daughter) and my wife were away on a women's retreat, I called and asked if he would help me with trucks. So we headed down to a local dealership. I told my son-in-law, Scott, what I needed, and they had three that fit my description. But as I was about to test drive the first one, the salesman said it had just been sold. So, we went for the second — sold. As we went for the third, word came that a sale was pending, so we got back in my car to drive away. As we were pulling out, the salesman came running up to the car and said, "My manager said a bird in the hand is better than two in the bush. The pending sale won't go through until Monday. If you can take delivery today, it's yours." Scot looked at me and said do it. Knowing I could always blame him, I bought the truck.

But as I was driving it home, all I could think about is the wrath of Betty — "You did *what*?" We aren't impulse buyers. She would never understand my making a major purchase in one day. Of course, she wouldn't be returning until Sunday afternoon, so I had some time to think and pray about how to handle this. When it was time for me to preach on Sunday morning, I still didn't have a plan. I got through the first service, but with the imminent return of Betty on my mind, I just couldn't preach the second service without confessing. So, I said to the whole congregation, "Folks, you're not going to believe what I did yesterday. I bought a truck." The entire congregation clapped and cheered (this is Texas). "But, you don't understand. I haven't told Betty. She is on the women's retreat and will be back in a couple of hours. I just don't know what to do. Pray for me." Then, with that off my chest, I was able to preach.

After the service, I was standing around in the foyer and a group of high school girls surrounded me. "Yes?" I asked. "Pastor Dave, looks like you're in trouble." Yes, I agreed. "We can help. We are women, so we know how women think." OK, I'm listening. "Tuesday is Valentine's Day. Give Betty the truck as a Valentine's gift." Ahhhh, the heavens opened; the light began to shine; wisdom from above. So, I parked the truck in front of our house, knowing Betty would park on the side (corner lot). Sure enough, and in she came. I walked right up to her, gave her a hug, and said, "Oh, I have missed you." But I guess I held her a little too long. She looked at me and said, "What did you do?"

"What did I *do*? What did I *do*? How can you suspect me of doing anything unusual?" *I sense it.* "Hmmm. Well, OK, you're right. I bought you a very special Valentine's gift." *Don't tell me you bought me a motorcycle?* "Betty, I know you don't like motorcycles. I would never do such a thing. But I did buy you something with wheels. It's out front." Together we walked to the front door. As she looked out, she began to smile. "Is that truck really for me?" *Of course, my darling.* "And I can drive it right now?" *Yes, my pumpkin.* "Where are the keys?" *Oh, the keys. Well, I am giving you the truck, but not the keys.*

Now, wouldn't that be *stupid* — to give her the truck, but not the keys? If I am going to give her the big thing, obviously, I will give her the little thing. Naturally, I gave her the keys, and she got in the truck and drove away. When she got back, she had a big smile on her face and said, "That is the nicest Valentine's gift you have ever given me. So while I was driving, I asked the Lord what I could give you. And He answered my prayer immediately." *Really, I can hardly wait. What is it?* "I am going to give you a beautiful, full length mink coat." Of course, I never got the coat. But what if she *had* given me the coat? Don't you think she would also give me the bag it came in? Of course, she would. If she is going to do the greater, she will do the lesser.

So will God. If He is going to part the Red Sea, He is also going to provide manna, quail, and water to keep the Israelites alive in the Wilderness. Likewise, if He is going to give us Jesus, He will take care of the smaller things as well. So much for His Provisions while we are suffering. But what about His Presence? Sometimes we feel the farthest from him when we are suffering. Has he left us? Will He ever?

II. God's PRESENCE

8:35-37

35*Who shall separate us from the love of Christ? Shall tribulation, or distress, or persecution, or famine, or nakedness, or peril, or sword?* 36*As it is written:*

> "For Your sake we are killed all day long;
> We are accounted as sheep for the slaughter."

37*Yet in all these things we are more than conquerors through Him who loved us.*

These verses deal with suffering in this life, and not surprisingly, with undeserved suffering. Paul has not quoted from the OT for three chapters. Then, suddenly, out of the blue, here comes a verse from Psalm 44, a psalm about undeserved suffering. The psalmist says, "All this has come upon us; but we have not forgotten You, nor have we dealt falsely with Your covenant. Our heart has not turned back, nor have our steps departed from Your way" (Ps 44:17-18). This is not discipline because of sin.

Yet right in the midst of this undeserved suffering the psalmist sits down to write one of the most perfectly organized portions of Scripture we have in the Bible. He has arranged the verses in Hebrew to look like a *ziggurat*. The ziggurat was a tower used for worshipping the stars in the Middle East. It was laid out with a square base. Each succeeding level was a square base built upon the one below. All sides were perfectly symmetrical. The psalm has four parts: Confidence, Complaint, Protest, and Petition. The Confidence (1-8) has ten lines of Hebrew poetry, divided five and five; the Complaint (9-16) has eight lines of Hebrew poetry, divided four and four; the Protest (17-22) has six lines of Hebrew poetry, divided three and three; and the Petition (23-26) has four lines of Hebrew poetry, divided two and two. Of course, the psalmist is communicating through both this structure and the words. Through the structure he is trying to tell us that right in the midst of this storm of undeserved suffering, he has not lost his balance. He can still think rationally. And in the words of the psalm he points to four facts about God that keep him afloat.

It reminds me of a time when my dad was flying my mother, my sister, and me to New York City from Nashville, Tenn. We were in a Bonanza, a single engine plane with a V-tail. When we hit the Appalachians, the "soup" set in — zero visibility. I was fourteen years old, but dad had taught me to take off and land a couple of years earlier just in case he had a heart attack while we were in the air. This time he wanted me to take the wheel and learn to fly in the soup.

Dad had been a flight instructor during WWII and studied engineering at Annapolis. I had complete trust in him. So he said we would be fine if I kept my eyes on three instruments. He pointed to the compass and said he would give me the setting. Then he pointed to the altimeter and said if we went too high ice would get us and if we went too low the mountains would get us. Finally, he pointed to the wing leveler and said this would tell us if we were in a turn — it would keep the wings level. We were in the soup for over three hours. There was a fair amount of turbulence, and my mother lost her breakfast more than once. But I was fine. Why? Because of my great courage? No. It was because I had complete trust in my father. I just watched those three instruments.

Years later I was asked to give the executives of Continental Airlines a tour of Israel to celebrate their inaugural flight to Tel Aviv. We were going to fly in their new 777, and everyone was excited. While we were over the Atlantic, the President and COO of Continental asked me if I wanted to see the cockpit (pre-911). He said it was even used to train some of the Challenger pilots. When we got up there, I saw an amazing assortment of screens duplicated on each side for the captain and co-captain. I couldn't make heads or tails of them. But right in the middle of all those fancy screens I saw three little instruments I thought I recognized. I asked the captain if those were what I thought they were. He said, "Yes, if the computers go out, we can still fly the plane with those."

The psalmist is telling us the same thing. Whether you are in the soup going across the Appalachians or flying to Tel Aviv over the Atlantic, there are four facts about God that will keep your wings level and get you to your destination if you focus on them in the midst of the storm. The first is His *power*, which we find stamped all over the Confidence section (1-8). God did all these things with His mighty right hand; He is fully able to control the circumstances of our lives. The second point of focus is God's *sovereignty*. His sovereignty shows up in the word "You" stamped all over the first two sections. It is clear the psalmist has complete trust in the sovereignty of God. Despite the current slaughter of the innocents (v. 22), God is in control. The third point of focus is God's *knowledge*. He knows what is in our hearts (v. 21) because He is all-knowing, omniscient. And because He knows everything, my personal situation has not fallen through some crack in His awareness. He is fully aware of what is happening to me.

But a cruel, capricious God could be in control, all-powerful and all-knowing, and still might not be *beneficent* toward those whom he controls. So, the fourth point of focus for the psalmist is God's *love*. We find this in the Petition (v. 26) when the psalmist makes his appeal based on the mercy of God. That word for mercy (*ḥesed*) was taken from the mother stork which would fight until death to protect her offspring. It is often translated "loyal love." It is a love that will never leave you. And that is the love in Paul's mind when he quotes from this psalm.

So these are the four facts about God that can get us through the storm of undeserved suffering: His Power, His Sovereignty, His Knowledge, and His Love. But especially His love, for it is this love in combination with the other three that tells us God will not allow anything to happen to us that cannot ultimately bring good to us and glory to Him. Yet we have to focus on these "instruments" He has provided.

Earnest Gordon, former Dean of Chapel at Princeton University, tells about the need to focus during his POW days in his book *Miracle on the River Kwai*.[2] The men were on starvation diets but still expected to work long hours on the bridge. As they got weaker and weaker, cholera swept through and killed thousands. Gordon himself got so weak they took his body and laid it in the death bin along with all the other corpses. There he lay, still alive, but they took him for dead. Just before Gordon would have died, two Christian prisoners decided to team up

---

2 Ernest Gordon, *Miracle on the River Kwai* (Carol Stream, IL: Tyndale House Publishers, 1984).

and perform a special ministry. They went around and began massaging the legs of other prisoners who were about to die, in order to get those feeble limbs going again. They massaged and massaged.

The spirit of the men in the camp began to rise because two people with a faith in God began to act in love. Then they began to make musical instruments (forty in all) and formed their own orchestra. They played Christian hymns and began to sing together. An agnostic became a Christian and began a Bible study in the midst of the camp. Soon love swept through the entire camp, right in the midst of their problems.

The Japanese didn't change; their cruelty continued. The diseases didn't go away; they still attacked from time to time. But in the midst of that camp they sensed *the presence of God,* and it sustained the lives of many of those men long enough to return to America.

When they were released, they thought they would come back with great joy and enjoy all the comforts of home again. But when they returned they said they lost the presence of God. In the midst of all their comforts they could not sense what they had back at the camp. They described their comforts at home as a sham covering the verities of life, the true things of God they had sensed back at that prison camp. Conclusion: *in the midst of the greatest suffering of life, we often sense the presence of God more than at any other time.*

We worry and worry and worry about our problems. It's like the two little birds flying in the heavens above that looked down at the Christians just trudging along, burdened with worry and concern over their problems. One little bird said to the other, "You know, I guess they just don't have a heavenly father like we do." The birds don't have to worry about the food they get. His eye is on the sparrow. How much more must He watch over us!

Paul picked a very apt term for Christians here. What would we pick as the most powerful animal on the earth? A whale? An elephant? Orca? A lion? None of the above. It is a sheep. "Aw, come on," we say. Well, that is what out text says. "We sheep are more than conquerors in all these things." The Greek text puts two words together to tell us we are "much more than conquerors" through Christ; but two things about sheep make them the most unlikely "super-conquerors." They're *dumb.* Ever seen a flock of sheep performing in a circus? Lions, bears, seals, snakes, elephants; but never *sheep.* Why? They are too dumb. Secondly, they *stink.* Ever been around the south end of a northbound sheep? For some reason sheep keep wanting to go off in their own directions. They keep getting lost and smeared with their own refuse.

What we are being told here is that all of our resources will come to naught when we try to find our way out of the pressure cooker. We are too dumb and all our own efforts stink. But we sheep have one thing none of these other animals has: sheep have a shepherd. They are totally dependent on the shepherd. We are more than conquerors through Him that loved us, the Great Shepherd. As sheep totally depend on their Shepherd and sense His presence in the midst of the pressure cooker, His Greatness is seen in His Provisions, His Greatness is seen in His Presence, and finally, His Greatness is seen in His Power.

III. God's POWER
8:38-39

For I am persuaded that neither death nor life, nor angels nor principalities nor powers, nor things present nor things to come, nor height nor depth, nor any other created thing, shall be able to separate us from the love of God which is in Christ Jesus our Lord.

Neither things present nor *things to come* can separate us from the love of God in Christ Jesus. That includes our sins. This is the "back door" way of saying that our future sins are also covered by the blood of Christ. The "front door" is Romans 4. Justification by faith at a moment in time tells us that *all* our sins — past, present, and future — are covered by the work of Christ on the cross. If one sacrifice for sin was sufficient to take care of the sins of the whole human race (Rom 5; Heb 10), then the cross can also take care of all *future* sins.

Many during the early history of the church knew only how to deal with *past* sins. They thought a person was born again at water baptism, and all their sins up to the point of water baptism were washed away. But sins committed after water baptism had to be dealt with by confession, repentance, penance, contrition, and the sacraments. In other words, there was no advance forgiveness for the sins we will commit in the future. This is why they lacked assurance of their salvation and did not believe in eternal security. How could they? They all knew they would commit future sins, and if these sins were not dealt with properly, one would go to hell.

But with the Reformation emerged a *forensic* understanding of justification. Melanchthon explained that justification was not a change in our character on earth, but rather a change in our standing before God.[3] God *declared* the sinner *righteous* in the courtroom of heaven based on the work of Christ on the cross and the sinner's acceptance of that work to pay the penalty for his sins. To fully develop this forensic aspect of righteousness we would have to go back to

---

3 P. Melanchthon, "Baccalaureate Theses," 10, in *Melanchthon: Selected Writings*, trans. C. H. Hill (Westport, CN: Greenwood, 1978), 17; cited in David Anderson, *Free Grace Soteriology*, Revised Edition (Houston: Grace Theology Press, 2012), 101.

Romans 4. Suffice it to say that because of the finished work of Christ on the cross, *no future sin or sins can separate us from the love of God in Christ Jesus.*

Not only are "things" like sins unable to separate us from the love of Christ; neither can "any other created thing" (*tis hetera ktisis*) like an angel or demon separate us from God's love. And "any other created thing" includes *me* — not even *I* can separate myself. Nothing I can say or do can separate me from the love of God. Oh, He may well be disappointed in the child. But we must distinguish between *acceptance* and *approval.* Approval is separate, and Paul takes up such "family matters" in Romans 12-16; however, we will always be accepted "in the Beloved" (Eph 1:6). We will always belong. Birth into a family is irreversible. He is our heavenly parent, and what can separate a child from a parent's love? Indeed, a mother's love is seen as one of the greatest constants we could imagine.

So, did Jane Fowler poison her child with ethylene glycol? Say it isn't so. As it turns out, Jane was seven months pregnant when she was convicted of poisoning her child and sent to prison. She had her second child in prison, and shortly thereafter, that child also died. Obviously, she did not poison the second child, so the obstetrician who delivered the second child began to suspect she did not kill her first child. They did an autopsy and found the same chemical in the second child that was in the first, a chemical quite similar to ethylene glycol. Four of seven labs made the same mistake and misidentified the chemical. It was not ethylene glycol, but a chemical that developed during Jane's pregnancy — a chemical that ultimately killed her children. So, Jane was released from prison. No, she had not poisoned her child. How could a mother do that?

Well, it does happen, doesn't it? Not that long ago, right here in Houston, a depressed mother astounded us by drowning her four children. Yet, as Isa 49:15 says:

> Can a mother forget the baby she nurses
> and have no compassion on the child she has borne?
> Though she may forget,
> I will not forget you!

This is God's promise. Though in some remarkable case a mother might have no compassion on the child she has birthed, God will never do that; He will never forget us. Romans 4:21 says God is completely able to bring to pass anything he has promised. And Jude 24 claims He is able to keep us from stumbling and to present us faultless before the presence of His glory. That is the Greatness of God, a consolation, a hope that can carry us through suffering in *this* world to our full inheritance in the world *to come.*

CONCLUSION

In the silver screen version of Andrew Lloyd Webber's *Phantom of the Opera* the Phantom lives a tragic life of hiding from the world in the catacombs below the Opera Populaire, the opera house in Paris. Born with a hideous birth defect on his face, the Phantom was part of a circus side-show as a boy, the object of scorn and ridicule from those who would pay to see the ugliness of this "Child of the Devil." One day he killed the man who had profited from his repulsive appearance and used to beat him on a regular basis. A young ballet student, who had witnessed the killing, helped him escape the police by hiding him under the opera house.

The young boy never leaves the opera house. As he grows up he discovers he has many natural gifts. He is a singer, composer, architect, designer, magician—a polymath, a genius in many arenas. But because of his ugliness he hides from the world behind a mask of his own making, a white mask that hides the half of his face which is so hideous to behold. He makes a home for himself in the labyrinths under the opera house and subsists by haunting the house and bullying its owners into paying homage to him lest he, the Phantom of the Opera, should bring them to financial ruin by frightening the patrons away.

In his loneliness the Phantom longs to have a normal life and a passionate love with a woman of his dreams, but instead he spends his time staring at his own ugly visage in the many mirrors he has erected on the walls of his lair. His only pleasure in life is his tutelage of the young Christine Daae, who shows promise of becoming a future diva. With his tortured soul the Phantom deceives Miss Daae into thinking he is the Angel of Music her late father promised would come to her after his death. As she blossoms into a talented ingénue the Phantom longs to possess her. He becomes insanely jealous when Christine's childhood sweetheart, Viscount Raoul de Chagny, comes on the scene as a patron of the opera and soon wants to reunite with Christine and have her for his wife.

In the climactic scene of the movie the Phantom has captured Christine and taken her below to his underworld haunt. Raoul discovers the hiding place but is not able to rescue Christine before the Phantom ties him to a grate to force Christine to choose between the two suitors. By this time Christine has ripped the mask off the Phantom to expose him as he really looks—nothing to hide behind. He hates her for exposing his ugliness, but at the same time he loves her and longs to have her as his bride. He puts her in a lose-lose situation. If she goes with the Phantom, Raoul lives, but she loses him and has to spend the rest of her life with this "Child of the Devil." If she rejects the Phantom, she loses, for then Raoul dies at the hands of his rival. What will she choose?

In her spell-binding response Christine slowly descends into the water and walks slowly, but deliberately toward the Phantom. As she approaches him, she is singing, "Pitiful creature, may God give me strength to show you that you are not alone." Then as she comes close and gazes into his eyes, beautiful Christine stretches up and gives the Phantom a passionate kiss on his lips. The Phantom is shaken. He has never experienced this kind of grace, this kind of love, a love that would reach out and embrace him in all of his ugliness, exposed for all the world to see, but most of all for *her*—his beloved—to see. How could she do this?

As though something within him has been set free, the Phantom sets Christine and Raoul free to live their lives together. He prepares to escape the police who are now descending into his hideaway. But before he goes, the Phantom goes around his bedroom and his dressing room breaking every mirror that has held him captive all these years. No longer is he a prisoner of his own ugly image. No longer will he behold his own repulsive defect in the mirror day after day, night after night, year after year. Christine has set him free. Her unconditional love has opened a door.

The Phantom escapes his dungeon. The police never capture him. But he lives on. And his love and gratitude for Christine Daae never dies. We know this because at the end of the movie when Raoul, now an old widower in a wheel chair, visits her grave to pay his respects, he finds a single rose with the ring of the Phantom on its stem, the ring the Phantom had intended for Christine, had they become one.

Of course, *The Phantom of the Opera* is pure fiction. But the truth of the matter is that each of us comes into this world with a defect (our Sin Nature). This defect is so ugly, so depraved and hideous, that we do our best to hide it from the world. We adopt various masks so people will not see how ugly we really are on the inside. But we know. And as we focus on our rotten condition day after day and month after month, our defect wraps its tentacles around us like a giant squid sucking the life right out of us. And we continue to hide, afraid that someone will discover our secret self and turn from us with loathing and disgust. This is the ugly truth behind Romans 1:18-3:20.

But Jesus comes along to love us in a way we have never experienced. While we were still ugly (Rom 5:8), He proved His love for us by giving His life for us, going to death row in our place. Our defect did not fool Him. He knew about it the whole time. We could not hide it from Him. Like Christine (is it a coincidence that the first part of her name is Christ?), He prayed that God would give Him the strength to show us we are not alone. There is One who loves us and wants us as His bride—all in spite of our ugliness.

We have no reason to believe the Phantom ever lost his defect. Half of his face would be ugly his entire life. But he was no longer a prisoner of his defect (Romans 6). Christine's love set him free. Just so, Jesus' love and the law of the spirit of life in Christ Jesus is setting us free from the ugliness of our defect (Romans 8), which never completely leaves us in this life. Because of his love we can smash the mirrors, which multiply our wretched condition in our own minds. We no longer have to focus on our miserable Condition; we are free to enjoy our wonderful Position as the betrothed of incomparable Son of God.

And as we focus our attention on this wonderful Position and the blessings that accrue to our Position, it begins to affect our Condition. Slowly but surely the Master Artist, the Holy Spirit, transforms our Condition until it conforms with our Position, all the while touching up His portrait until we look more and more like the Son of God who lives in us. As the beggar responded when the artist painted a portrait of the man he saw *inside* the homeless man with his rags and his filth, "If that's the man you see, then that's the man I'll be," we too can become like the God-Man who lives inside of us. And that, my friends, is how we are delivered from the power of sin to become *Portraits of Righteousness*.

APPENDIX

What Does the Righteousness of God "Look" Like?

I f Paul's readers are convinced that the main goal of the gospel is to reveal the righteousness of God in this life by faith (1:16-17), then we are bound to wonder just what this righteousness "looks" like. In one sense, Romans 12–16 is Paul's template for how God's righteousness should "look" in the way Christians treat each other. However, this theme of "righteousness revealed" is not only relevant to Romans, it also surfaces throughout the Scriptures.

Soon after Abram's call by God (Gen 12:1-3), he was set apart among the nations as a "Hebrew" and blessed by the priest of God Most High (14:13, 18-20). A key goal of Abraham's commission to "be a blessing" (12:2) emerged later, after Abraham enjoyed "table fellowship" with the Lord, and he and his descendants were given this charge:

> "Shall I hide from Abraham what I am doing, since Abraham shall surely become a great and mighty nation, and all the nations of the earth shall be blessed in him? For I have known him, in order that he may command his children and his household after him, that they keep the way of the Lord, *to do righteousness and justice*, that the Lord may bring to Abraham what He has spoken to him." (Gen 18:17-19, emphasis added)

Implicit in the Lord's charge to Abram is the realization that we, the Body of Christ, the *spiritual* seed of Abraham, are in fact "his household after him." So his commission "to do righteousness and justice" passes down to us. We are well-advised, therefore, to pay more attention to this notion of "doing righteousness" as it is developed in the Old Testament. This God of Abraham brought the Hebrews out of Egypt to be a people "holy unto His name" — a people *separate* from the gentile nations insofar as they behaved differently. The whole Law of Moses can thus be seen as their "template" for *how to treat each other* and *maintain "table fellowship" with God.*

In this light it is therefore not surprising that when Moses became so frustrated with the Israelites following their all-too-hasty departure from God's commandments (Ex 32:8) he pleaded with God to show him His glory so he might be able to tolerate them in the wilderness (Ex 33). God responded to Moses' request by agreeing to "proclaim His name" as He passed before Moses to show him His "goodness" (33:19). When God fulfilled His promise, it turns out that His "goodness" — His "name" — had everything to do with compassion towards the people, and it is clear that Moses was to demonstrate that same kind of "goodness" toward them. Thus, the righteousness of God "looks like" mercy, compassion, and longsuffering, yet it is displayed in such a way that it does not overlook iniquity (34:6-7): God also promotes *justice*.

When we get to the New Testament, we see that the purpose of the law does not change; therefore, Christ's first priority is to teach the same high standard of righteousness or "template" for behavior that the Law of Moses was designed to exemplify (Matt 5:17-20). Not surprisingly, this disposition reflects the Lord's self-revelation to Moses in Exodus 34:6-7: for Jesus' disciples to "be perfect as your Father in heaven is perfect" (Matt 5:48), they must model *His* righteousness in the way they treat each other (6:33). So, it will "look like" incredible patience and tolerance for one's brethren in a variety of situations when our natural inclination would be to *objectify them* and treat them with sustained anger and resentment, especially in our speech (5:21-47).

James is fully conscious of Jesus' teaching in Matthew 5 and promotes this same standard when he describes his "brethren" as "the firstfruits of His creatures" — they are to be "swift to hear, slow to speak, slow to wrath; for the wrath of man does not produce the righteousness of God" (Jas 1:18-20). Epitomizing the very "soul" of Torah, James then says this about a way of life that claims to "do" the righteousness of God: "If anyone among you thinks he is religious, and does not bridle his tongue but deceives his own heart, this one's religion is useless. Pure and undefiled religion before God and the Father is this: to visit orphans and widows in their trouble, and to keep oneself unspotted from the world" (1:26-27).

For Matthew and James, therefore, righteousness is revealed in the world by a "separate" or "holy" people in what they openly *do* and *speak*; so, the Matthew 5 teaching that James calls "wisdom from above" will produce "peaceable" speech toward one another, such that "the fruit of righteousness is sown in peace by those who make peace" (Jas 3:13-18). For the author of Hebrews such wisdom is the hallmark of mature believers: those who are "skilled in the word of righteousness" by "having their senses exercised to discern both good and evil" (Heb 5:13-14). Paul reveals that this mature wisdom only comes with a humble sensitivity to the daily leading and teaching of the Spirit of God (Rom 8:14; 1 Cor 2:6–3:4; compare Jas 4:5-6).

John echoes the same preeminent concerns about "looking" righteous "out in the open." John 3:21 affirms that the work of God has to do with "deeds" that "come to light." John clarifies that these "deeds" are done by those who "walk in the light" because they know God as light and therefore love one another boldly as *people* of light (1 Jn 1:5–2:11; Jn 12:35-50). Just as the *sons of God* who are "revealed" will suffer with Christ (Rom 8:17-19), John is clear that recognition "at his appearing" depends on boldness in this life (1 Jn 2:28; 4:17-18) as righteous children of God (2:29–3:3); and that in turn entails sacrificial, righteous *behavior*, especially in the way we treat the brethren (3:4-18). Righteousness is thus "worked out" in love for one another, so that we "keep His commandments," showing love for God rather than love for the world (Jn 14:21, 23; 1 Jn 2:15-17; 4:7–5:3; compare Jas 4:1-4).

John's caution about our potential censure at Christ's appearing (1 Jn 2:28) echoes Paul and James in warning of future judgment by Christ when contempt is shown in this life for one's brother. Even believers under persecution are held to the same impossibly high standard that God desires a "righteous one" (*dikaios*, Jas 5:6; compare Rom 1:17b) to display before the world: it is our speech and behavior *in suffering* that is especially subject to judgment by Christ (Rom 14:10-13; Jas 5:9, 12). This is precisely the subtext of Romans 8:18-30, where we see the ministry of the Spirit so essential to sustain speech and behavior during suffering that is worthy of a "son" to be rewarded with co-inheritance with Christ in the Kingdom (8:14, 17b); this is because a "son" under duress has the best opportunity to reflect the Father's righteous character before the world. It is a Spirit-mediated "hope of righteousness," as Paul describes in Galatians 5:5—a hope realized by "faith working through love" (5:6).[1]

John thus best summarizes how we "perfect" the righteousness of God: "If you know that He is righteous, you know that everyone who *does* righteousness is born of Him. ... we are now children of God; and it has not yet been revealed what we shall be, but we know that *when He is revealed, we shall be like Him* ... love is *perfected* among us, so that we have confidence on the day of judgment, *in that we are like him in this world*" (1 Jn 2:29, 3:2; 4:17, emphasis added).

---

1   It is therefore shortsighted to see the righteousness in view in Gal 5:5-6 as nothing more than a final verdict, or "future justification." See e.g., John Piper, *The Future of Justification* (Wheaton, IL: Crossway, 2007), esp. 203-206; and N.T. Wright, *Justification* (Downers Grove, IL: InterVarsity, 2009), esp. 138-39. See also our Excursus, "Relying on the Spirit to Display Righteousness," in Chapter 18, "The Groaning of God."

This, then, is how our righteousness "exceeds in glory" (2 Cor 3:9). For in appropriating the righteousness of Christ in the way we treat one another, we "are being transformed into the same image from glory to glory, just as by the Spirit of the Lord" (3:18). And in anticipating greater glory at the Judgment Seat of Christ (4:17; 5:10), we become ambassadors of Christ to the world — the righteousness of God *in Him* (5:20-21). Our "crown of righteousness ... on that Day" (2 Tim 4:8) is a "crown of life" that correlates with the impartial love we display toward one another in this life as "firstfruits" or "portraits" of the Father by the "faith of Christ" (Jas 1:12, 18; 2:1).

SCRIPTURE INDEX

(Page entries listed in *italics* are found only in footnotes)

CPSIA information can be obtained
at www.ICGtesting.com
Printed in the USA
BVOW11s1705090317

478086BV00004B/55/P